I0759898

Flipping Capo

Flipping Capo

How the FBI Dismantled the *Real* Sopranos

SÉAMUS McELEARNEY
with BARBARA FINKELSTEIN

In accordance with my obligations as a former FBI employee pursuant to my FBI employment agreement, this book has undergone a prepublication review for the purpose of identifying prohibited disclosures, but has not been reviewed for editorial content or accuracy. The FBI does not endorse or validate any information that I have described in this book. The opinions expressed in this book are mine and not those of the FBI or any other government agency.

—Séamus McElearney

Published by Chicago Review Press Incorporated
814 North Franklin Street
Chicago, Illinois 60610
ISBN 979-8-89068-016-7

Library of Congress Control Number: 2025939913

Typesetting: Nord Compo

Printed in the United States of America
5 4 3 2 1

Séamus:
To my dad, James McElearney.
Thank you for the hard work ethic you instilled in me.

Barbara:
To Max Hockley

"Enter, but I warn you—he
who would look back, returns—again—outside."

Dante's *Purgatorio*, Canto IX

CONTENTS

AUTHOR'S NOTE

As an FBI employee, I wasn't at liberty to talk about what my squad did to bring down the "real Sopranos." I retired in April 2019 after twenty-one years with the Bureau, and now I can reveal how we dismantled the DeCavalcantes—a New Jersey organized crime family that eluded law enforcement for more than a century. The DeCavalcantes were well on their way to becoming as brutal as New York's "Five Families" when I met Anthony Capo, a mob soldier so violent even his fellow mobsters didn't want to work with him. Capo and I were an odd couple, but we stopped the DeCavalcantes dead in their tracks.

Note on Names and Sources

The names of some individuals have been fictionalized. These names are indicated by the use of **boldface** on first mention. Any similarity between the fictionalized names and the names of real people is strictly coincidental.

Direct quotations from sources, which include public records (including court documents, transcripts, and proceedings), interviews, and various publications and other media, appear between open and closed quotation marks. When no quotation marks are used, the sources have been paraphrased.

1

I'M GOING UP, HE'S GOING DOWN

January 1, 2012

ANTHONY CAPO WOULD BE the first to admit he was a mama's boy. Witness Security Program rules mandated that he steer clear of every last person from his previous mob life. His wife and three kids didn't follow him into his new anonymous life, and if not for his mother's devotion, Capo would have been completely alone in the world. He could be on a Himalayan mountaintop, inside a Kansas haystack, even in WitSec—or "Witness Protection," as Hollywood calls it—and Capo's mother would find him. She always knew how to give her son courage, before and since my FBI team and I arrested him on December 2, 1999, in a predawn sweep of thirty-nine alleged members and associates of the DeCavalcantes and other organized crime families. Whaddaya gonna do? A mom wants to see her boy happy.

Capo was committed to becoming a law-abiding citizen, for me if not for himself. I'd be lying, though, if I said I never worried about him flouting WitSec protocol to make a human connection again with someone he loved. If the federal marshals who monitored him discovered the smallest breach of the rules, Capo would be out on his ear. Then he would be fair game for mobsters with a grudge who swore they would kill him or die trying. The list of Capo haters was not short.

Getting into WitSec had been a complicated process. Government witnesses like Capo didn't just sign on the dotted line and pole-vault into a beautiful new life. It involved me preparing a threat assessment to assure the US Marshals Service, which runs WitSec, that Capo didn't pose a threat of violence to anybody. This document was not an academic exercise. Mafia retribution against law enforcement and snitches was an open secret. Six years before I joined the FBI, the Mafia blew up a bridge in Sicily frequented by mob-buster Judge Giovanni Falcone—while he was on it. Around the same time in New York, the Lucchese organized crime family shot the sister of their former captain* turned government witness Pete Chiodo. She was an innocent bystander, but in the 1990s, even in America, certain Mafia elements resorted to old-world retaliation. She didn't die . . . but still.

WitSec candidates go through an extensive vetting process to make sure they're capable of following US Marshal guidelines. A candidate has to take his new life seriously, as Capo did when he turned his back on organized crime to become a car salesman. I gave him a lot of credit. By 2012 he was too sick to work, but for years he had been on his feet all day—a danger for a diabetic and, until his arrest, a lifelong drug abuser. He really did try, and all vanity aside, he wanted to be a success story for me.

From the moment we met inside an FBI-issued Pontiac Grand Prix, Capo enjoyed ribbing me about the Pittsburgh Steelers, my team. I gave it right back to him about his team, the Dallas Cowboys. When we began sparring with each other, neither of us would have guessed that he would voluntarily become a witness for the government he despised and testify against the men he had sworn a blood oath to defend to the death.

Those men were members of the DeCavalcantes, the New Jersey crime family that took its name from Simone "Sam the Plumber" DeCavalcante—and that many believe served as a model for the fictional crime family of HBO's *The Sopranos*. Back in the '60s, Sam the Plumber was a Newark-based mafioso notorious for bribing Jersey's politicians,

* *Captain* is the term for a midlevel leadership position in the Mafia. *Caporegime* is the Italian word for *captain*. *Capo* is a shortened form of *caporegime*. These terms are interchangeable. The captain oversees a crew of soldiers (made members) and associates.

judges, and businessmen while also funding the San Giuseppe di Ribera orphanage back in Ribera, Sicily. In his own small but comprehensively vicious way, Capo followed in Sam the Plumber's footsteps by committing murders, shaking down contractors and small businesses, and infiltrating labor unions and petroleum plants. In short, stopping at nothing to prove his loyalty to La Cosa Nostra—"this thing of ours," the term of art for the Italian Mafia. As the first made man in DeCavalcante history to turn against his companions, Capo no longer experienced the thrills that had characterized his decades of criminal adventures. But he didn't succumb to any new disasters either. It's fourth and goal and he's going for it.

By 2012, Anthony Capo had testified at seven trials, prepped for countless others, and helped put away dozens of high-level mobsters, but now the day he had been waiting for was three weeks away: on January 25, he would stand before Judge Jed Rakoff in the Southern District of New York and await sentencing. Capo definitely would have gotten LIFE* if he hadn't cooperated. But cooperate he did, and his service as a government witness qualified him for a sentence of "time served." For that hoped-for outcome, though, we had one more hoop to jump through: the government prosecutors and I had to prepare a so-called 5K letter,† an appeal for leniency on Capo's behalf.

After New Year's, I contacted the US Marshals to schedule a phone call with Capo. When my desk phone rang and a special number popped up on the screen, I knew it was him.

I picked up on the second ring.

"Hey, kid, you just made your favorite snitch's day," Capo said.

"It's been a while, Anthony. How's it going?"

"It'd be great to see you, kid."

---

* At the FBI, we always referred to a life sentence as "LIFE"—in all caps. It meant the defendant was going to leave prison in a box.

† Technically, it's called a 5K1.1 letter. It's given to a defendant who provides substantial assistance to the government in the investigation of others for criminal conduct.

Nearly impossible. Even us good guys were off limits to him.

"I've been missing my mom," he said. "The kids too, but I'm realistic. I ain't seeing them." Capo's wife had long since moved on.

I didn't want to be a hard-ass, but I had to remind Capo that nobody from his pre-WitSec days could see him without the marshals' intervention. He was in the psychological boondocks, and he may as well have been living on the moon.

"It's too late. I already saw—"

"I cannot know anything about this," I said. But I heard Capo loud and clear. He was lonely, living God knows where, and he had seen his mom.

Capo wisely changed the subject and asked me about my wife. When I was single, I didn't mind talking about my romantic exploits. Now that I was married, though, I was ultra-protective of my personal life. Bond or no bond, I had to be on guard against saying anything to Capo that could potentially harm me or my loved ones. No law said that once in Witness Security, Capo had to stay in it. I sincerely believed he had reformed himself. But what was to say that if he left the program he wouldn't go back to his old neighborhood? Other witnesses had gone back and resorted to their old ways.

I was the luckiest guy in the world talking to one of the unluckiest guys in the world. Even if Capo did get "time served," his life would still be on a downward spiral while I got to ride high in the best years of my FBI career.

"We should talk about your sentencing date on the twenty-fifth," I said.

"It's all I think about, Séamus."

"You're going to do great."

"I know I've got to give a speech to the judge," Capo said.

"I know you remember what to say. But it doesn't hurt to overprepare."

"I'm giving you all the credit," Capo said.

"There's no need for that," I said.

"I can't throw a pity party for myself."

"Right. It's not about you. It's about having remorse."

"'If it wasn't for Séamus, I wouldn't be standing before you now, Your Honor,'" Capo elucidated for my benefit. "'I'm responsible for the misery and heartache I brought into the lives of my victims' families.'"

"What do you want to tell the judge about our relationship?" I asked.

"'Your Honor, Séamus stuck with me through thick and thin. After my arrest, when the DeCavalcantes threatened to kill—" Capo choked up. He always did when he reminded himself that DeCavalcante captain Frank Polizzi had ordered a hit on Capo's family. And on law enforcement.

Throughout my FBI career, I had seen government witnesses screw up at sentencing. They were *Me me me me me*. The judge doesn't want to hear how your family missed out on having you the past three years. The family whose loved one you killed doesn't get to have them at all.

But I wasn't worried about Capo addressing the court during his sentencing. In thirteen years, I had witnessed his transformation firsthand. He was remorseful.

"I'll be in the courtroom with you, Anthony," I promised. "I'm going to have a big contingent of FBI agents on hand to support you in front of the judge. I'm praying you walk out of that Manhattan courtroom a free man."

Before we hung up, Capo told me his life was in jeopardy. His formidable enemy now was not the mob. It was diabetes. He had already lost three toes to it.

Capo had not officially been my problem for years. The first made man I ever flipped was on the verge of becoming a free man with an asterisk: except for an occasional scheduled visit with his mom and kids, he was never going back to his old life. Rules are rules.

Everyone makes choices in life. Capo had once chosen a life of crime. As a government witness, he chose to rehabilitate himself. Now my choice was to stand by him.

2

FROM THE BRONX TO THE BUREAU

Anyone who grew up in the Bronx, like me, knows the law of the streets is fight or flight. You got a problem with me, we'll settle it with our fists. Growing up on Bainbridge Avenue alerted me to the lawlessness that lives just beneath the surface of civilized life. I saw friends do illegal drugs. Steal from mom-and-pop shops. Get stabbed. Some Bainbridge punk used to braid an iron chain through his fingers and smack it against people's doors. Why? Because. Maybe my sentimental education wasn't the stuff of a personal college essay, but it was my life. The Bronx was vocational training for the psychological rassling I was born to do.

I'll never stop thanking my parents for moving to the New York City borough that schooled me in self-defense and split-second thinking. Jimmy, my dad, and Christine, my mom, moved from the Republic of Ireland to the Bronx fresh off farms in County Monaghan and County Longford. As children they never knew anything but hard work and diminished horizons. I myself might be heaving burlap sacks of wheat into a silo or lugging glass milk bottles into a cold cellar today if these two brave kids hadn't gotten on airplanes more than sixty years ago. They were at the tail end of a great Irish immigration that began in 1848 and was largely over by 1960, when they disembarked, separately and alone, from Aer Lingus at Idlewild Airport.* They traveled by public transportation to apartments waiting for them in the South Bronx.

My parents met at Gaelic Park, the Irish sports facility in the Bronx four blocks south of Manhattan College. By the time I was born in 1967, Jimmy and Christine McElearney were settled into a prewar brick walk-up two miles east in St. Brendan's parish—a major move from the poor South Bronx. Their lives remained Irish. The *Irish Echo*, the *Longford Leader*, and the *Argus* were my parents' newspapers, and they read them religiously. County Monaghan, where my dad was from, bordered on Northern Ireland, so he sympathized with the Irish Republican Army, especially in the days of Bobby Sands's hunger strike to protest the end of the IRA's privileges in Northern Ireland's British prisons. I think he, like many of my friends' fathers, dropped money off for the IRA at one of the many Irish bars on Bainbridge Avenue. On our annual family trips to Ireland, he instructed us kids to keep quiet when we went through checkpoints on dark dirt roads. Nobody even knew for sure who was manning them: the IRA, the Republic of Ireland's Gardaí, the English, or the Northern Ireland Protestants. I myself never fathomed the dangerous political maze that defined the "Troubles," a war of attrition that rippled along the edges of my entire youth. I was an American kid, and seeing soldiers and rebels with guns was, frankly, beyond my comprehension.

In fact, I was so determined to be an American that my mother's well-meaning efforts to instill Irish culture into her children pretty much fell on deaf ears and deaf feet. My accordion education ended when I forgot to bring the instrument to my lesson, and an episode involving Irish dancing concluded with me kicking my shoe across the dance floor in the middle of a jig. There would be no Riverdance in this American boy's future.

Only one thing in our family was not negotiable: our Catholicism. Both of my parents were devout. The Lenten season stands out in my mind as particularly church-filled. For one, we observed the Stations of the Cross, the fourteen-step devotion commemorating Jesus Christ's last day on earth as a man. It could all get a bit much for my taste, what with the interminable praying and visits to the confessional booth. But

* Idlewild Airport was renamed JFK International Airport in 1963.

I took the story to heart. Several stations concerned Christ's struggle to carry the heavy wooden cross on Calvary. I wouldn't admit it to anyone, but I had my own cross to bear. If Christ could trudge, fall three times, and stumble toward His fate, I could march on too in the face of my tormentors. I must confess, though, I was not meek as a lamb when a neighborhood kid was stupid enough to mock my childhood stutter.

The ground-floor apartment my parents moved to on Bainbridge Avenue a couple blocks from Montefiore Medical Center and O'Meara's Greentree Restaurant was close to the string of gas stations my father owned in and around our working-class neighborhood, a midcentury Irish enclave of Catholic churches, pubs, and dollar stores set against the blare of ambulance sirens. More important for me, Bainbridge Avenue gave me my American life. Around the corner were the Williamsbridge Oval track and field, the Whalen Playground, and St. Brendan's School. Hard to believe my childhood home is now a bodega, and the bedroom I shared with my kid brother Liam is the frozen food section.

My Bainbridge Avenue days were full of school, friends, and pranks. Like all good St. Brendan's School students, we worked overtime to torture the nuns, such as when we dropped our potted-plant science projects out the third-story window. Not that the nuns couldn't give as good as they got. Sister Michael Marie, for one, would light you up in a heartbeat. Brian Schumacher, or "Shu," as we all called him, punched her right back in the gut. In the 1980s, if you hit an Irishman—or Irishwoman—they'd hit you back harder.

After school I would rush home, dash off my homework, and meet up with my friends at the Williamsbridge Oval to play sports. Baseball was paramount. Bainbridge Avenue boasted talented sports dynasties, and we waited all year for spring so the Goldens, Caseys, and Coffeys could display their athletic gifts. We played football in the fall and basketball whenever we felt like shooting hoops. By my teens, I was big into hockey. My one childhood grievance is that my parents didn't give me skating lessons so I could play ice hockey. I played floor hockey instead. I loved sports and I loved hitting people. In my early twenties, a fan reached over the boards at Murray's Skating Center in Yonkers and punched me while I was fighting a player. When the game ended, I fought the fan in the hallway. He got his price of admission. Good times.

Some of my Bronx memories are not rosy. The brother of my friend Brian Corrigan drowned at Tibbetts Pool just north of the county line in Yonkers. Both of Shu's parents died while we were in grammar school. Right after high school, my friend Lee got shot and killed. And **Vicki Drapes**, twelve years old—twelve!—pretended she was pregnant. In Catholic school, we were taught to draw a straight line between good behavior and a good life. But this was the Bronx. Out on the streets and in the privacy of people's homes, we saw the good die young. Later on, as an FBI agent, I learned from one of the DeCavalcantes we flipped that mob guys could live past a hundred—and receive a letter from the president of the United States congratulating them on reaching that milestone. They might not be healthy, but they hung in there, and when that letter arrived, the mobsters found it hilarious. I still puzzle over our earthly rewards, just and unjust, meted out like savory pie and Guinness on St. Paddy's Day.

Church of St. Brendan, Bainbridge Avenue, the Bronx.
Photo by Barbara Finkelstein

My freshman year at Cardinal Spellman High School, my parents dropped a bombshell on me: we were movin' on up to a private house in suburban Westchester County. But I wouldn't even consider switching to Roosevelt High School, a mile from our new house.

What was once a short bus ride from St. Brendan's parish was now an ordeal. Traveling from Westchester back to the Bronx involved catching a ride in the morning with my father to his gas station and then taking two buses to Spellman. Door to door took an hour and a half. Coming back home was even hairier: three buses and a mile-long walk to my house. Another hour and a half.

If I missed a bus, I risked running into the Bloods, Black Spades, or whatever other gangs had marked the Cardinal Spellman neighborhood as their turf. With my fists, I could defend myself, but I was no match against guns and knives.

Sports were out of the question. My sport was getting to and from school. Missing out on high school athletics was a huge sacrifice, but abandoning my Bainbridge Avenue friends? No way.

One of the benefits of having a dad who owned a gas station: I was behind the wheel of a car as soon as I turned sixteen. Shortly after a guy T-boned me in my mom's Mercedes, and nearly killed my best friend Dave, I bought a 1978 Pontiac Firebird Formula with my own money. My first car. Sweet!

After Cardinal Spellman, half of my friends went to Manhattan College in the tony Riverdale section of the Bronx, and half went to Iona College in affluent Westchester County. I went to Iona, but I kept coming back to the Bronx to hang out with my Spellman crowd, mostly at the local bars. The Pinewood, Dorney's, Greenleaf, Terminal, and Characters are gone now, but the bonds I formed with my pals continue to this day. About twenty of us meet for our annual Christmas dinner at our favorite Japanese steakhouse in Westchester, five miles as the crow flies from Bainbridge Avenue. We'll be friends for life.

My parents paid 100 percent of my college tuition, but I had to get a night-shift job for my non-school expenses. I worked a 6:00–10:00 PM shift with no breaks, unloading trucks at United Parcel Service in Elmsford, a working-class village that was a twenty-minute car ride from Iona. I had just started hitting the weights really hard, and I viewed my job as another workout. Great for chest expansion. I loved it.

I graduated with a BBA in finance, but I didn't go straight to the FBI. No one does. The Bureau wants the workplace, preferably the financial sector, to test your mettle. It won't hire a college grad whose biggest achievement to date is lining his bedroom walls with empty Coors Light cans. The working world breaks you in. The FBI turns you into a bloodhound.

I had worked part time at my dad's gas station since I was ten, but after I graduated, I went to work for him full time. It was the least I could do to thank him for getting me through college without racking up student loans.

Working for my father was no picnic. It was one thing for him to treat Jimmy Butler, one of his gas jockeys, like a hired hand, but he also treated me, and Liam, like that, not like his sons. Work started at 8:00 AM. If we were ten minutes late, he sent us home without pay. Lunch was a fifteen-minute break, barely time enough to cram a sandwich down our throats. If a car pulled up for gas, you put your food down and waited on them. I can still hear my dad yelling, "Gas!"

I credit my father's strictness for the work ethic he dinned into Liam, my two sisters, and me. If you could work for my father, working for anyone else was a walk in the park.

After two years of indentured servitude to my dad, I heard about an opening in the audit department at East River Savings Bank in New Rochelle, near Iona, from a good friend. My last interview was with the director of internal audit. Turns out it was Jimmy Butler, the gas fellow who'd once worked for my dad on Bronx Boulevard. Needless to say, Jimmy jump-started my adult working life: I got the job.

After a couple of years at East River—including one memorable day when my coworker Bill O'Meara and I happened to sit out a robbery*—I

* It was Christmastime, and Bill and I were down in the Cortlandt Street branch vault conducting an audit. Jimmy Butler called us and asked where we were. "In the vault," I

moved on to internal audit at AIG, the insurance company. My résumé boasted that I knew how to use Excel and WordPerfect. A bit of an exaggeration. East River's computers were grossly out of date, and I hadn't gotten around to learning any new programs. I didn't want to get fired, so I enrolled in a weekend computer programs crash course at my own expense.

I'd worked at East River Savings Bank, AIG, and then Crédit Agricole for nearly six years. Never loved a day of it. Who likes to admit they never felt 100 percent confident in their industry? During my auditing career, I was always treading water in the deep end of the pool. I did not want to go through the next thirty or forty years of my work life out of my depth. I swore I'd find meaningful work. For work I loved, I'd be a sponge and soak everything in.

Not for nothing, but first- and second-generation Irish Americans have been drawn to law enforcement since the middle of the nineteenth century. I can see why. You're not tied down to a desk and a calculator all day long. You're out watching for trouble, and you're ready to tangle with it. You're the guy people call when they're in trouble.

Bingo. That's what I wanted to do. Help people in trouble.

You may be scratching your head. The bruiser guy wants to help people? As the firstborn son in an immigrant family, I was already the de facto helper for my parents. With all due respect to them, they were clueless about life in America, and they needed a lot of help. That's not a put-down. Nothing in Ireland had prepared Jimmy and Christine to pay phone bills, energy bills, doctor bills, and school tuition, or get a Social Security number for me. Even my birth certificate turned out to be problematic. In my teens I found out my legal name was James. Uh-uh. I was Séamus. I gathered up documentation, drove downtown to the city's health department, and got my emended birth certificate in the mail three weeks later.* Not such a big deal for me, but handling such tactical matters was too much for my mom and dad. A scary

---

said. Jimmy asked, "Are you drinking or working?" I said, "Working." He said, "Well, get upstairs. The bank just got robbed." We went up and saw all the bank tellers crying. Eventually the FBI got involved.

* I went through all that trouble, and all the health department did was cross out "James" and write in, by hand, "Séamus." Welcome to government bureaucracy.

thought considering the lives of six people—more if you count our relatives in Ireland—depended on my dad's business savvy for sustenance.

The work I had done at East River, AIG, and Crédit Agricole was a far cry from helping people the way I wanted to help them. I had gotten on the wrong road. I had to get on the right one. I needed a mission.

I knew enough from TV and movies that the FBI's mission was to protect the country from attack and public corruption. I wrote away for a job application, filled out all fifteen pages before the due date, and mailed it off to FBI headquarters in Washington, DC.

I waited. In a few months I got a letter saying I had to take an SAT-type test with math and verbal sections. I passed it.

I waited again. In a couple more months, I was invited to 290 Broadway in Lower Manhattan for a panel interview with three special agent (SA) assessors. The same day I had to take a timed written exercise designed to assess my analytical abilities. Talk about stress!

In due time, I received a conditional letter of employment, pending a polygraph test,* a drug test, and an extensive background check. I could have fallen out of the application process at any point. All somebody at work or in my neighborhood had to do was say one damning thing about me. Thanks to my dad, who threatened me at a young age about the perils of doing drugs under his roof, I wasn't worried about passing the drug test. I never experimented with drugs at all.

Even so, I cannot tell you how many times people said, "Séamus, you'll never be an FBI agent." My friends and family knew I had no military or law enforcement background. In their eyes, I didn't have the bona fides. I get it. People fix you in their minds as the Bronx boy or the bank auditor. They didn't know my personal motto was "Persistence beats resistance."

In January 1998 I proved them all wrong. Two years after sending in my application, I received a letter telling me I had been selected from among 100,000 applicants in New York to attend agent training at FBI

* FBI agent Mike Templeton administered my polygraph test, after rescheduling numerous times. When I became an agent, Mike and I worked on the same floor. He told me the candidates who accommodated his requests to reschedule always failed. Thankfully, I broke that trend.

headquarters in Quantico, Virginia. I was among the mere 2 percent that got in. This Bronx boy with no military service and no experience with firearms was headed to the FBI.

A friend told me about an agent named **Tricia Harris**. I was intrigued when I found out Tricia, a Bronx girl, was on an FBI criminal squad. We got together at Rory Dolan's Bar in Yonkers and I plied her with questions (not drink). *How many people were in your FBI class? How do you make a phone call from Quantico (in pre-cell phone days)? Can I drive down? Will I be assigned to the New York office? Will I learn how to use a gun? How do agents get paid?*

What? You think Inspector Lewis Erskine on *The F.B.I.* didn't ask about his paycheck? The World Wide Web was brand new in the 1990s, so I never even thought of using a search engine to find the answers.

Tricia was a walking advertisement for the Bureau. She was over the moon working there. Her job sounded fascinating. Prestigious. I was hooked. I wanted to work out of the NYO. Look at me: I was already talking about the New York office like an FBI employee.

Once I got my acceptance letter, I had a new hurdle. How was I going to hold on to my dream job through the shitstorm that followed me down to Quantico?

3

TRY RUNNING WITH A BUM KNEE

In the weeks before my four-month FBI training program, I was a perpetual motion machine. By day I worked at Crédit Agricole, and by evening I played pickup games in a city basketball league as a member of the Bainbridge Avenue Narrowbacks. I figured running up and down the court was a good way to get into shape.

Wrong.

One night I got into position for a rebound and my knee popped out. Hurt like hell, but I didn't dare complain. How easy would it have been for the FBI to bypass me and select a more fit physical specimen? I wasn't throwing away my shot! I iced my knee every chance I got, and when February rolled around, I said goodbye to my girlfriend Millie, filled my Mitsubishi 3000GT with boxes and suitcases, and drove five hours on I-95 South to Quantico, Virginia, to be part of FBI class 98-05—the fifth class of trainees in 1998.

I was just past thirty and heading off on my own. I figured I had seen it all, done it all. But I was about to experience several firsts.

A. I had never set foot on a military base before Quantico. I wasn't surprised by the presence of twentysomething military police. My recruiter had warned me not to speed or I'd attract the attention of these kid cops. But I did have a moment when I envied these boys: so young and already they had made the decision to go into uniform.

B. My roommate was a former Chicago cop who walked around in his purple underwear and called his girlfriend "Booger." The only roommate I'd ever had was Liam, and the only other people I had ever lived with were my parents and sisters. Chicago wasn't my only roommate. I had two additional suite mates, and the four of us had to share one bathroom. When this gang found out I was from New York, I could feel the oxygen leave the room. They hated New Yorkers. It's a thing the rest of the country has about us. And these guys were my band of brothers?

On day 2, I got down to serious business with my first physical fitness class. One instructor was perfect for me. He liked to box and do martial arts. The other one liked to run. I wouldn't know which regimen I was getting until I walked into the gym.

"Good morning, class," said the other one. "My name is **Mr. Hucklebee**, and I'm your fitness instructor." Five foot three inches and 120 pounds of him soaking wet—a runner. Shit.

I had been taking over-the-counter glucosamine and chondroitin supplements to restore the cartilage in my bum knee. On our first two-mile run, I started out fine. I remember seeing this classmate, Dennis Langkos, fly past me. He had arrived at Quantico with a reputation for running a five-minute mile. I was nearing the end of my first quarter mile when I had my next setback: my knee gave out. I fell to the ground and had to be carried off the track on a stretcher. Mr. Hucklebee wanted to send me home.

Inside I had a sinking feeling: I'm going to end up an auditor back in some Wall Street office. Outside I wasn't having any of it. I punched the stretcher and said, "I can stick this out! I'm not leaving!" I prayed the FBI saw steely resolve in me, not insubordination.

The doctor told me I needed surgery for a torn anterior cruciate ligament, or ACL. Not what I wanted to hear. Surgery would get me sent home. I swore to the two class counselors, the instructor, and the doctor on everything holy I would get physical therapy.

PT helped a little. I also wrapped and iced my knee every day. If the truth be told, though, I knew my knee was an old injury. I'd dislocated it the first time years earlier playing hockey. Stupid me, I used to nudge the kneecap back where I thought it belonged. One time it popped out during a bare-knuckle karate belt test. I saw it hanging off the side of my leg, and I had to push it back into the correct position as I'd always done. I could feel it scraping against bone. Now I had to find time in a no-free-time schedule to put it through physical therapy.

I didn't find a miracle cure at Quantico, but at least I got to stay. I was not going to be "recycled" into class 98-06 or 98-07 as I had feared. I was going to graduate on time with my 98-05 class. But now that I was semi-handicapped, I had to distinguish myself in some other way. I stumbled upon—literally—three other areas where I could rehabilitate my name.

My first effort came in the classroom. Given that we only had sixteen weeks to get through our material, the academics were rigorous. Our classes included Behavioral Science, Legal I, Legal II, White Collar Crime, Communications, Foreign Counterintelligence, Laboratory/Fingerprinting, Organized Crime, and Ethics. I had read the US Constitution at Cardinal Spellman, but I never pored over it the way I did at Quantico. And until my training program, I didn't know anything about courtroom procedure. I loved the course work in a way I had never loved my previous studies. I knew they would have practical applications for the rest of my work life. In fact, I was intrigued by organized crime. The violence. The history. These city boys were into everything.

Not that my finance education was a waste. I brought my work experience to bear in an orientation session about life insurance. Our facilitator told us we could pay $20 every two weeks for a $40,000 term policy with Federal Employees Group Life Insurance. Coming from the private sector, I knew the math made no sense: I used to get $50,000 worth of life insurance at no cost to me. The government's plan was a joke. Twenty dollars every pay period may not sound like a princely sum, but we rookie agents were only getting a base salary of $36,000 a year. Why do healthy men and women in their twenties and thirties need to shell out so much for so little?

I stood up and told the class, "You can get a million dollars' worth of coverage at your age for forty dollars a month. Go get a term life insurance outside of this class." James Bond didn't have to worry about his finances, but Séamus McElearney and the FBI class of 98-05 did.

The second area where I could excel was in a monitored boxing match between two FBI candidates called the Bull in the Ring. The only things standing between you and your opponent are boxing gloves, mouth guards, and headgear. In our first sparring sessions, we were told to hit at 50 percent strength. I hit Dennis Langkos, the runner, lightly but right between the eyes and immediately pulled back when he got woozy. Occasionally we sparred with women, but I would barely tap them. We had heard horror stories about guys hitting women harder than they should have. For me, hitting them at all was unacceptable.

For our last class, I was matched up with a classmate named Carlton Peeples. Carlton had begun his work life as a combat engineer in the mid-1980s. So, not a Caspar Milquetoast. He was a big kid, like me. I, born, bred, and buttered in the Bronx, with a fifty-inch chest and 225 pounds of meat and muscle on my frame, was not a shrinking violet either. Everyone was ordered to watch Carlton and me go at each other in the opening round of our final class. The instructors wanted to see the big boys fight. They called us the Clydesdales, after the famous Scottish draft horses. We weren't thoroughbreds, just workhorses that could go the distance. We were deliriously happy hitting each other. Ultimately, the Bull in the Ring would give us both the muscle memory to defend ourselves against slap-happy bad guys. Carlton would go on to hold various titles in his twenty-plus years at the Bureau.

My third shot at repairing my reputation lay in Hogan's Alley, a ten-acre Potemkin village of sorts where the FBI stages criminal situations so we grunts can learn what to do in a bank robbery, a hostage-taking, or a standoff. The facility mimics a small high-crime city, complete with houses, trailer park, stores, banks, post office, pawnshop, motel, movie theater, and a pool hall attractive to Hogan Alley's seediest fictional residents. Locals get hired to take on roles as terrorists, bank robbers, or innocent bystanders, and we trainees learn how to interpret what's going on before our eyes. To participate in these simulated crimes, we are taught by firearms experts how to fire weapons in surprise "shoot-don't-shoot" scenarios—something I had never done until I came to Quantico. We used training weapons called "red handles" that didn't have live ammunition. The FBI made sure it never had a Brandon Lee or Alec Baldwin debacle on its hands. We had to carry the red handles on our persons all throughout training, because we were going to carry actual weapons once we became bona fide agents.

During a surveillance class, I was behind the wheel and my female partner was riding shotgun as we followed an actor-perpetrator down a street just outside Hogan's Alley. We realized too late that he'd led us into a dead end. If this had been a real event, the guy would have burned us. I realized what had happened and pulled over. Sure enough, he turned his car around and headed back to where my partner and I were parked.

"Follow my lead," I said.

I leaned in toward her and pretended we were making out. When the "bad guy" drove past us, he saw two people locked in a lover's embrace. He couldn't conclude, *Law enforcement doing surveillance.* We left with a takeaway: you have to think fast to outsmart a criminal.

In a pool hall scenario, a role-player put his hands on me and I body-slammed him like I was Bob Backlund in the wrestling ring. Thank you, Characters, thank you, Terminal, for those barroom brawls of yesteryear!

"You're an animal!" the actor yelled, and crawled away.

I asked my legal instructor if I had overreacted.

"Nobody's got any business laying a hand on you," he said.

Finally, someone who thought like a Bronx boy.

Weeks into the program, our FBI instructors caught a trainee in a lie. He had withheld relevant personal information. The FBI rarely forgives such an infraction. Here's why.

With or without eyeglasses or contact lenses, an agent had to have 20/20 vision in one eye and no worse than 20/40 in the other. In the late 1990s, the FBI did not allow for LASIK surgery to correct vision problems, yet **Bill** had had the procedure and didn't tell anyone.

As part of our training, we were subjected to mace full in the face. The experience was unpleasant but necessary: agents were expected to stand up in court during trial to tell a defense attorney we knew exactly what getting sprayed felt like. A person with normal vision can cope with the discomfort, but recent LASIK patients like Bill risk going blind. Unless he wanted to accept a horrible, irreversible outcome, Bill had to fess up to his instructor.

He got kicked out.*

I'd had a private matter to conceal too . . . in addition to my long-time knee injury. As with Bill, the crime might not get me fired, but the cover-up could.

When I first started at Quantico, I was still, technically speaking, an employee of Crédit Agricole. I hadn't told my bosses I'd left for the FBI. My employer knew I had applied to work at the Bureau. As part of my background check, the FBI had spoken to my managers in person. But I hadn't yet given notice for a basic financial reason: I was waiting to get my bonus for the previous year. It wouldn't hit my bank account until the Saturday before Quantico.

Don't forget—this was 1998. There was no way to get in touch with your boss on a Saturday. There was no smart phone, no texting, no 24/7 access to your laptop. So even when I found out my bonus was in my bank account, who was I supposed to call?

On Monday, my first day at Quantico, the very first break we got, I found a pay phone and called Crédit Agricole to say I was now working at the FBI. They weren't happy about my bailing on them, but they took my sudden departure like champs and wished me good luck.

Because I was the guy from New York with a fancy sports car, and because I felt about as popular as ants at a picnic, I wanted to humanize myself in the eyes of my fellow trainees. I told some of them about the stress I was under: how I had stood to lose my bonus—money due me—if I gave my employer the customary two weeks' notice.

Some honorable pain in the butt went and told our class counselors what I had done.

Believe me, I could see my infraction from the FBI's point of view: I appeared to be deceitful. I only hoped my superiors remembered the story I'd told the FBI interviewers during my panel interview about the time I was in a bank vault and could have walked off with a dozen gold bars and tons of cash. I'd never have gotten caught, but I left all the stuff behind.

* Over time, the FBI relaxed its rules, and I got LASIK surgery myself.

Here I was with a screwed-up knee I should have taken care of years ago, unresolved questions about my dealings with Crédit Agricole, and anxiety that a perfect storm of stresses would resurrect my childhood stutter. I was always conscious that the FBI had been testing us from the moment we became candidates—and that I was about to flame out.

I put my case before my class counselors: I had taken a $40,000-a-year pay cut to join the FBI, and I needed my bonus money—all of it earned—for living expenses. If I was guilty of anything, it was of having a big mouth. I promised that one day my willingness to confide in people would serve the criminal justice system well. I don't know if it was my dumb luck or the FBI's sense of fair play, but I got to stay.

By the time I saw Mr. Purple Underpants and my three other dorm mates, word had spread that I had duped my former and current employers and then, true to my devious New York ways, bamboozled my way out of trouble.

My first days at Quantico did not turn out the way I had hoped. At the very least, though, I wanted to tell Mr. Hucklebee, Mr. Blabbermouth, and everyone else: you can't keep a boy from Bainbridge Avenue down.

4

THE FUCKIN' NEW GUY FINDS A HOME

Come May 1998, I graduated as a member of the class of 98-05. I had already undergone several nasty educational incidents, including one where I was spritzed with mace, thrown into a shower, and told to rinse my eyes out. Gross, but I was so grateful to be in the program that I told my instructor he could throw me into a shower even if I was wearing a three-piece suit. I found my cloud, and nobody was pushing me off it.

Getting our office assignment was one of the FBI's unique hazing moments. All the trainees met up in a classroom. Our instructors called us up one by one and handed us an envelope with our office destination inside. None of us knew for sure where we'd end up. I decided that if I landed in, say, the El Paso FBI office, I'd spend half my time wondering how the hell I got there and the other half wondering how the hell I was going to get out.

Hey, I have nothing against El Paso, Texas, or Anchorage, Alaska, or any other small town in our great country. For me, though, a damn Yankee, Backwater USA was not where the action was. The Bronx gut runs on rush orders, don't waste my time with explanations, I want this yesterday, and I prayed my assignment would be the flagship office in Lower Manhattan. Meanwhile, for a lot of 98-05 graduates, New York City—my plum assignment—was Dante's nine circles of hell rolled into one. Nobody wanted to go there except us New Yorkers. But as we heard time and again, it's all about the needs of the Bureau. If that meant I'd get stuck in Podunksville, I'd think seriously about jumping ship.

I needn't have worried. The FBI genie granted my wish: I was going home to NYC.

We "fuckin' new guys," or FNGs, as probationary agents were known, got sent to 290 Broadway, across from FBI headquarters at 26 Federal Plaza. There we joined one of two applicant squads, which put us through a rotation of the Bureau's various administrative functions. I was assigned to Applicant Squad A-4.

Yes, more training on top of Quantico. You wouldn't know your arse from your elbow if you didn't go through an applicant squad first. Like many big organizations, the FBI is a matrixed operation, with headquarters in DC, field offices in all fifty states, satellite offices, undisclosed locations, and task forces run jointly with other law enforcement agencies. In the late 1990s, the Bureau was also divided into three investigative divisions: Criminal (CRIM), Counterintelligence (CI), and Counterterrorism (CT). Each of these was broken down further into branches with areas of specialization (white collar, organized crime, cyber, drugs, etc.). Just try to figure all of this out on your own. Impossible.

One of our earliest assignments had us conducting background checks into FBI applicants. I was taken aback when I realized that one year earlier, I'd been interviewed by newbies like me. I thought you had to be a seasoned agent to perform that task. Nope. Applicant investigations were considered entry-level work. It makes sense. No one's going to ask you to do a criminal investigation while you're still wet behind the ears.

It's the needs of the Bureau first.

A second rotation had us working for two weeks at 26 Federal Plaza in the operations center. That's where the Bureau keeps track of arrests, surveillances, tips and complaints from citizens, and related activities. It's where people—a.k.a. headcases—call during the 10:00 PM–6:00 AM shift and ask you to investigate the UFO hovering over their house.

A third rotation taught us how to do surveillance. My days were spent driving around dozens of neighborhoods and highways in New York's five boroughs. The point was to get familiar with the routes, demographics, cultures, businesses, and buildings I would come upon on a typical surveillance operation. We inhabitants of the late 1990s didn't have GPS to show us the way. The FBI gave each of us some NYC Hagstrom road atlases. Nowadays you can only find them on eBay, but right up until the end of analog times, we depended on them to get us from, say, a mobster's house in Elizabeth, New Jersey, to a mob boss's strip club in Queens, New York.

I was assigned to Surveillance Operations 2, or SO-2. Sounds like more matrixed bureaucracy, right? Turns out SO-2 was dedicated to surveilling the DeCavalcantes. It took no genius or cunning on my part to land on a team that was just starting to investigate one of the oldest and most secretive mob families in America. By a stroke of dumb luck, my desires and the FBI's needs coincided.

Nothing is etched in stone, though. I knew that at the drop of a hat, the Bureau could send me anywhere. If I wanted a permanent place on an NYC organized crime (OC) squad, I still had to build my reputation. I heeded the call to help with additional assignments. We got requests every day to aid in an arrest or search warrant or "sit a wire"—listen in, with court authorization,* on a real-time conversation between suspected bad guys. I volunteered as much as I could, even on Saturdays and Sundays. My thinking was, if I made myself useful and took overnight, weekend, and holiday shifts, I'd look more appealing than the agent who just did the minimum.

Don't get the idea I was some toady. I nixed a couple of options right off the bat. No white collar. No cyber. I was aware of them from my banking and insurance days, and I wasn't looking to be bored batshit.

I also tried to ingratiate myself to my higher-ups, and a little chutzpah paid off. I spoke to assistant special agents in charge (ASACs), supervisors, and seasoned agents on OC squads. I was enthralled by what I heard. I went looking for books about La Cosa Nostra and the FBI. At the Barnes & Noble near 26 Federal, I picked up *Underboss: Sammy the Bull Gravano's Story of Life in the Mafia* by Peter Maas. Gravano's Bensonhurst neighborhood in Brooklyn wasn't really like Bainbridge Avenue, but the story spoke my language. Bensonhurst was full of immigrants and second-generation Europeans, nearly all of them

---

* It's called a Title III (Wiretap Act) order.

Catholic, nearly all of them churchgoing. Bar culture was key. Fists and fast on your feet were the law of the streets. That's where the similarities ended. My Bainbridge Avenue friends were working stiffs in white collar and public service jobs. Guys like Sammy the Bull didn't know what W-2 employment was. Still, I was riveted by Maas's account of a mobster so valuable that the US government backed him for a reduced sentence. Whatever Sammy the Bull knew, I wanted to know too—but from the other end of the telescope.

On August 7, 1998, three months into applicant purgatory, we got news about the bombings of American embassies in Nairobi, Kenya, and Dar es Salaam, Tanzania. More than two hundred people were killed, including twelve Americans, and forty-five hundred people were wounded. Like a giant aircraft carrier changing direction, the Bureau shifted its attention to counterterrorism. Rumors went 'round that new agents would be sent to Africa.

Theoretically, I liked the idea of seeing far-flung places, but I had reservations about going to countries that served cornmeal porridge and collard greens at one end of the food spectrum and curry and cilantro at the other. Look, I've been tormented my whole life about my "restricted palate." I'm a chicken-and-steak guy. Ask my mother about all the times I hid the potatoes in my glass of milk or fed them to the dog. I thoroughly exasperated her whenever we were in Ireland: hold the colcannon and champ, please! For me, it's egg whites on whole wheat toast with ketchup. It's hamburger with steak sauce. I didn't want to get on a plane at 225 pounds and come back a bag of bones.

I also had a bred-in-the-bone connection to the city where I was currently assigned. I wanted to do a deep dive into New York, not acquire superficial exposure to cultures I would never effectively penetrate. Hadn't I just abandoned one career because I knew I could never truly excel at it? I didn't want a repeat of my auditing dead end.

Plenty of agents accepted the counterterrorism assignment, but a couple of New Yorkers like me who didn't want to work in counterterrorism finagled a way to stay in the city. One probationary agent managed to extend his SO-2 rotation and hung on for months until he got a permanent assignment in organized crime. He rolled the dice and it paid off. Maybe that's what you had to do.

Anybody who tells you that combating organized crime is strictly a patriotic duty is disingenuous. It definitely is a patriotic duty, but it's also setting sail for uncharted territory with a crew, a compass, and courage. I had never met a mobster and probably wouldn't know one if he flashed his gold pinkie ring in my face. But with my street smarts, I felt I could be of use on an OC squad. I wanted to help unravel a criminal enterprise that might have been my path in some alternate universe.

I sought out Kevin Donovan, the ASAC in the NYO's organized crime branch. Kevin, relatively new to his post, went to bat for me with his higher-ups. He drafted me in December 1998 and assigned me to C-10, the OC squad dedicated primarily to investigating the Bonanno crime family. *Grateful* doesn't even begin to describe how I felt. I wasn't going to let Kevin down.

Cue the *Dragnet* music. No sooner did I get to the squad of my dreams than Jack Stubing, my supervisor, asked me if I wanted to go to cyber instead. The Bureau was engaged in a major cyber trial and, with my background, I was seen as an asset. Again, the needs of the Bureau.

It's a miracle I didn't laugh in Jack's face. That weekend course I took in Excel and WordPerfect convinced my superiors—mistakenly—that I was a computer whiz. Look, in 1998, all you had to do was log on to a console running on MS-DOS and you just about qualified for a Turing Award. C-10 had one computer for the entire squad. People hardly touched it.

I didn't want to come off as high maintenance, but I had no trouble telling Jack, "I want to work with you." He was happy to hear it, and I was happy to stay.

My relationship with my girlfriend Millie had been on again, off again for months, while my romance with OC at the FBI was just beginning. The beauty of OC? As each day passed, I was learning the mob was into everything. Drugs. Murder. Public corruption. Sure, white collar and cyber too. Wherever they can make money. That's their bottom line. I was going to find out how NYC really rolls.

The Bureau was the new love of my life.

5

I LEARN FROM AN FBI LEGEND

THE ORGANIZED CRIME BRANCH at 26 Federal had about three hundred people working on a handful of gnarly cases. One involved Sammy "the Bull" Gravano, the confessed murderer and government witness I'd read about in Maas's *Underboss.* Another involved the January 1998 slaying of DeCavalcante associate Joseph "Joe Pitts" Conigliaro, a sixty-seven-year-old wheelchair-bound loan shark with a decades-long reputation as a ruthless SOB. Another case had Jack Stubing direct my squad mates Jim McGoey, Kim McCaffrey, and Jeff Sallet to take down Bonanno crime boss Joseph Massino and gut his loan-sharking and money-laundering empire.

I was excited to pull the curtain back on a world of Vinny Gorgeouses and Carmine the Snakes whose mob empires were largely built on loan shark practices. I didn't understand any of it yet, but I would.

It wasn't exactly balls-to-the-wall when I arrived at C-10. Early days were so quiet you could have installed pews and celebrated mass. The squad's cases, overseen by longtime agents, had hit a brick wall. The FBI was coming off a hiring freeze, and new agents hadn't had time to hit their stride. But things were changing fast. You can't know this when you're a rookie, but you are about to change the workplace culture. Young people can do that. They're energetic. Ambitious. Impatient. They want to leave their mark. They're just waiting for the right moment to pounce. My entry into C-10 couldn't have been better timed.

First, I got matched up with Stacy Bowery, a take-no-crap agent who became my partner. Stacy graduated from Quantico training in 98-06—one class behind me—and I was always busting her chops about my unsurpassable one-month seniority over her. A more fearless agent I never saw. No agent, no prosecutor, no mobster could rattle her.

Second, in my initial month at C-10, I got word that George Hanna was coming by. Hanna was an FBI legend. As a brand-new agent in the late 1970s, Hanna was packing up to move from Brooklyn to Jacksonville, Florida, his first post-Quantico assignment. En route from his house to a dry cleaner's one Monday, he walked past a bar. Through the window, he saw the owner and stopped in to say hello. Talk about luck: Hanna chanced upon a robbery. He had his FBI-issued gun on him and shot one of the robbers dead. He persuaded the other one to throw down his weapon.* William Webster, the FBI director, got wind of Hanna's heroism and rewarded him with his choice of assignment. Hanna asked to stay in New York and was assigned to C-31, a Queens-based squad tasked with bringing down violent truck hijackers.

He couldn't unpack fast enough. One more New Yorker who was too in love with the city's sinners and saints to work anywhere else.

Hanna had gone to high school with guys who went the wrong way and fell under the mob's sway. By the time I met him, he had relationships with agents, NYPD detectives, neighborhood merchants, and truck hijackers themselves. He was sharp as a razor and all street. He understood that but for a twist of fate, he might have ended up on a truck-hijacking crew too. I was going to make George Hanna my mentor.

In January 1998, eleven months before I got to C-10, Hanna got a phone call from Ralph Guarino, a longtime FBI informant and small-fry criminal who made a living stealing stuff out of warehouses on the

* Years later Hanna convinced the surviving robber to become a cooperating witness for the government.

Brooklyn and New Jersey waterfronts. A lot of Ralph's loot came from trucks held up at gunpoint by members or associates of New York's Five Families: the Bonannos, Colombos, Gambinos, Genoveses, and Luccheses. Ralph, however, was primarily "with" the DeCavalcantes, the organized crime family so under the radar they were generically known as the North Jersey Mafia. As an informant, he'd had voluntary chats with Hanna—his FBI handler—and given him intel about the underworld activities of his fellow criminals.

"I got a problem," Ralph told George Hanna from a pay phone in Brooklyn.

Hanna listened.

Ralph had gotten the brainy idea to rob a Brink's truck making a scheduled cash delivery to a Bank of America branch office on the eleventh floor of 1 World Trade Center. Ralph was forty-one and he was "tired of fucking earning," as he put it.* Walking off with an easy $1.6 million haul would pave the way to a swell life of broads and fun.

If Ralph had gone into the North Tower with his three partners in crime, he would have made damn sure they all executed the gambit as planned. But Ralph was off in La La Land picturing his merry men laden with riches. He couldn't know that the New York papers were about to dub his fellow robbers "the Three Stooges" for taking their masks off in front of the WTC cameras. One robber was caught within hours, the other two within days. Ralph's accomplices were either true blue or scared shitless, but they'd refused to dime him out.

Ralph was smart enough to call Hanna. He wanted to get ahead of a potential arrest.

Hanna had a solution.

Ralph would become a full-time cooperating witness for the FBI. He had no choice. If he got caught and was hit with RICO, the federal Racketeer Influenced and Corrupt Organizations Act used to pass long sentences on OC members and associates for crimes ordered or committed, he'd be looking at life in a federal penitentiary. No longer just an informant, Ralph had now become a *proactive witness*. Under Hanna's

---

* Ralph's quotation comes from *Made Men: The True Rise-and-Fall Story of a New Jersey Mob Family* by Greg B. Smith (Berkeley Books, 2003), 27.

direction, he would wear a wire and make consensual recordings the FBI and New York federal district courts could use as evidence against other organized crime figures at trial. If Ralph provided us with "substantial assistance," he'd get a 5K letter and avoid life in prison.

For most of 1998 and 1999, nobody ever suspected Ralph of working with the feds. Wired up, our inside man could help the FBI pull down the veil on the Five Families of New York—and possibly the DeCavalcantes in New Jersey, whose century-long union tampering, loan-sharking, and extortionist activities were about to get attention from both the FBI and HBO.

When George Hanna stopped by C-10, he was looking for help. He was great with people, not so great with paperwork. Hanna often drove from Queens to 26 Federal to ask the FNGs—like Stacy and me—to join other agents in transcribing Ralph's cassette tape recordings. Hanna took the two of us into a twenty-second-floor rear office. He pointed to a shitpile of recordings and surveillance logs. I was like, *Oh my God.*

Hanna asked if Stacy and I would make transcriptions, get them into the case file, track them, submit the recordings to ELSUR—our electronic surveillance unit—and make copies for the assistant US attorney (AUSA). A lot of Ralph's three-hundred-odd recordings had been done in nightclubs and diners, places full of laughter and slamming doors and clattering dishes. Mobsters often spoke in whispers and passed notes to each other. They code-switched: they'd move from recognizable conversation to euphemism and hints. It would be challenging to make out what they were saying. A two-hour-long tape could take five times as long to transcribe.

If anybody at my previous jobs had asked me to organize, decipher, and transcribe a mountain of tapes—if my father had asked me to do that—I'd have mutinied. When the FBI legend asked for help, Stacy and I looked at each other and said, "When do we start?"

Working on these tapes was a great way to learn a case. You listen to a mob guy on a recording and it hits you: *Wait, I just saw a surveillance photo of him. Now I've put a name with a face with a voice. Wait, did he just admit to committing a crime on tape?*

In the department of "You Never Know What's Going to Be Useful," I leveraged my friendship with a Manhattan College pal, Kevin Frawley, to help C-10 evaluate Ralph's heist. Kevin worked on the eighty-fourth floor of the World Trade Center's South Tower for Euro Brokers, a financial brokerage company, and he was able to tell us approximately what Ralph's stolen foreign currency was worth.

I was never so happy to do shit work until now. Thanks to the work ethic I inherited from my dad, I was working with Stacy to bring order to the law.

6

BASICALLY, IT'S A SEASON OF HELL

In late March 1999, just as Stacy and I were getting our tracking system in place, my dad suffered a seizure at the gas station. He was about to test-drive a customer's car but collapsed before he got behind the wheel. Thank God. A close friend of his happened to stop by and found him lying on the floor. He got him over to Our Lady of Mercy—the Bronx hospital that had tried unsuccessfully for years to buy the land underneath the gas station.

We didn't want to jump to conclusions, but each of us in the family had been making our own observations for a while. My dad was still going to the gas station every day, but I for one noticed that the man with the steel-trap mind had become forgetful. After his collapse, my mom made an appointment with a doctor in the city. The diagnosis was swift: my father had a brain tumor. A second medical opinion at Memorial Sloan Kettering was even more nonnegotiable: Dad had three months to live.

My dad's response to his diagnosis was adamant: no chemo, no radiation. We set him up in the living room and made him as comfortable as we could. We shut the gas station down immediately and took stock of the money situation. On top of being devastated, we now had to face some unpleasant truths.

Even in the best of times, my dad had been good-hearted to a fault. If you came into his gas station and needed a new transmission for your car, he'd let you pay it off in installments. Time and again, he got beat that way. I'd made a manila folder for him labeled DEADBEATS, and it was yea thick. But in recent months, when his customers "forgot" to make payments, he hadn't been going after them at all.

Unbeknownst to any of us, my father had also stopped making mortgage payments on the house. He had let his overpriced whole-life insurance lapse. Once I joined the Bureau, I didn't have time to help my parents manage their finances, and for all intents and purposes, nobody had been minding the store for months, maybe a year. My auditor brain went into high gear. How much did my dad owe in back taxes, interest, and penalties?

To our alarm, Jimmy and Christine McElearney were tens of thousands of dollars in arrears with their mortgage payments. Their bank pounced like a panther on prey: we were in imminent danger of losing the house. You want to see someone come unglued? Picture my mom contemplating the loss of her home and her husband at the same time.

As if one wave of financial turbulence weren't enough, another one of long standing surfaced to deal us a double blow. This problem originated in 1987 when my grandmother passed away. My grandfather rewrote his will two months later and disclosed its contents to all his children. The family learned that my father, the eldest son, would inherit the farm in County Monaghan, Ireland, upon my grandfather's death.* From that moment on, the inheritance hung over us like a storm cloud ready to burst.

My father's family—Aunt Bridgie in upstate New York, Aunt Alice in Queens, Aunt Kathleen in Ireland, and to a much lesser extent Uncle Peter in England—were in a fury. The sisters thought the farm should pass down to Kathleen, because she lived in Ireland. Every so often, my

* Within days of my paternal grandmother's death, my mom lost both of her parents as well. I flew with her to Ireland and we rendezvoused with my dad at JFK Airport on his way back from his mother's funeral to Yonkers. Three deaths in twelve days.

aunts would gather to hold family meetings where they would pressure my dad to say the farm would go to Kathleen upon their father's death. Some of these meetings were at our house in Yonkers. The aunts could pressure away till the cows came home. My grandfather was adamant that the property go to his eldest son.

I had nothing to do with any of it. This wasn't my generation's headache.

Shortly after my dad got his cancer diagnosis, his father died. Suddenly, his generation's headache became my headache: my dad asked me to handle the Irish property affairs. He had his own battle to fight.

Kathleen back in Ireland couldn't understand why her "well-off" American brother wouldn't come and pay his final respects to their father. Of course, he was under doctor's orders not to fly. She didn't see him the day of the funeral, sitting up on the sofa, a blanket over his shoulders, his chin trembling. All she knew was that her father's will was about to become a reality: brother Jimmy was going to inherit the farm.

My dad could barely concentrate long enough even to say "Monaghan." Sometimes the pain got so bad he had to be rushed to the hospital. A couple of times the priest came to the house to administer last rites. How could Jimmy McElearney handle the legalities of a will? He turned the big ball of wax over to me.

Here was my situation in a nutshell: I was a rookie agent on an organized crime squad and spent every waking hour loving my life and learning the ropes. But my dad had been diagnosed with terminal cancer. To stave off the bank repo of our house, my twenty-six-year-old brother and I suddenly had to contemplate taking on $250,000 worth of our parents' debt. Despite my vaunted career as a bank auditor, what did I know about assuming a mortgage? And my crowning glory? I was about to get tangled up in a binational legal knot I was in no way competent to unravel. It crossed my mind that I might have to leave the FBI. How else was I going to manage my finances and the family's on public-sector peanuts?

Whatever sympathy I might have had for my aunts and uncle flew out the window when Aunt Kathleen splurged on a plane ticket to the States to plead her cause. It was bewildering. Kathleen knew our family was about to lose the roof over our heads. Why didn't *she* try to help *us*? People say you're only as good as your last good deed, and that was sure true about my dad's relatives. They didn't remember how generous Jimmy had been whenever any of them fell on hard times.

Only my Uncle Peter in England was emotionally disengaged, because he had another swath of land coming to him in the will. What I couldn't respect about my aunts was the deviousness. Even as my father lay on his deathbed, they congregated at our house to try to bamboozle him into signing the farm over to Kathleen. A couple of them would ambush my mom in the kitchen while Kathleen tried to coax my dad into signing.

Death brings out the worst in people.

One evening my mom came into my bedroom and told me to wake up. I'd gone to bed early because I had an early-morning surveillance, so if my mom dared to wake me, the news couldn't be good.

She was furious. "They're ganging up on me," she said. "They want me to get your dad to sign over the farm."

I stormed downstairs and slammed my hand on our glass coffee table.

"Get the fuck out of here," I yelled at the lot of 'em. They scattered like geese. They had never heard dear nephew Séamus talk like this before.

Now we had another job on our hands: one of us had to stand sentry over my father 24/7 to make sure no one coerced him into signing away his parents' bequest.

What was I supposed to do? Leave the FBI and do guard duty at the house in Yonkers? I couldn't help but think back to my days at Quantico, when I feared getting kicked out of the program. Only this time I wasn't pounding a stretcher after my knee gave out or defending my integrity to my class counselors. My decision was easy: I wouldn't let the family's domestic and financial troubles deter me from my life's purpose. I'd hold on to C-10 until my knuckles bled red, white, and blue.

7

IN THE MIDDLE OF CRAP, I GET MY EDUCATION

With the help of a lawyer my mom knew, Liam and I purchased our parents' house in May 1999. Two months into our dad's diagnosis, my kid brother and I were business partners. Real adults, the two of us, but that didn't stop Liam from razzing me about starting my day with sit-ups. "You need a strong core to transcribe those monster cassette tapes," he said.

"Fine, kiddo," I said. "But just so's you know, those cassette tapes are going to become the core of C-10's case against a bunch of some pretty bad guys."

A few bright spots: Millie and I got back together, and she was a real sweetheart with my dad. He adored her. She would bring him spareribs and just hang out with him. In June we sold the gas station. And Liam sent an application in to join the FBI as a mechanic. He'd been working alongside our father since he was a little kid—like five, six years old—and he had to be the most experienced mechanic in New York State. He couldn't join the Bureau as an agent, because he didn't have a college degree.

Liam wasn't entirely wrong about the back-office nature of my work on C-10. To be honest, watching water boil can be more fascinating than transcribing a recording. And sitting with a Dictaphone device in my ears was not what this contender signed up to do. But George Hanna wouldn't have asked Stacy and me to tackle those recordings if so much weren't riding on them. For one, the prosecutors needed transcriptions to help them prepare indictments. Two, the words in those transcriptions could convince a bad guy to flip.

Hanna operated Ralph Guarino as a proactive witness from January 1998 to December 1999. Stacy and I began culling through Ralph's recordings in December 1998 to transcribe only what the AUSAs would need to prosecute a case. That meant accurate but not always word-for-word transcripts. It took us hours to produce a single one of them. But the effort was worthwhile. As we began to learn, the combination of photo, recording, and witness testimony was the perfect formula for a conviction.

Instead of feeling shunted away in a back room doing grunt work, we came to see our job as a blessing in disguise. First, we showed our bosses we could be trusted to get the work done. Second, we got a crash course in what it takes to develop a government witness.

For instance, Hanna gave us a heads-up on a key problem: when jurors hear that the FBI is working with a witness and that the FBI is supporting him in the lifestyle to which he has become accustomed, they get their backs up. The government has its hands full explaining that a witness cannot suddenly live on, say, $1,000 a month after indulging a $10,000-a-month lifestyle with his mob partners.

Take Ralph himself. As a mob associate—an individual connected to a crime family but not an official member of it—he was the kind of low-man-on-the-totem-pole schmuck that mobsters love to abuse. He was always eager to ingratiate himself to the higher-ups in the hopes that one day he might become a made man. For a mob wannabe, no criminal act was too horrible, no dinner tab too high, no pleasure trip too costly. Ralph couldn't say, "Hey, fellas, I'm having a cash flow problem. Can you stand me a C-note?" The FBI had to fund Ralph to keep him a credible asset. And wouldn't we have loved for a witness to get made and capture the induction ceremony on tape!

Defense attorneys tell the jury that this means the FBI buys testimony—and that it's a sign of our corruption. The defense needs to discredit us so they can deliver a not-guilty verdict for their client. They're just doing what they get paid to do. It's a fallacy, though, to accuse us of buying testimony. We're paying the witness to *stop* committing criminal acts while giving him cover to get the bad guys on tape. You can't expect a witness to record mobsters by night and steam lattes for $11.64 an hour by day.

Listening to Ralph's tapes gave Stacy and me a de facto master's degree in mob mentality. We also got a de facto PhD in mob surveillance.

Hanna made it job one to safeguard Ralph 24/7. SO-2 surveillance team leader Joe Sconzo, an agent and attorney by trade, was responsible for watching Ralph. Hanna asked Stacy and me to compile all of SO-2's surveillance logs. Sometimes the surveillance team tailed Ralph more than once a day, and over the course of two years, we had about a thousand logs.

Remember that Excel course I took on my own dime? I knew the program well enough now to generate a month-by-month spreadsheet detailing every single surveillance we did on Ralph. Let's say Ralph was meeting with person A at Pinocchio's Restaurant in Elizabeth, New Jersey. Ralph might not know the true names of the other two people at the meeting. So inside two Excel cells, I would write "UNKNOWN MALE." Those same two unknown males would pop up at another meeting and Ralph would get their names and pay attention to the cars they drove. I'd ask the operations center to run their license plates and find out their legal names. I'd get their DMV photos and make sure the plates and photo matched the person in the restaurant. When I was sure of the identity, I'd go back to my spreadsheet and type in the legal name and "Johnny Two Times," or whatever nicknames they had. I'd note what clothes they were wearing. I'd jot down whether or not we had them on a recording. Without ever meeting these guys face to face, Stacy and I were tracking every player involved in the various crime families Ralph worked with. My spreadsheet got us up to speed.

Once an auditor, always an auditor.

I went from thinking my transcription work was a drag to seeing it as Thor's hammer. We would use it to crush the DeCavalcante family. The fact is, for me, the tedium of transcription was an antidote for that sick feeling in the pit of my stomach that said, *Your dad is dying, boy, and your mom's about to become homeless. What in God's name are you going to do?*

I arrived super early at 26 Federal Plaza on Mondays and put in twelve-hour days. I came in on weekends. Saturdays I worked all day. Not so different from the seven-day-a-week schedule I used to have at my father's gas station, except for taking off half of Sunday. Not quite enough time to sustain my relationship with Millie, who lived more than an hour from Yonkers. For better or worse, I had a one-track mind. I ate, drank, and breathed transcription.

Liam wasn't the only one razzing me about it. John DiCaprio, an NYPD detective working with C-10, used to tease me about "Séamus and his binders." Nobody was laughing, though, when Stacy and I could tell the prosecutors what a government witness said, where he said it, and who he said it to. The prosecution could depend on us to quote chapter and verse.

As part of the legal "discovery" process, we also had to share what we knew with the defense attorneys. They couldn't dispute their client's misdeeds and whereabouts when we had a surveillance picture, a recording, and witness testimony as evidence we could present at trial. The transcriptions and our spreadsheet helped spur mob defendants to plead guilty.

All of this we learned before we even set foot in a courtroom.

Best of all was watching George Hanna handle a government witness. In addition to protecting Ralph's identity as the WTC heist architect, he had to make sure Ralph didn't crack under the pressure of wearing a wire. Moreover, Hanna had to guard against his witness committing crimes without our knowledge. He was allowed to continue with some criminal activities, such as gambling and selling illegal cigarettes. We couldn't let his mob connections wonder why this schmuck was suddenly walking the straight and narrow. But these activities had to be authorized—and directed—by the FBI and the AUSA to build a case.

Life's complicated. So is working at the Bureau.

Hanna also took advantage of Ralph's jaunts to Florida. He would head down there with his surveillance team and bug the mob guys' hotel rooms with video and audio. It's hard to dispute camera evidence in court.

You could forgive someone with Hanna's success rate for boasting. But George Hanna was not that kind of man. He never forgot that things can go wrong. With your cassette recording device, for example. You can record a three-hour conversation in which the mobster divulges incriminating information, only to have your recording device go on the fritz. You have no record of anything. You can't exactly have your government witness go back and say, "Can we talk about everything we talked about yesterday?" To recoup your losses, you might have to coach the witness to say, "I can't believe what you told me yesterday about X." It might take several conversations for you to recapture the gold lost in that original excavation.

In my first year as an FBI agent, I never once saw George Hanna be anything but respectful to Ralph. In fact, he would give Ralph as big a monthly stipend as possible. It wasn't easy to do that. He had to fill out a lot of paperwork, jump through hoops to get approvals, and go pick up the money himself at our financial management unit, or FMU. But Hanna didn't mind sweating the small stuff. He knew being decent to Ralph would result in evidence at trial.

It was easy to like George Hanna. And he liked us. He loved Stacy. When he introduced us to other law enforcement people, he would play us up. Like "Stacy's great. She's really good at surveillance" or whatever. Stacy and I wanted to live up to the reputation this legend created for us. No way would we let him down.

Despite all the precautions Hanna took, Ralph's mob contacts began whispering that Ralph was working with the government. Rumors began flying that he had masterminded the bank heist in the World Trade Center. Why was he still out on the street? It doesn't take more than suspicion for a violent criminal organization to eliminate a possible rat. For Ralph's own safety, Hanna pulled him off the street. Ralph Guarino's days as a proactive witness were over.

The time had come for the government to make a move. The Southern District of New York would issue arrests for thirty-nine alleged members and associates of the Gambino, Bonanno, Lucchese, Colombo, and DeCavalcante organized crime families. Thanks to George Hanna and Ralph Guarino, the Southern District indictment included the names and "ranks" of many alleged DeCavalcante made men: "soldiers" Joseph "Tin Ear" Sclafani and Jimmy Gallo; "captain" Anthony Rotondo; and acting boss Vincent "Vinny Ocean" Palermo, among others. Ralph said they were all big fish.

The arrests were scheduled for December 2, 1999. C-10 was going to find out who was a minnow and who was a whale.

I fully expected to keep transcribing recordings and filing surveillance logs into the new millennium. There was no end to them. Maybe I would be like the bureaucrats who felled Al Capone by getting him charged with tax evasion. No shame in that. But I knew myself. I wouldn't be completely happy making an arrest from behind a desk. Was I ever going to meet a bad guy face to face?

To my surprise and delight, Jack Stubing named rookie me as team leader for one of the December 2 arrests. Becoming a team leader was a big deal. Team leaders are often seasoned agents, and I had been on the squad less than one crazy year. My target: a DeCavalcante soldier named Anthony Capo.

Capo had already been in prison a couple of times and had a reputation with law enforcement for being an asshole. And here I, a graduate of three Catholic schools, had gotten the ticket to arrest him. I made a conscious decision to bring in a violent hater of cops and G-men while treating him with respect, as I had seen George Hanna do. I was worried, though. I wouldn't admit it to anybody, not even to Stacy, but I wondered whether I was up to the task. Would I be emotionally distracted by my personal issues? The family was still reeling from the sale of Dad's gas station. Dad's own condition continued to deteriorate. He'd been admitted to St. John's Hospital in Yonkers and then transferred to hospice care in Hawthorne, New York. On top of these disruptions in my family, we still had the ordeal in Ireland hanging over us.

You know what's interesting, though? Despite all the chaos rocking my life, when I accepted the assignment to arrest Anthony Capo, the words rolled off my tongue like I was Seneca. I was going to do what I was born to do.

8

IT'S PRIME TIME: THE COWBOYS VS. THE STEELERS

On Thanksgiving Day, a week before our big arrest, George Hanna, Stacy, and I sat in a hotel basement across from a Brooklyn contractor named Americo "Mike" Massa. Nearly two years earlier, the Manhattan District Attorney's Office had sent Javier Solano, one of its assistant DAs, to interview Massa about the murder of Joseph Conigliaro. Joe Pitts, as Conigliaro was known, was the brutal DeCavalcante associate, loan shark, and narcotics trafficker who spent a couple of decades in a wheelchair after a gang-that-couldn't-shoot-straight fiasco. The story went round that in the 1970s, Joe Pitts and a DeCavalcante soldier named Jimmy Gallo tried to shoot one of their loan shark "customers"—a suspected informant—during a shakedown. In the fog of war, Pitts and Gallo shot each other. The shakedown victim ran off, Gallo walked away with barely a scratch, and Joe Pitts ended up paralyzed from the waist down.*

Massa had given ADA Solano what he thought was an airtight alibi about his whereabouts on the night of January 23, 1998, when Joe Pitts

* Once Joe Gallo got out of prison, the shakedown victim turned up dead with a single bullet in his head. Gallo used to boast about having gotten away with killing a rat.

got shot for the second time in his life, drove himself off to Methodist Hospital in Brooklyn, and died on the operating table. That day at the hotel, Stacy, George, and I were even more suspicious. The word on the street was that Joe Pitts had been extorting Mike Massa. To us, Massa appeared to have a motive to kill Joe Pitts. Our goal was getting this turkey to cooperate.

I must have listened to Massa's recorded conversation with ADA Solano fifty times. No two ways about it. Massa was lying. I knew where the hole was in his story.

Massa had told Solano something like "I drove over to the home of Joey Brideson. He was in Joe Pitts's crew too. He wasn't there. I spoke with Joey's wife. Mrs. Brideson said Joe Pitts had pulled up to the curb a little while ago. Joey ran out to talk to him, got into his car, and the two of them drove off together."

Massa told ADA Solano, "I'm surprised Joe Pitts was even alive and driving."

Bingo. That was Massa's self-incriminating comment. Mrs. Brideson had no idea that Joe Pitts was bleeding from a gunshot wound. How could Massa have known?

Can't say I knew my rookie ass from my rookie elbow, but I felt I could flip Massa.

"I don't blame you for hating Joe Pitts," I told Massa. "He was extorting the crap out of you. He'd have killed you himself for one late payment. If you tell us how he was murdered, you're likely to get a shorter prison sentence. Otherwise, man, you're looking at LIFE."

I tried to convince him: numbers are better than letters. Any prison term is better than LIFE. LIFE means you're coming out in a box.

I felt bad for the guy. He was forty-three years old. Illiterate. Scared. Try as I might, I could not reason him into becoming a government witness.

God knows I was itching to flip some weak link that would ultimately lead to a bigger story. But Massa wasn't it.

Eight days later, Mike Massa was irrelevant. I didn't need him anymore.

By December 2, 1999, my dad had been in the Dominican Sisters of Rosary Hill Home,* a nearby nursing facility and hospice, for two months. He could die at any moment. I knew that. But I had to lead an OC team in the arrest of a violent made man. I'm remembering a few words from a poem we read at Cardinal Spellman that goes, "Because I could not stop for Death—"

In the days before the arrest, I conducted a site survey of Anthony Capo's home, a red split-level house in the South Beach neighborhood of Staten Island. I needed to gather information and head off possible obstacles. I had a lot of administrative checks to make too.

First I had to run Capo's rap sheet to see what kind of criminal he was. I had to know precisely the charges against him. Then I had to assemble an arrest team of eight people that would descend upon Capo with utmost efficiency. A complicating factor was an alternate arrest team organized by the Eastern District of New York. Those guys were competing with the FBI and the Southern District of New York to make the arrest and flip Capo for the sake of their future mob prosecutions. As usual, George Hanna was wily. He said I could defuse the competition by absorbing an EDNY person into my team.

I didn't know much about Capo's domestic life. I had to verify who else might be living in the split-level house. Could somebody have an active warrant out for their arrest? The FBI ran these checks to ensure our safety and the safety of everyone in the house. I went out a couple days before the arrest to do surveillance. The last thing I wanted was to face some armed crazies who thought I'd come to arrest them.

I also had to choose a staging area. I settled on the entrance to South Beach at Father Capodanno Boulevard and Sand Lane five minutes south of the Verrazzano-Narrows Bridge and several blocks from Capo's house. My team and I would depend on our Hagstrom maps to navigate our way to a parking lot before dawn. Eight cars. No lights.

I was so anxious about oversleeping that I got out of bed at two thirty in the morning. I washed up, shaved, and headed out from

* Rosary Hill Home in Hawthorne, New York, was founded by Mother Mary Alphonsa Lathrop, the younger daughter of American novelist Nathaniel Hawthorne.

Yonkers to Staten Island. I stopped off to buy coffee and donuts for my team, because they were doing me a favor that day.

It was pitch black when I pulled into the parking lot at 4:00 AM and the kind of cold you get when Satan flaps his wings. An icy mist from Gravesend Bay tormented my team as we huddled in a tight knot to organize the arrest of Anthony Capo.

I wasn't personally acquainted with most of the members on my team, except for Kenny McCabe, a fabled mob investigator for the Southern District of New York, and I didn't know him well either. One guy, Mike Campi, was a well-respected agent on C-5—the Genovese squad. An agent named Paul Tambrino came over from C-16—the Gambino squad. He was the agent I coopted because he was leaguing with the EDNY to arrest Capo first. Only one team member, Brian Getson, was a friend. He'd gone through Quantico with me. All of these guys, plus a Drug Enforcement Administration agent and an NYPD detective, were more seasoned than I was. I wasn't concerned only about being strong in front of Anthony Capo. I had to be tough in front of my colleagues.

I wasn't a complete newbie. One of my first surveillances was at the wake of Gerlando Sciascia, a Sicilian-born mobster nicknamed "George from Canada" because of his alignment with the Montreal mob. Jim McGoey, Kim McCaffrey, and Jeff Sallet, my C-10 squad mates investigating the Bonannos, knew Sciascia had been a big cheese in the crime family. Our federal government indicted him in the early 1980s for moving heroin from Canada to the United States. Rather than stand trial, Sciascia gave the slip to our authorities and managed the Montreal–New York heroin trade from Canada. Even though the Canadians eventually extradited him to the United States, Sciascia wriggled out of a guilty verdict allegedly by bribing a juror with $10,000. To all external appearances, Sciascia went legit when he established a construction company in the Bronx. On March 18, 1999, shortly before I learned about my dad's brain tumor, Sciascia was found shot to death on Boller Avenue, a dead-end street four miles east of Bainbridge Avenue.

A whole lot of spiffily dressed people showed up to pay Sciascia their last respects. I was still new at surveillance the day I went to his wake at the McMahon, Lyon & Hartnett Funeral Home in White Plains, a town fifteen miles north of my parents' house in Yonkers and two blocks from an FBI satellite office. Winter was over and I had a clear view of the unabashed mourners streaming into the funeral home. I was surprised to see so many of the Bonannos among them. Unlike former Gambino crime boss John Gotti, famous for his public strolls in his double-breasted suits, this family kept a low profile. Bonanno boss Joe Massino understood that showboating had gotten Gotti way too much attention, and he steered clear of Italian life cycle events. He had even gone so far as to shut down all the Bonanno social clubs to stymie the government's eavesdropping. But for reasons yet unknown to the Bureau, Massino must have wanted his high-level people to show up to Sciascia's wake in White Plains.

The Bonannos who came had Kenny McCabe to thank for documenting their presence. Kenny used weddings, christenings, and funerals as a portal into the mob's intricate social network. He'd park his van as close to the church or funeral home as he could get and start snapping pictures. Thanks to his sharp memory and his quick draw on the camera trigger, Kenny helped identify hundreds of mobsters. He used to put cooperating witnesses in front of his La Cosa Nostra photo albums and ask them to identify made men and their associates. Prosecutors depended on Kenny to help them build a case.

From my vantage point in an FBI van, I watched Kenny and watched the gangsters watching him through the tinted glass of his van. The mob guys would bang on the hood as they walked past, but Kenny was unflappable. He just kept taking pictures of them and the license plates on their cars. Kenny had encountered every species of gangster in his eighteen years as an NYPD detective and in his twenty-plus years as a Southern District investigator, and he had no illusions about the depravity to which these guys could sink. Yet he did his job without a trace of condescension. In fact, former acting Lucchese boss and government witness Al D'Arco told his biographers that Kenny "was like a friendly enemy, always out there in his white

Dodge taking notes on us. . . . One wedding they brought a piece of cake out to him."*

Without my surveillance experience, and without learning from the best pros involved in an arrest, I would have been sweating bricks at the thought of confronting Anthony Capo. Instead, I leaned on protocol. I could show my team a sketch of Capo's house; you don't want to approach any building in ignorance. I could go over the FBI's deadly force policy and explain that agents who reasonably believe the arrestee poses a serious physical threat can defend themselves.

I was nervous, but I knew I had prepared a full year for this arrest. With my transcription knowledge of the arrestees named in the Southern District indictment, they were almost as familiar to me as . . . family. I was ready to lead my team to Capo's red split-level house and do my job.

Just before we drove out in a phalanx of FBI cruisers to Anthony Capo's home, I called the NYPD's 122nd Precinct to let them know we were going to be in their area.

5:55 AM. A light fog. The smell of petrochemicals and fish.

We'd execute at 6:00 AM.

We pulled up to Capo's house. I sent a couple of agents to the rear of the ground-level garage to make sure nobody inside the house left out the back door. Everyone else in my crew followed me up the raised concrete walkway to five oddly diagonal steps. I unclenched my jaw and knocked hard on the front door.

Fortunately, nobody could hear my heart pounding when a petite bottle-blonde woman came to the door. She was wearing a robe and looked wide awake, as if she had been expecting an entourage of law enforcement. In fact, I barely got "FBI" out of my mouth when she said, "Anthony's at his mom's house." She introduced herself as "Anthony's wife" and gave us her mother-in-law's address. My team and I decamped to a two-story gray house several blocks away.

* *Mob Boss: The Life of Little Al D'Arco, the Man Who Brought Down the Mafia* by Jerry Capeci and Tom Robbins (Thomas Dunne Books, 2013), loc. 2614–2819, Kindle.

Now I was flying blind. I had no sketch to go by. My whole team, every last one of us, was just a little bit more wired.

Soon we were heading up a concrete driveway lined by a wire-mesh fence and a flat-top boxwood hedge. We waited at the door of a neat aluminum-sided house. I took note of the teapot in the left ground-floor window and a wreath on the front door. *Holy Mother of God, it's like normal people live here*, I thought.

The door edged open. It was him.

Because of Kenny's photos, I recognized Anthony Capo by the haughty slant of his eyes. Standing before me, though, in flannel pajamas and T-shirt, he wasn't the same intimidating guy in the pictures. This man looked frail, probably on some kind of drug. He didn't put up any resistance. Neither did his mom and stepdad huddled together behind him.

If you're trying to be a tough guy and you're not, the mob guys will figure you out in five minutes. I was a sort-of-nice Catholic boy from the Bronx, unless you pissed me off, and I wasn't going to pretend otherwise. I would approach Capo with respect, just as I'd seen George Hanna do with his collars. If the shoe had been on the other foot, I'd want someone to treat me like that.

I asserted my leadership by assigning an agent to go watch Capo change into street clothes. Capo came out dressed in jeans, sweater, and a Dallas Cowboys football jacket. He was underdressed for the weather. Capo knew the drill: No jewelry. The less clothing, the better.

I handcuffed Capo and guided him into the backseat of my Bu-car,* a Pontiac Grand Prix. I got in behind Brian Getson, our driver, and slid in next to Capo. I told him he was under arrest by the Southern District of New York on RICO charges. I didn't go into detail about RICO. I simply identified Brian and myself and read Capo his Miranda rights.

Capo invoked his right to remain silent and obtain counsel. I kept my fists balled up so I could punch him in case he tried to reach across me and strangle Brian, kick out a window, or wriggle out of the handcuffs. The perps on TV cop shows always do stuff like that. It can happen in real life too. You never know. *Don't be complacent*, I instructed myself.

---

* Short for the FBI's "Bureau car."

I reached inside my FBI flak jacket and pulled out a Hershey bar and a cardboard pint of orange juice. Ralph Guarino told us Capo had diabetes, a fact that had gone straight into my Excel spreadsheet.

"You don't miss a thing," Capo said. But he thanked me and drank down the OJ.

Polite. Respectful. I'm thinking, *What's wrong with this picture?*

A sugar hit sufficed for now, but Capo said he needed his meds: metoprolol at 10:00 AM and a Humulin insulin injection before lunch. This man was chronologically thirty-eight years old, only six years older than I was. But years of hard living had made him flabby and a little slow moving. I could take him if I had to.

I nodded at Capo's Dallas Cowboys jacket. "I'm a Pittsburgh Steeler fan myself," I said.

Capo took the bait. "The Cowboys mopped the floor with the Steelers in '96, 27–17," he said.

I said, "America's team, my ass."

I could swear a bolt of electricity rattled Capo's bones.

"Pittsburgh came back that year after a long drought," I said.

"Yeah, well, Dallas had them for breakfast."

"They'll be back next year."

"The Cowboys'll have a second helping."

"Easy, tiger. We still beat you in two other Super Bowls." I was busting his balls.

The FBI radio was on, and we heard several agents complain to the operations center that their targets were on the lam. Capo relaxed into his seat. He said, "We knew you were coming."

I thought, *Oh shit.* I said, "Uh huh."

Capo quirked an eyebrow at me and I thought, *He didn't have to say he knew we were coming. Did he just throw me a bone? Maybe he wants to open up to me.*

Could I flip him?

What was I thinking? I had just met the guy.

Look, Capo was still a cipher to me. But he was nothing like what I'd been warned about. He wasn't confrontational. He wasn't rude. And I had just seen evidence of his close relationship with his mother. I did not see a crazed hater of law enforcement.

We were back on the Verrazzano-Narrows Bridge, headed to 26 Federal Plaza, when I released my fists and began filling out FBI paperwork and US Marshal intake forms—the latter of which annoyed the crap out of us agents. I did keep a good grip on my ballpoint pen. Hey, the criminal imagination is innovative, and so is mine. If needed, I could use that pen as a weapon.

"Mr. Capo, when is your birthday?" I asked. Before he could answer, I said, "It's August 17, 1961, right?"

Capo didn't know what I was up to, but he played along. "August 17," he said. He waited to see what came next.

"And your phone number? Isn't it—" I rattled off the ten numbers of his home phone.

"Right again," he said.

"I need you to confirm your Social Security number." I gave him the last four digits.

He nodded. I could tell by his body language he already thought he said too much.

I paused. *Yeah, Anthony. Chew on the tidbits I just gave you.*

"Mr. Capo, you're lawyered up. Just listen. Don't say anything."

I had his attention. Perfect. Let the mind games begin. I wasn't one of those Harvard-trained agents who don't know shit about the streets. Capo was going to find out my brain was as criminal as his.

"You have been charged with conspiracy to murder Charles Majuri," I said.

Capo laughed.

I said, "Too bad a cop lived on Majuri's block. You decided not to go through with the plan."

Capo wasn't laughing anymore.

I made some small talk with Brian Getson to let the seedling I planted in Capo take root.

Then I reiterated, "Do not say a word. Just listen. . . . Regarding the RJF Trucking stock fraud, you rented a mailbox to receive checks in the city," I said. "Your 'suite.' That's cute."

He looked at me deadpan. I knew he was thinking, *What else does the FBI know?*

Capo already had a lot on his plate. Hershey bar. Pint of OJ. Food for thought.

In one of our earlier Bonanno-related enforcement actions, we'd executed a search warrant for a basement gambling den. We went in early one Monday evening. Monday Night Football. Big betting night. I was with a bunch of guys from C-10. I looked around and thought, *There's got to be money here. Where would they put it?*

Not that my dad was a criminal, but he used to leave money in his jacket pockets all the time. At the gambling den, I opened up a closet. I reached into a pocket and voilà, pulled out a handful of fives, tens, and twenties.

Almost on cue, the phone rang. Maybe somebody was calling to place a bet? I picked up the receiver. Bingo. I pretended I was a bookie and, even without access to my trusty spreadsheet, I wrote down the caller's name and his bet. From my pre-FBI betting days, I knew "times" meant ten dollars. Five times is fifty dollars. Twenty times a hundred. I did this every time the phone rang. I wish I could remember which teams were playing.

"How many times do you want?" I'd ask. I was half amused, half on edge. But I like taking a risk.

We gathered enough evidence that night to bust a Bonanno gambling ring wide open.

I was learning to look at every situation for its breakthrough moment.

Law enforcement had had a hard-on for Capo for a long time. We knew he was a mob somebody and he had to know other La Cosa Nostra thugs. I had no idea if Capo's criminal history began and ended with his rap sheet or if his rap sheet was only the tip of the iceberg. I wanted to be the one to find out.

9

I'LL MAKE YOU A PROFFER YOU CAN'T REFUSE

THIS WASN'T CAPO'S FIRST RODEO. He could practically tell *us* the protocol for getting fingerprinted and photographed.

I completed my arrest paperwork and then, with members of my squad, transported a handcuffed Capo from FBI NY headquarters to the Southern District courthouse at 500 Pearl Street. I had to wonder what Capo was thinking as we passed signs pointing to the various civic institutions he must have encountered in his thirty-eight years in New York City: the BUREAU OF VITAL STATISTICS, the CITY CLERK'S OFFICE, the CITY HALL WEDDING PHOTOGRAPHER, and the NEW YORK COUNTY SUPREME COURT. Even in my auditing jobs, I saw how the government enters our lives every step of the way. I hoped the Southern District would be one of Capo's final stands in the criminal justice system.

Eight thirty, nine—I was already wiped out when I arrived with Capo at the courthouse. I had barely shut an eye all night for fear I would sleep through my alarm clock. Fortunately, Capo was one guy in a big arrest, and the judge arraigned him as part of the group. Still, the day promised to be extra long. I had to keep myself sharp to see if David Ironman, Capo's attorney, could convince the judge to release Capo on bail. The government would be vehemently opposed.

"When you meet the pretrial people, don't lie to them," I advised Capo in my low, confidential voice. "You lie to them, it'll affect you getting bail. If they ask you if you have assets, just tell them."

The expression in Capo's eyes revealed his stupefaction: *Is law enforcement trying to help me or scam me?*

"You don't know me from a hole in the wall, but I have no reason to lie to you," I said. I told Capo he would be handcuffed to his seat, likely alongside other people he knew. "Loose lips sink ships," I said. "Be careful what you say."

I was waiting for Capo to give me his haughty look. All he did was nod.

He did not get bail. The judge decided Capo was a flight risk. He also observed that Capo had committed his most violent acts when he was on probation.

Nice to know.

I repeated George Hanna's mantra: Don't make it personal with the mob. I asked myself, *What's my goal?* It was to get Anthony Capo to cooperate. Everything else—the Cowboys versus the Steelers, orange juice and a Hershey bar—were a means to that end. I had to convince this guy that cooperation was preferable to spending ten or twenty years or a lifetime in an American prison far from everyone he cared about.

Even a hardened criminal had to have a soft spot.

I met Capo's stepfather in the lobby of the Southern District of New York and handed him Capo's Dallas Cowboys jacket. In the presence of FBI agent Brian Getson and attorney David Ironman, I counted out $285 Capo had brought along with him and gave that to his stepfather as well. NYPD detective Steve Kaplan had purchased Humulin over the counter at Duane Reade for Capo, and Capo's stepfather took home whatever was left.

Word got back to Capo: *That agent who arrested you? He was respectful to your stepfather.*

Just as George Hanna taught me: you catch more flies with honey than with vinegar.

Anthony Capo. *Department of Justice Trial Exhibit, US Attorney's Office, Southern District of New York / FBI*

For now, the roof over Capo's head would be the Metropolitan Correctional Center on Park Row, an echoing underground walk from the Southern District courthouse. Judging by what I knew about MCC, this place was going to be different from FCI Danbury in Connecticut, where Capo once spent six months. Danbury is the federal prison where Leona Helmsley—the hotel magnate "Queen of Mean"—and Unification Church leader Sun Myung Moon did time for tax evasion in relative comfort. One longtime mob watcher observed that MCC was so wretched that inmates sent over from New York's Rikers Island at the beginning of their trial ask to go back to Rikers—itself a harrowing place. The arrestees who lodged at MCC could be crime family bosses, drug traffickers, stock scammers, weapons dealers, or terrorists. Gambino boss John Gotti was there in 1986. So was Sammy "the Bull" Gravano, for conspiring to murder Paul Castellano, Gotti's predecessor. MCC has since been home to Mexican drug lord Joaquín "El Chapo" Guzmán and Khalid al-Fawwaz, an al-Qaeda operative found guilty of conspiracy in the 1998 embassy bombings. With Boy Scouts like these as your dormmates, you could be motivated to get the hell out of there.

You might even give serious thought to collaborating with the feds.

Capo was already familiar with RICO and the likelihood that he could receive "extended criminal penalties" just for being in the same room with a mob guy. If he went away for two decades, who was going to provide for his stay-at-home wife and their three kids?

One day went by. One long, sobering day.

Late Friday afternoon Capo's attorney called me. "My client would like to cooperate with the government," Ironman said. The man had a hurried way of talking that implied he had bigger fish to fry elsewhere.

I was still green and I didn't fathom the import of what Ironman was saying. I thanked him for calling and said I would be in touch.

I was about to get on the phone with Maria Barton, a seasoned AUSA in the Southern District. She had spearheaded the indictment. I once tried to get her to sign an FD-597 property receipt form when she took possession of some of Ralph's consensual recordings that Stacy and I had duplicated. Maria was insulted. I didn't understand why. For me this was Auditing 101. She refused to sign and complained to my supervisor. I was hoping this call would get our relationship back on the right footing.

"Just received a call from Capo's attorney," I told her. "Capo wants to cooperate."

"Hey, that's great news, Séamus," Maria said. But she was caught off guard. Her lawyerly instincts kicked in, and she was immediately concerned about what I had said to Ironman.

"I only said I'd let the government know and we'd be in touch," I assured her.

Maria would coordinate with Ironman. She urged me to talk to my supervisor about initiating a proffer. I had not yet been involved with this aspect of legal proceedings.

I brought it to Jack Stubing. "You flipped the guy!" he said. "How'd you do it?"

I laughed. "I insulted the Cowboys."

"For real. How'd you do it?"

I think my banter with Capo bonded us. But I said, "Capo's diabetic. I fed him some OJ and some hard truths."

Jack gave me a tutorial in initiating a proffer, the contract between a federal prosecutor and a defendant in which the defendant tells the government everything he knows about his own criminal activities and the criminal activities of others. In practice it's a Q&A between, say, an FBI agent and the defendant. The payoff for Capo: nothing he told us would be used against him, as long as he didn't lie. In fact, the more useful Capo's information, the more likely the government would offer a cooperation agreement with the possibility of a reduced sentence.

In Capo's circumstances, a proffer sounded like a good deal, right? Yet it wasn't without risk. The guys in prison are smart. They see you leave your cell and they want to know where you're going. If you tell them, "I'm going to court for a status conference," they'll insist on seeing your paperwork. If you're proffering, you won't have any, because you're not going to court. You're blabbing to the feds, and for your fellow inmates, that's tantamount to treason. You're a snitch and you're going to get hurt. Or killed.

One time you might get away with saying, "The bus picked me up, but it turns out I got called to court by accident." But proffering is not a one-time deal. You might proffer numerous times, because the government needs to know if you're trustworthy and valuable. You only get so many bites at the apple before the other inmates figure out something's up.

Proffer day arrived. Capo sat across from Maria Barton, Ironman, George Hanna, Kenny McCabe, and me in a featureless SDNY interview room. No handcuffs. He was more alert than the day I arrested him. Steering clear of controlled substances really does get you your mind back.

Maria explained in detail that during the proffer, the prosecutor was going to ask Capo questions and follow-up questions. Capo had to answer truthfully. He'd also have to offer up any criminal information he was aware of—including his own culpability. If we could verify everything Capo said, the proffers could lead to a cooperation agreement.

Ironman had cautioned Capo that proffering was no joke. Capo would have to be a hundred percent truthful. No games. No mind-fucking.

"Don't be that guy who holds on to the golden nugget until the very end," I told Capo in the presence of his attorney. "Tell us the worst first."

"Agent McElearney will compile notes that he'll use later to create a summary of our conversation," Maria said. "Your words won't incriminate you, but your actions might."

Anthony cocked his head to the side. He didn't understand.

"Let's say you robbed a bank yesterday at eleven o'clock," I said. I spoke up only because my example was the one FBI agents typically use in a proffer. "You tell me the name of the bank. I can't use your admission against you. But I can go to the bank and request the bank video. I review it and sure enough, you did the robbery. If the proffer falls apart at any time—if you lie to us—I can use the video evidence against you."

"I ain't lying to you," Capo volunteered.

"The proffer is your 'queen for a day,'" I said. "Use it and it'll help you."

"I'm making my life an open book," he said.

At this point, I didn't know if Capo was going to be honest or half-ass it. But I was going to act on faith. I wanted him to believe I had confidence in him.

And I did.

Capo, a made man, had no choice but to remake himself.

10

ANTHONY CAPO SPILLS HIS GUTS, BRIEFLY

You know how they say it was the best of the times, it was the worst of times? That's what my life was for me. On the one hand, I was thirty-two years old and had just flipped the very first member of a hundred-plus-year-old crime family—even though I didn't fully grasp the import of what I had just done. On the other hand, I was watching my father slide into a painful death, and my mother into a financially constrained future. On top of everything, I started to hear rumblings at 26 Federal that I was too young to run Capo, too know-nothing. But Jack, my supervisor, believed in me. He gave me the opportunity.

I cut myself some slack. My father was fading in and out of consciousness. The truth is, my family was waiting for a merciful end to come. The closer my dad got to dying, the more I took refuge in C-10. My work lifted me out of my personal life and set me down in the life and death of the DeCavalcante crime family.

At the first proffer, Anthony Capo had to do two things. He had to "eat the indictment" he'd just been arrested on. And he had to tell us about any bodies, dumped, buried, or burnt. We needed to get to them before they got moved.

Capo didn't skip a beat.

First, he ate the indictment: Capo admitted to conspiring to murder Charles Majuri, then a member of the DeCavalcantes' three-man ruling panel. He admitted to engaging in stock fraud too. In short, he confirmed that everything we'd charged him with was accurate—and that Ralph Guarino was right on the money with everything he told us.

Second, Capo told us about the bodies. Three of them. The FBI knew about one, a newspaperman turned real estate investor named Fred Weiss. September 11, 1989. Bullet-riddled body. Corpse dumped on a Staten Island sidewalk. The New York papers called the slaying a mob hit but never reported whodunit. Now Capo told us, the way I might tell you what I had for lunch: it was him, Vinny Palermo, and Jimmy Gallo. Capo—a DeCavalcante associate at the time—drove them to Weiss's apartment building. Palermo and Gallo—both made men—pumped the lead. Several other DeCavalcantes played supporting roles.

"Word came down from 'the Bull' that 'John' wanted to kill Weiss to keep him from talking to the feds," Capo said.

"John" was John Gotti, the flamboyant boss of the Gambino crime family. "The Bull" was Sammy Gravano, the mobster whose book I read when I wanted to learn about the FBI.

I was two degrees of separation away from John Gotti and Sammy Gravano. I had gone from reading about them to dealing with the people around them. How awesome was that?

For the moment, the remaining two bodies were more important to us than Fred Weiss. We didn't know about them at all. If Capo wanted a cooperation agreement, he'd have to spill his guts, ASAP. It looked like we were going to start digging.

"Mr. Capo," Kenny said. "Kenny McCabe. Investigator for the Southern District of New York."

Capo got up from his folding chair. He wasn't handcuffed but he didn't immediately extend his hand. He narrowed his eyes to slits and deadpanned, "I don't know a Kenny McCabe. I know a Fuckin' McCabe."

"The one and the same," Kenny said. A moment of levity and we all had to chuckle.

"You used to come by my house once, twice a year. You brought pictures and prints to show me."

"I didn't want to see you get hurt."

"I appreciate that," Capo said. He shook Kenny's hand.

I didn't know what Kenny and Capo were talking about.

Kenny arched an eyebrow. "Treating you well here?" he asked.

"I'd like it better if Paulie was doing the cooking," Capo said. He didn't have to explain the *Goodfellas* reference to us.

Next, George Hanna introduced himself. He'd been dealing with mob characters forever. I took note how he put Capo at ease.

Me, I was reserved. I didn't want to say the wrong thing. I just took everything in.

Kenny, George, and I sat across from Capo so we could read his body language top to bottom. Capo rested his elbows on his thighs and leaned forward.

Ironman moved his chair into a corner. He kept jiggling his foot to let us know he was in enemy territory. He didn't want to be known as a lawyer who cooperated people. If Capo went on to become a government witness, he'd be given a court-appointed lawyer, and Ironman would leave so fast he'd be a Nike swoosh.

"Should I begin speaking?" Capo asked. He'd picked up on Ironman's discomfort too.

Ironman stopped shaking his foot. He was still Capo's attorney and had to fulfill his legal obligation to him. "Like we talked about," he said.

George gave Ironman a sideways glance and leaned forward to carve out an alarmingly intimate space between himself and Capo.

"You mentioned three bodies," George said. "We don't know chapter and verse about Fred Weiss, but of course we saw his body. We'll get to him. Let's hear about the other two."

Capo didn't hesitate. "There was a guy, John D'Amato," he said. "He was the official underboss and acting boss in the DeCavalcante family. Me and Victor DiChiara did him."

"Who's Victor DiChiara?" George asked.

"An associate in the DeCavalcante family," Capo said. "Looks like Séamus."

"What do you mean by 'did'?"

"Victor drove. I shot Johnny Boy. That's what we called D'Amato. Johnny Boy."

"You and Victor DiChiara killed John D'Amato?"

"Yes."

"Why?" George asked. "Briefly, for now."

"A lot of people didn't like the way Johnny Boy was running things," Capo said. "They said he was greedy. He owed money. One day his girlfriend calls me up. She's crying. She tells me Johnny Boy is a sexual deviant. He engages in group sex and homosexual acts."

"The two of you decided to kill Johnny Boy on your own?" George asked.

"No. What happened is, I told Rudy Farone and Vinny Palermo. They gave me the assignment to kill Johnny Boy. We couldn't have such goings-on in the DeCavalcante family. What would people think? I did say I wouldn't do nothing until I got the order from Anthony Rotondo, my captain."

"Did you get that order?" George asked.

"Yes. Victor and I told Johnny Boy we were taking him out to a meeting and dinner. Like I said, Victor drove. I was in the passenger seat and Johnny Boy was in the back. I turned around and shot him in the face. Victor starts yelling, 'He's groaning! Hit him again.' So I shot him two more times."

"He was dead?" George asked.

"Stone cold," Capo said.

George gave the floor to Kenny.

Kenny brushed back a lock of hair from his forehead, the only sign that he had just heard evil reduced to indisputable evidence presentable at trial. He crossed a long leg over his knee and asked, "Where's the body?"

Capo exhaled from deep inside his gut. The most emotion I saw him express to date. "We drove it to Rudy Farone's garage in Brooklyn," he said. "Uncle Rudy and Vinny Palermo instructed my captain to take it to Marlboro in upstate New York. Phil LaMela—he was a DeCavalcante soldier—he has a garbage dump there. We always called Phil 'the Undertaker,' because he let us bury bodies on his property."

Kenny said, "By 'captain' you mean who?" Capo had just said, but Kenny was checking to see if Capo could keep his story straight.

"That's Anthony Rotondo," Capo said. "Anthony didn't like to get his hands dirty. He said, 'My wife's waiting for me. How come Anthony and Victor can't go?'"

George: "Then what happened?"

"Vinny and Uncle Rudy said they'd take a drive up to Marlboro. The next morning, Victor, Anthony, and me were supposed to meet to clean the car. Anthony never showed. Victor and I mopped up, but we still had to get rid of the car. Vinny had gone through Johnny Boy's suit and found five grand on him. He gave it all to Victor to compensate him for his car."

Kenny felt the urgency to keep Capo talking. He said, "You mentioned a third body."

Capo drew a breath and said, "There's another body up there. In Marlboro."

Was I in a movie or what?

We waited for our potential government witness to keep going.

He dropped his voice. "Joey," he said. "Garofano."

Kenny was known for being courteous even with the worst of the worst. As if Capo were a delicate flower, Kenny said, "Do you need a minute?"

Capo said he was fine. But his eyes looked glassy. "There's a lot to say about what happened," he said. "I have to go back to Fred Weiss."

George knew we had to move faster. He tried to focus Capo on Garofano and D'Amato. "Both bodies ended up in Marlboro at the same time?" he asked Capo.

"D'Amato in 1991," Capo said. "Joey in '89 a week after we did Fred Weiss."

Kenny asked, "Can you tell us in a sentence or two the connection between Fred Weiss and Joey Garofano?"

"Joey was in on the Weiss murder," Capo said. "No sooner do we kill Weiss when Joey tells me, 'I ain't doing time for nobody.' I warned Joey he had to stop talking like that."

George and Kenny asked, "Why?"

"We were afraid Joey was going to rat us all out," Capo confessed. He mumbled, "I went to my captain. I said Joey might cause us a problem."

"Did Joey become a problem?" Kenny asked.

"Yes," Capo said. His voice had a catch in it. "He vanished."

You know how Eskimos have a hundred words for ice? The FBI should have a hundred words for silent. The moment was silent. I'll call it solemn. But we didn't have a solemn moment to waste.

We talked a bit longer with Capo to see what he could tell us about the LaMela property in Marlboro. He'd never been there, and we didn't get much. George and Kenny stood up. They thanked Capo and shook hands with him again.

A federal marshal escorted Capo out of the room and led him through the underground maze connecting the Southern District of New York to the Metropolitan Correctional Center. Capo would sit in general population until we called him.

If we called him. We had to determine if he was telling us the truth or not.

The team went into a huddle. We believed Capo. Every single one of us.

For Capo's safety, we had to move him. And we had to talk to his family about possible danger to them.

Our next step was getting a search warrant. Marlboro was in the Northern District of New York. George told me to prepare for a drive up to Albany, the state capital, within the next few days to secure the warrant.

George, Kenny, and I left the SDNY together.

"Did you catch what Capo said?" Kenny asked.

"You two know each other?" I asked.

Kenny nodded. "I drove out at least once to tell him he had a target on his back."

Reality check: *Séamus, you're dealing with a serious player.*

On my way home later that day, WFAN Sports couldn't block out the replay of our SDNY Q&A in my head. I'd seen people get more exercised over killing a spider than Anthony got over killing John D'Amato. Homosexual acts bad, but murder fine?

Who put the target on Capo's back?

I was starting to understand: What Capo was charged with was just the tip of the iceberg.

And what was that about ratting out his friend Joey to Anthony Rotondo?

Dad, I prayed. *Hold on. Please just hold on.*

11

WE FIND A BULLET, BUT NO BODIES

I SPENT THE WEEKEND after Capo's first proffer corroborating his story with AUSA Maria Barton. Maria also had to coordinate with her counterpart in Albany so I could get a court-ordered search warrant for the LaMela property. Once she activated the legal bureaucracy, the burden was on me to make sure everything Capo told us was on the level. Come Monday, it would be me driving up the New York Thruway to the state capital with John DiCaprio, the NYPD detective who teased me about my binders; me swearing out the warrant in front of a judge; me giving the go-ahead to start digging in Marlboro.

Meanwhile, Capo was transported from MCC to an undisclosed prison facility for his protection.

Eleven days had passed since Capo's arrest—eleven days in which the DeCavalcantes could have moved whatever was left of John D'Amato and Joey Garofano. I was about to embark on a grisly mission in Hudson Valley wine country.

It was a sentimental journey for me.

I pulled onto the Tappan Zee Bridge and thought back to the times my father drove us up in his Ford station wagon to the Catskills, or, as we knew them, the "Irish Alps." My dad was a work machine, but he carved out a weekend or two every summer so he and my mom could transport themselves back to the old sod. They were like two Irish wrens, basking in Irish music, céilí dancing, and Gaelic football. The Catskills were perfect for my sisters, brother, and me too. We used to stay in East Durham—the "Emerald Isle of the Catskills"—and the four of us would be out all day unsupervised. We divided our time between sports and amusement centers. Pinball machines had been around for decades, but video games were new. We'd play ourselves into a frenzy with Asteroids and Pac-Man. Our mom wanted us to go read a book, but those amusement centers were great meet-up places. To this day, I run into people I met in the Catskills as a kid.

We were little heathens, but our mom never lost sight of our Catholic instruction. On Sunday, my dad drove us to St. Mary's Sacred Heart Church on Route 145 to hear Mass. So many Irish attended that the service had to be piped through loudspeakers to the overflow parishioners outside, the McElearneys among them.

The Thruway had also been the on-ramp to my extended family life. My Aunt Bridgie and Uncle Eddie and their seven kids lived in Kingston, and we spent a lot of happy weekends with them. Thanks to my uncle's job with IBM, we went swimming at the company pool. With the recent rancor over my grandfather's will, though, my relationship with Aunt Bridgie was in the tank. Thinking about my dad, semicomatose in Rosary Hill Home, I wouldn't be surprised if steam was coming out of my ears. John picked up on my agitation and asked if I wanted him to take over the wheel.

I knew Albany a little. Once I got my driver's license, I would drive up there from time to time to procure inspection stickers for my dad's gas station. Lots of car owners in the Bronx and Westchester came to my dad for inspection. He had a reputation for overlooking a cracked windshield, bald tire, or broken headlight.

However sad I felt about my father, I was grateful, and dumbstruck, by how my life as a bank auditor had moved into the rearview mirror. The ledger I was balancing now—a ledger of crimes confessed to and repented—was of a different order from the profit-and-loss columns I used to audit in my not-too-distant long ago. Now I got to ponder the balance sheet of Anthony Capo's life. How could somebody with his vicious renown become putty in the hands of the New York Southern

District? RICO had a lot to do with getting Anthony to heel, but something else was afoot here too. I couldn't put my finger on it yet.

A team of FBI, NYPD, New York State Police, and NYS Department of Environmental Conservation excavators received a fax of the court-approved search warrant, and they were already digging when John and I pulled into Marlboro. I had seen pictures of the LaMela property and assumed the place was small. Eyeballing it now, I guessed it was big as a football field. A wee bit of anxiety infiltrated my optimism. How much digging did we have to do to find even a fingernail?

The size of the place wasn't the only problem. Between September 1989, when Garofano was killed, and December 1999, when we started digging, LaMela had done major construction on his building. One or both of the bodies could have been dumped beneath it and shifted over time. One or both could have been moved accidentally during excavation and brought to a dump. They could be bonemeal. It doesn't take ten years to disappear without a trace.

The excavators kept at it for three and a half cold days. With the aid of backhoes, K-9 sniffing dogs, and ground-penetrating radar, they uncovered a spent bullet casing but not so much as a sifter of bone dust. Too bad for us. A DNA test on any remains would have given credence to Capo's allegation that Joey Garofano and John D'Amato had gone to their eternal reward in Marlboro's gangland graveyard. As it turned out, we were looking for a needle—two needles—in a haystack.

Phil LaMela never showed his face, not while John and I were there. It didn't matter. We had no evidence of foul play, so we couldn't charge him with being an accessory after the fact.

That last day in Marlboro was anticlimactic. More vivid is my memory of driving home to Yonkers and tormenting myself with questions: *Is Anthony Capo full of crap? Is he playing me? Did I let this guy get the better of a brand-new agent?*

At the same time, I could justify finding nothing. The area we excavated was extensive, and the construction of a new building had probably overturned the soil. I didn't know I was driving myself nuts for nothing. When you're looking for a body, even in a contained area, chances are slim to none you'll find anything.

My bigger surprise that day was my mom's premonition. After the dig, the family drove over to Rosary Hill Home to see my dad, as we had done many nights. I arrived with Liam, now an FBI mechanic, and we were both tired. We were hoping to rest up for work the next day. But as my brother and I were getting ready to leave the hospice, my mom said, "I think you boys should stay." Christine McElearney had a religious sixth sense I respected.

My mom, Liam, my sisters, and I got to see Jimmy McElearney take his last breath. Official time of death: 12:55 AM, December 17, 1999. We'd made wake and funeral arrangements, but when he died, none of us were ready.

We called my dad's siblings in New York and Ireland and relayed the news. Believe me, those were difficult calls to make because of the anger we still felt. But letting them know immediately was the right thing to do.

12

IT'S A HORRIBLE CHRISTMAS

My mom and sisters were up the rest of the night, but I sacked out when we got home. As I drifted off to sleep, that line I learned at Cardinal Spellman popped back into my head: "Because I could not stop for Death"—and suddenly the next line: "He kindly stopped for me—" Not for me but for my father. My dad, the man I revered, was gone. Strange how only fifteen days ago, I was afraid to sleep lest I sleep through Capo's arrest. My dad's death was different. Jimmy Mac would rest for eternity, and I would rest too, if only for a few hours.

Friday morning, I drove my mom to the Hodder Farenga Funeral Home in Yonkers to arrange the two-day wake on December 18 & 19 and the funeral on December 20. Hodder's was across the street from Rory Dolan's. Convenient for the Irish, who go to wakes and then hit up the bar. For me, Rory Dolan's was a milepost. It's where I used to see my friends and where I met Tricia Harris, the FBI agent who talked to me about joining the Bureau and getting on an organized crime squad. I'd like to say I wasn't giving work a second thought, but my mind strayed back to it. Capo hadn't entered Witness Security yet. He had to take a polygraph test. I had to file paperwork. And I had to tell him the dig yielded nothing that could help him.

My mother and I spent a good amount of time preparing for the wake and funeral. I called the local papers to post my dad's obituary announcement and then coordinated with the Yonkers Police Department to give my father a proper send-off. My dad's last journey on earth would start at Hodder's on McLean Avenue, move on to his gas station on Bronx Boulevard, continue to our house in the Colonial Heights section of Yonkers, and come to a stop at Annunciation Church nearby. My brother, sisters, and I put together a photo collage of my mom and dad and us kids over the years to display at Hodder's. We asked my dad's good friend Gerry Finlay to sing "Shall My Soul Pass Through Old Ireland." It was an Irish rebel song my father loved.

Dad's sisters were on their way over, Kathleen from Ireland, Bridgie from Upstate New York, and Alice from Queens. Uncle Peter had flown over from England a couple months earlier to pay his final respects. We knew the reunion with our aunts would be tense, but our anger at Dad's family notwithstanding, we suffered through it.

I figured I'd left nothing to chance.

Which is why I was flabbergasted when my work cell phone rang at Hodder's and I heard Anthony Capo's voice in my ear. I had told Capo's mother I'd be out of commission for a couple of days because my dad died, and evidently she conveyed the news to her son. It was decent of Capo to offer me his condolences, but weird considering only two days ago I'd been digging around in the dirt for two bodies he helped put there.

Life made no sense! On the one hand, I've got cruelty coming at me from my dad's family. I'm worried about the legal mess they've created for my family's future. I'm freaked out about my mom. How's she going to survive? On the other hand, I'm thinking a cold-blooded killer, a notorious douche to law enforcement, has a heart. I could rationalize that Capo was strategically polite to me. I was what stood between him and a life sentence. But I'm not a piece of wood. I was grateful to him for a word of kindness on the worst day of my life.

Don't think I was going all soft on Capo. The FBI agent in me was overjoyed this made guy had done what no other DeCavalcante in history had ever done. Good that Capo saw me as his friend. Good that I was on my game. I needed information from him for prosecutions.

Agents forget at their own peril the fine line between enlightened self-interest and friendship. The more I got Capo to relax, the more he was going to say something he hadn't planned on saying to anybody.

At the funeral, I was stunned by the many FBI colleagues who showed up. I'd been with the Bureau for only a year and a half, and I didn't expect this kind of support from agents and supervisors. In my eulogy, I said it was a lot easier to work for the FBI than for my father—a line that prompted a few knowing laughs. Afterward, we had the customary Irish luncheon to celebrate my father's life. What better place to reminisce about Dad's run-ins with the law than Mannion's, the Yonkers restaurant-pub where he was known to have a pint or two. More than once, Jimmy McElearney had been pulled over for test-driving a customer's car above the speed limit. He would have enjoyed seeing the Yonkers Police at the front of his funeral cortege instead of bearing down behind him with lights flashing. My family had a good laugh.

The next day was my mom's birthday.

Christmas was four days after that.

Nobody was feeling festive.

The rest of the world wasn't on an even keel either—not with Y2K breathing down its neck. We tech ignoramuses were afraid a "99" to "00" turn of the millennial calendar would hobble computing systems and throw banks, businesses, health care, and schools back to some pre-IT Stone Age. Whatever. I didn't have the mental real estate for any of this stuff. With my dad's health taking a nosedive over the past nine months, and then with his dying a painful death, my world had already fallen off a cliff.

No dad. No decorated pine tree. No lights.

It would have been the worst Christmas ever but for my Cardinal Spellman friends. Out of respect for my father, they canceled our annual Christmas dinner. In the ten years we'd been celebrating our school ties, 1999 was our only cancellation. In spite of the horror I had experienced over the past three days, I felt joy mixed in with my grief. I had my immediate family, friends, and FBI colleagues to thank.

Now, in the new millennium, my squad and I could get down to the business of debriefing Anthony Capo.

13

I DEBRIEF A PROFESSIONAL CRIMINAL

Capo had to give us a 360-degree picture of his crimes, and his word alone wouldn't be good enough. We had to corroborate every last piece of information he gave us. Only if Capo's story was kosher would the government offer a cooperation agreement. Capo would also have to plead guilty to all his crimes, tell us the truth, and agree to testify at trial. Moreover, the judge at the plea proceedings could ask questions about his crimes and Capo would have to answer them. If the government discovered that Capo lied or withheld information—*psht!*—they'd rip up the agreement. For a thirty-eight-year-old man who got out of bed every day for the past twenty years raring to scheme, threaten, and cheat, the cooperation agreement was a tall order.

The government held all the cards. But Capo stood to benefit significantly. Naming all his crimes in this document would protect him against anybody else looking to charge him with a crime. The cooperation agreement was the ace up Capo's sleeve.

It was a chance for Anthony Capo to get a second chance.

While we were waiting for Capo's acceptance into the Witness Security Program, the Monmouth County prosecutor's office in New Jersey let us know Capo was a suspect in two recent murders. We had to address the allegation ASAP.

Monmouth County was investigating the October 1999 murders of two stockbrokers in Colts Neck, an affluent township near the Jersey Shore. FBI agent Dave Shafer was working with an informant who speculated the cut on Capo's right hand between his thumb and index finger could have come from discharging a gun. Because of Capo's association with the DeCavalcantes, and his propensity for violence, the Monmouth County prosecutor wanted a chat with him.

On January 6, Stacy and I transported Capo from a local prison facility to the Southern District Attorney's Office in White Plains. This was only the third time Capo and I had seen each other. In the car, he again expressed his condolences about my dad. I told him I appreciated his words. And I did. In turn, I let Capo know Colts Neck wanted to talk to him.

He didn't speak right away. "Is this about those two murders?" he asked.

I nodded. I couldn't question him, because Tom White, his newly appointed attorney, wasn't present.

"They came and talked to me just before I got arrested," Capo said.

"They," I repeated. I was asking without phrasing it as a question.

"A couple of New Jersey detectives."

"Looks like Jersey's escalating its investigation," Stacy said. "Not a question," she added.

"Are they going to try and pin this on me?" Capo asked. "I had nothing to do with it."

I believed him. He had already been forthcoming about the murders of Weiss, Garofano, and D'Amato—and we'd known nothing about the latter two. Think about it: If we discovered Capo was lying about Colts Neck—*finita la commedia*. The government would put him away for life. Why would Capo take that risk?

Not that I was going to depend on gut feelings or logic. Nobody at the FBI would. We'd have to substantiate Capo's claims through every means possible: collaborating with law enforcement, talking to informants, obtaining hotel and airfare receipts, reviewing phone bills and toll records, locating traffic tickets, and examining victim reports and surveillance video.

"You have nothing to hide from Monmouth County, Anthony," I told him. "Admitting to murders you committed will protect you from being charged with murders you didn't do."

I knew I was beating a dead horse, but mob guys are always trying to manipulate you for their benefit. That's why I reminded Capo, "Don't hold anything back. This is not a sit-down."*

Stacy and I led Capo into a room in the Southern District. Tom White, Capo's lawyer, got there just after we did. Stacy and I left the room so Capo and White could discuss the allegations about Colts Neck. We returned in a bit and led Capo and his attorney to an interview room, where two detectives, an ADA, and AUSA Maria Barton were waiting for us. Capo was wearing prison garb the same beige as the walls. We sat down at a long wooden table.

What a difference from the day I arrested him. Now Capo looked alert. He didn't appear particularly worried about Colts Neck either.

"Good morning, Mr. Capo," one of the detectives said. "We're investigating the murders of two stockbrokers in Colts Neck, New Jersey. We have information leading us to believe you were the shooter."

Capo was pissed off. "I had nothing to do with that," he yelled. Nice! This was the Anthony Capo I had been warned about. He got his dander up if you accused him of a crime he didn't commit. I'd have gotten angry too.

The detective persisted. "What do you know about those murders?"

Capo flung his haughty look at them. "Whatever I read in the papers," he said.

"What was that?"

"I know the victims were Jewish fellows."

"How do you know that?"

"I read it in the papers," he repeated slowly, as if talking to morons.

Tom White intervened. "My client had nothing to do with Colts Neck," he said.

* A sit-down is a mob meeting to resolve a dispute.

The ADA asked Capo, "What were their names?"

Capo was practically frothing. He said, "I don't have a clue and I could care less." For good measure, he threw in, "They obviously pissed somebody off."

Monmouth County collectively rolled their eyes. "Obviously," they said.

I only knew a little more than Capo. One of the stockbrokers was a guy named Albert Alain Chalem. He had a pump-and-dump stock scheme going.* Chalem had a reputation for burning everyone he met. Not cool when you're burning members of the Russian or Italian mob. Plenty of people thought Chalem had it coming to him. As for Meier Lehmann, the other victim, probably just an unlucky guy in the wrong place at the wrong time. But who knows?

Monmouth County might have been overzealous in linking Capo to the murders, but they weren't reckless. Early days revealed that Phil Abramo—a DeCavalcante "person of interest"—controlled Toluca Pacific Securities, a shady brokerage Chalem worked for. It was in the realm of possibility that the DeCavalcantes killed him.

The ADA was smug. He was exactly what George Hanna would never be: hostile toward the subject, and toward me too.

The Monmouth County detectives requested samples of Capo's blood to compare with blood found in Chalem's house.

"Gladly," Capo said.

DNA testing was still pretty rudimentary, and we'd have to wait a while for the results.

One thing was certain: Chalem knew his killers. The Jersey prosecutors found no sign of forced entry into his gated mansion.

---

* This sort of scam goes back to the 1920s, when a team of investors—the Radio Pool—bought Radio Corp. of America (RCA) stock at $100/share, talked up the company's value to gullible buyers who bought at $500/share, and then watched these buyers go broke when the market crashed in October 1929. A congressional committee on banking and currency investigated pump-and-dump manipulations—legal until the crash—and worked to outlaw these practices in the 1930s.

In the midst of all the Colts Neck commotion, we kept working to get Capo into the Witness Security Program. WitSec is designed to protect government witnesses, especially from convicts in the general prison population eager to harm a "rat." Ordinary people often think it's a get-out-of-jail-free card: in exchange for testimony at trial, the government gives the cooperating witness everything from a new Social Security number to a new face—and off goes the witness to a sunny American suburb, like the Steve Martin character in *My Blue Heaven*.

Not quite.

WitSec consists of prison (Phase I) and relocation (Phase II). In the prison phase, the government houses the witness in a protective custody unit (PCU) at one of seven US prisons. As part of Phase I, I had to compile a threat assessment. I highlighted the mob's propensity for violence and its attempted reprisals toward witnesses in similar circumstances. Case in point, the attack on anti-Mafia crusader Judge Falcone by Sicily's Corleonesi crime family,* and the shooting of former Lucchese captain Pete Chiodo's sister—an innocent bystander—after he turned government witness. Shooting the ex-captain twelve times in the stomach, chest, legs, and arms a year earlier hadn't satisfied the Lucchese appetite for retaliation.

Next, Capo had to pass a polygraph exam and an interview with the US Marshals. The marshals had to be sure Capo wasn't going into the program to retaliate against another witness. Capo passed. Fortunately, George had a great relationship with the US Marshals and the Bureau of Prisons. He expedited Capo's entry into Phase I.

The WitSec relocation process Hollywood loves doesn't actually occur until Phase II. That's when the witness gets a new identity. But that's getting ahead of the story. There's no saying the witness will want to become Steve Martin's "Todd" living "somewhere in America," at a safe distance from his old neighborhood, family, and friends. A witness can decline to enter Phase II and go off on his own. But then he won't get a new ID from the government.

Even if he didn't go beyond Phase I, Capo would be safer in a WitSec prison than anywhere else in the country.

* Three police escort agents were also killed. Fifty-seven days later, the Corleonesis murdered Paolo Borsellino, an anti-Mafia judge and prosecuting magistrate, and his five police escorts.

The preliminary interviews continued as we waited to hear from WitSec. To keep bonding with Capo, I talked sports with him.

"In our lifetime, Joe Torre," Capo said. "Hands down, the Yankees' greatest manager."

"Hey, Torre took over a team that was already built to win after Buck Showalter was fired," I said. "But I do give him credit for winning the World Series in '96 and back-to-back titles in '98 and '99."

"Pettitte, Clemens, Cone," Capo counted off on three fingers. "With a pitching staff like that, you can't lose."

"Don't forget Mariano Rivera," I said. "He's lights out as a closer. Remember his ERA?"

Capo gave me his heavy-lidded glance. Once upon a time, that face would have made a deadbeat debtor wet his pants. Weird to think it was a sign of camaraderie with me.

"It was 0.00 in the '99 World Series," I said. "Rivera recorded one win and two saves."

Capo mimed one of Rivera's cut fastballs. "Unstoppable," he said. "The Yankees swept the Braves that year."

"Break out the brooms!" I said.

We both had a good laugh.

And why not? The FBI's game of taking down the New Jersey DeCavalcantes was just getting started with Colts Neck and WitSec, and I was pretty sure we were in for extra innings. I just prayed Capo could bring all the heavy hitters home.

Capo was accepted into a WitSec facility. It was a world with its own rules and regulations designed to protect the identity of government witnesses.* The government's interviews with Capo continued there.

In a prison room with chairs, couch, table, and vending machines sat Capo, his lawyer, an AUSA, and me. Sometimes other FBI agents

* I am not at liberty to disclose WitSec protocol.

attended. I was Plato to Capo's Socrates. He talked and I took notes to prepare my FD-302 interview reports.

First, we needed details about Capo's crimes charged in the indictment. "Vinny [Palermo] wanted to kill Charles Majuri in 1998," Capo began. "He had to. Majuri was planning a power move on Vinny. Vinny recruited me, Victor DiChiara, Joseph 'Joey O' Masella, and Jimmy Gallo, a soldier, to do the job.* Gallo wanted to ring the doorbell and shoot Majuri as soon as he opened the door."

Capo remembered that nugget I threw at him on the day of his arrest. He confirmed a cop lived on Majuri's block. "That's why we couldn't kill Majuri in front of his house," Capo said.

Capo told us about Giovanni "Uncle John" Riggi, the crime family's official boss, arrested for labor racketeering† in New Jersey a month after the murder of Fred Weiss. Almost three years later, Riggi pled guilty and began a twelve-year prison sentence in Butner, North Carolina.

"But prison doesn't end a mob boss's authority," Capo said. To ensure executive continuity, Riggi named John D'Amato acting boss. A fateful decision for all concerned.

"You know D'Amato's girlfriend told me he was a homosexual 'swinger,'" Capo said. "Who would take us seriously if our gay acting boss sat down to discuss La Cosa Nostra business with John Gotti or Joe Massino? Jake Amari, our underboss, didn't even consult with the Five Families the way he was supposed to. He ordered Johnny

---

* Joey O Masella advised calling off the hit, because it was poorly planned. In October 1998, Masella was shot several times as he sat in his car, likely because he owed thousands of dollars to various LCN families. Masella lived long enough to tell the police that the shooter was a dark-haired man with a mustache. Anthony Greco, a former Las Vegas casino dealer, fit the description and was arrested in the December 2, 1999, LCN sweep—but all charges against him were dropped on January 7, 2002. Las Vegas gaming regulators have never granted Greco's request to reinstate his casino work permit. "Charges Dropped, but Ex-mob Hit Suspect Can't Get Work Card" by Henry Brean, *Las Vegas Review Journal*, November 2, 2008, https://www.reviewjournal.com/news/charges-dropped-but-ex-mob-hit-suspect-cant-get-work-card/.

† According to the US Department of Labor, *labor racketeering* refers to the infiltration, exploitation, and/or control of a union, employee benefit plan, employer entity, or workforce. It is carried out through illegal, violent, or fraudulent means for profit or personal benefit.

Boy killed. John Riggi rewarded Amari by promoting him to acting boss."

Amari held on for five years. Like the fictional boss in season 1 of *The Sopranos*, he got stomach cancer and died. Amari's death in 1997 prompted a DeCavalcante reorg. The family established a three-man ruling panel made up of Vinny Palermo, Charles Majuri, and Girolamo "Jimmy" Palermo (no relation to Vinny). Capo said all three had equal power.

"But Vinny had the stronger personality," Capo added. "We all saw him as the real acting boss."

Capo went full tilt and exposed the DeCavalcante family structure. He gave us the names of the seven captains directly answerable to the ruling panel, as well as the names of the twenty-one soldiers divvied up among them. He also gave us a mini lesson in DeCavalcante history. The family originated in Ribera, Italy, and ultimately ended up in Elizabeth, New Jersey.

"I was part of the family's Brooklyn faction," Capo said.

Before Ralph Guarino, the FBI didn't know about a Brooklyn faction.

I had to ask, "How were they different from New Jersey?"

"We were willing to do work."

Capo explained. In this context, *work* meant killing.

Anthony Capo was leading us into the inner sanctum of the "real Sopranos."

Capo moved on to crimes we knew nothing about. He was as matter-of-fact as I was at a job interview.

He couldn't possibly recall every robbery, assault, or extortion he'd racked up since the early 1980s. There were too many of them. He did recall clearly, however, an incident at a bar in which he stuck a fork in the face of a guy going after a girl they both wanted. And he remembered that one of his earliest robberies involved a haul of $1,500. Capo and a partner executed a plan drawn up in part by Anthony Rotondo, the DeCavalcante captain who was starting to loom large in Capo's life. Capo and his partner tracked a pharmacy delivery truck to a public housing project in Brooklyn, threatened the driver with a loaded pistol, and turned over the entire heist to Rotondo.

"The robbery took place around Christmas, and all I got was a stocking full of coal," Capo complained.

Capo's other robberies used the same template. In one case, Capo waited for closing time at **Tony's**, a Woodbridge, New Jersey, pizzeria. After the owner locked up and got in his car, Capo stuck a gun in the driver's-side window, carjacked him, and stole the day's take.

"My partner and I ditched him by the side of the road," Capo said.

But get this: ten years after this robbery, Capo and a Bonanno made guy were hanging out at Hipps strip club on Staten Island when they chanced upon Tony's owner—the very guy Capo and his partner robbed.

Tony recognized Capo. "I had $15,000 in my socks," he boasted.

Tony asked the name of Capo's partner. Capo wouldn't say.

Capo also told us about a robbery he did at a Robert Hall clothing store in the early '80s.

"I was working with my childhood buddy, Joey Garofano," he said. "A friend of Joey's heard the store was easy pickings. Early one morning we got into my Ford Thunderbird and headed out to Woodbridge. I carried a .25 caliber pistol. Joey had a toy gun. Once we were inside the store, I tried on some suits. Then I put his gun to the salesman's head. Joey herded the other workers into a closet. We walked off with as many suits and ties as we could carry. We emptied the cash register too. Our takeaway was only $2,500."

Not much of a haul, especially as Capo had to hand all the suits over to Anthony Rotondo. Rotondo, who took credit for the score, gifted the suits to John Riggi. That's the way it was with the mob: the owners ate the cane and the workers ate the weeds. Riggi, whom Capo hadn't met until this point, let the two robbers keep the cash.

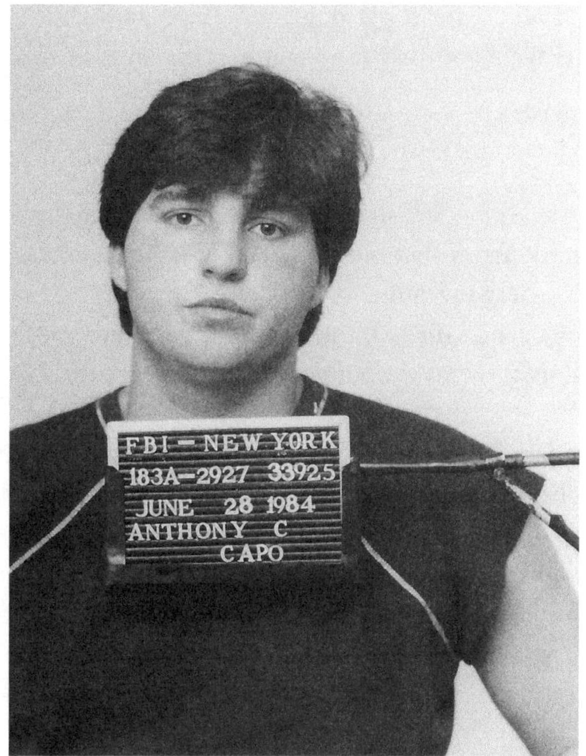

Anthony Capo in 1984. *Courtesy of the FBI*

No business was too small for Capo's schemes. Take **Pet Utopia**. The Staten Island pet store was owned by **Dino Sarducci**, a brother-in-law of Capo's landlord. Sarducci's shop was regularly robbed and vandalized by the Bonanno family. Sarducci asked Capo for help. Capo intervened, and ultimately Sarducci had to pay Capo to "protect" Pet Utopia's puppies, kittens, hamsters, and fish.

"I made at least $8,000 on Pet Utopia," Capo told me. He joked, "We were getting paid to protect goldfish."

Actually, Capo did better than goldfish. He made Sarducci pay off the *vigorish*, or extortionate interest, on a "shylock loan" Capo took out with a Bonanno captain.

"I asked Sarducci for a pet dog too," Capo said.

Aw. Some deals you just can't put a price on.

Why was loan-sharking, or "shylocking," as Capo called it, such a draw for the Mafia? Think about that old joke. Why did Willie Sutton rob banks? Because that's where the money is.

The DeCavalcantes, like all the mob families, liked easy money. Once loan sharks start preying on people's weaknesses, they can easily make a bundle.

A loan shark, or a shylock, is a moneylender who offers loans at extremely high interest rates. Terms of repayment are strict and nearly always operate outside the law. The threat of violence, or actual violence, is typically used to enforce repayment.

Here's how it works in practice.

Let's say I'm a loan shark. I loan you $10,000 at five points. A point is the same as a percentage of the original amount, assessed weekly. Hence:

$$\$10,000 \times 5\% = \$500$$

Your interest payment to me every week is $500.

By the end of the month, you will have paid me $2,000 in interest—but you still owe me $10,000. The principal amount is not reduced until you pay me back in full. Until I get my loan back, you keep paying me $500 a week. This loan arrangement can go on for a long time. After a year, for example, you could end up paying me $24,000 in interest, which, of course, is more than twice the amount of the loan.

The loan shark determines what points to charge you based on your "street credit," or your ability to repay in a timely way.

Now, let's say you have a gambling addiction. You're not going to go to Chase Bank for a loan. You very well might seek out one of these extortionate loans to cover your gambling debts. As the debts mount and you can't repay them, the loan shark can extort you for some kind of equity, such as your business. If your debt exceeds your total financial worth, the loan shark can hire people to beat—or kill—you.

In the late 1980s, Capo took up home invasions on Long Island. They started when a guy named Darren tipped him off that a Jewish couple had a safe in their house.

"A home invasion requires more planning, more manpower than a suburban store robbery," Capo informed me.

For his inaugural break-in, Capo would be part of a team that included Joey Garofano, Anthony Rotondo, Vinny Palermo, Joseph "Joey O" Masella, and Frank "Frankie the Beast" Scarabino. Like Capo, Joey, and Joey O, Scarabino was a DeCavalcante associate.

No single role in a home invasion was more important than another. My mind flashed to a famous verse from 1 Corinthians: "The eye cannot say to the hand, 'I don't need you!' And the head cannot say to the feet, 'I don't need you!'"

Capo dressed up in a police uniform. Scarabino, a tattooed hulk of a man, drove Capo and Joey Garofano to the Long Island house in a stolen car. Anthony Rotondo drove the "crash car," a legitimate car to crash into the cops if they arrived on the scene. Masella drove yet a third car as backup. Vinny Palermo brought along his pet dog to look like a local dog walker.

"We used walkie-talkies to communicate with each other," Capo said.

When the big night came, Capo, suited up to look like an NYPD officer, rang the bell. An elderly man came to the door.

"Sir, you've got an intruder in your backyard," Capo told him.

The homeowner let the "police officer" in. Capo whipped out a set of handcuffs and an unloaded .38 caliber pistol.

"Open your safe," Capo ordered.

Once the safe was open, Capo handcuffed the man and his wife, both in their seventies.

Capo radioed Joey Garofano to come into the house. Joey figured he didn't need the walkie-talkie anymore and left it with Scarabino.

"I didn't see nothing valuable in the safe," Capo said. "Joey and I got the hell out of there. Outside, Scarabino was nowhere to be seen. The friggin' car doors were locked. How were we supposed to escape?"

Scarabino justified locking the car and leaving it because it was a stolen vehicle. He went out looking for a place to dump it.

Joey O's job was to dispose of guns and clothing.

Anthony Rotondo drove Capo, Joey, and Vinny Palermo back to Palermo's house on Long Island.

"Vinny went berserk on Darren," Capo said.

"'Jack shit!' Vinny yelled at Darren over the phone. 'We walked away with jack shit! Get your fucking ass over here. Now!'"

"Darren was shitting bricks. He told Vinny, 'I swear I know a better mark.'"

The same pack of DeCavalcantes, minus Scarabino, went out on the next sortie. Frankie the Beast was "on the bench" for jeopardizing the previous operation. With the mob, the eye really does need to remind the hand, "Hey, I need you to pay attention!"

"I used the same playbook on the next victims," Capo said. "They were an Indian couple and I made like I was NYPD."

Masella drove the crash car. Vinny Palermo left the dog home and arrived in another car. The invaders kept in touch via walkie-talkie. Once the male victim was handcuffed and lying facedown, Capo radioed Palermo to come inside.

"Darren was back in Vinny's good graces," Capo said. "We collected cash, jewelry, and half a dozen jars of medical cocaine."

After the heist, the robbers convened at Palermo's house to assess the loot. The jewelry was fenced by a jeweler across the street from the 122nd Precinct police station on Staten Island.

Masella once again got rid of the guns and uniforms. He dumped the cocaine too. There wasn't enough of it to sell.

"I was happy with my take," Capo said. "For both break-ins, I took home $20,000. Joey O Masella was pissed off, though. He only got $5,000."

Scarabino was lucky Vinny Palermo let him live.

Capo recalled some more home invasions. Quite a few, including a mom-and-pop bakery, he did with Darren. Others he did with Palermo and Joey Garofano. In one instance, Capo drove them all to a house in the Bensonhurst section of Brooklyn. Joey and Palermo rang the front doorbell. When nobody responded, Palermo kicked in the door. Nothin' worth stealing. Damn!

Maybe they were overthinking it. Palermo decided to try a home invasion in Queens with only Capo in tow. Capo donned a postal worker's uniform and rang the doorbell. He could hear a woman inside. She wouldn't come to the door.

"I didn't force my way in," he told me. "I heard kids."

I thought to myself, *If Capo had gotten in, this could have gone really bad. I mean, terrorizing people in their own home?* FBI agents are trained not to judge—and George had told me not to get creeped out—but I was thoroughly disgusted.

My disgust registered with Capo. The next time we met, he expressed remorse.

Maybe Capo was changing.

But that's not what I cared about right then.

Capo had done the majority of his violent crimes with the DeCavalcante acting boss. Vinny Palermo's goose was cooked. He'd have to cooperate with us or spend the rest of his life making license plates.

If Vinny flipped, Capo would get all the credit, the way Ralph did when Capo cooperated. With Capo's information, we could supersede on the initial indictment and charge the acting boss and other DeCavalcantes with three murders.

What would Vinny do?

14

THE ACTING BOSS SINGS AND COOKS

JACK STUBING LEFT C-10 to become coordinating supervisory special agent (CSSA) and now oversaw all OC investigations. Our new supervisor was John DiStasio, a "philosophical" FBI agent we nicknamed "the Doctor." I recall reading a paper of John's that linked globalization, banking, mass migration, economic uncertainty, and US tourism. Yeah. Smart. I believe he spent some time in Russia. No idea how he came to supervise an Italian organized crime squad. We were all stunned and then amused by his short fuse when it came to Bureau bureaucracy. Within weeks of becoming our supervisor, John would storm about, ranting and raving—"Motherfucker this agency, motherfucker management"—and then retreat into his office. We were curious one day when John called the squad into the organized crime conference room.

George Hanna took the seat next to him. "George has some news," John said.

Something big was breaking. I jotted down "March 21, 2000" on my yellow legal pad.

George levered himself up and announced, "Vinny Palermo wants to join Team America."

What? The acting boss wants to cooperate?

While we got our bearings, George went on: "The court will release Palermo on bail into FBI custody," he said. "He'll need round-the-clock security at a safe house. Get ready."

The entire OC branch in 2000 was about three hundred agents strong. Four agents would do eight-hour security shifts on Palermo instead of working their regular cases. Even the C-10 agents dedicated to the Bonanno crime family had to make time for the DeCavalcante acting boss. The needs of the Bureau.

For Séamus McElearney, Bronx boy, the news was surreal. One minute I'm pumping gas off the Bronx River Parkway. The next I'm keeping a mob boss under lock and key so the mob doesn't kill him.

F'ing amazing.

Somebody asked where the safe house was. George was discreet. "It's in an isolated area," he said. "We'll let you know."

"Isolated" was not my "area." Yonkers had a harness racing track, a planetarium, sculpted gardens, a historic manor, two malls, and a Division of Motor Vehicles. Not to mention it was famous as the home of serial killer David Berkowitz, a.k.a. Son of Sam. Whatever desert island Vinny was being held on, I was going to rack up hundreds of miles a week driving there, to Yonkers, to Lower Manhattan, to Capo's prison . . . My nerves were already jumping between exhilaration and exhaustion.

George was an ace people person, and he had connections all over the metropolitan area. Thanks to him, our new source was placed in an isolated safe house with 24/7 FBI protection.

I'd seen Vinny at the arraignment on December 2. I was wrapped up in Anthony Capo, but I remember looking at Vinny, in his dress pants and black pullover sweater, and thinking, *So, that's what an acting mob boss looks like.* With his prominent eyebrows, thin lips, and salt-and-pepper hair, he looked like any number of guys I used to pass on Bainbridge Avenue without a second thought.

In his early days at the safe house, Vinny kept to his bedroom. He was in the middle of nowhere, surrounded by law enforcement. He had just made a life-altering decision that put him into a super-elite fraternity

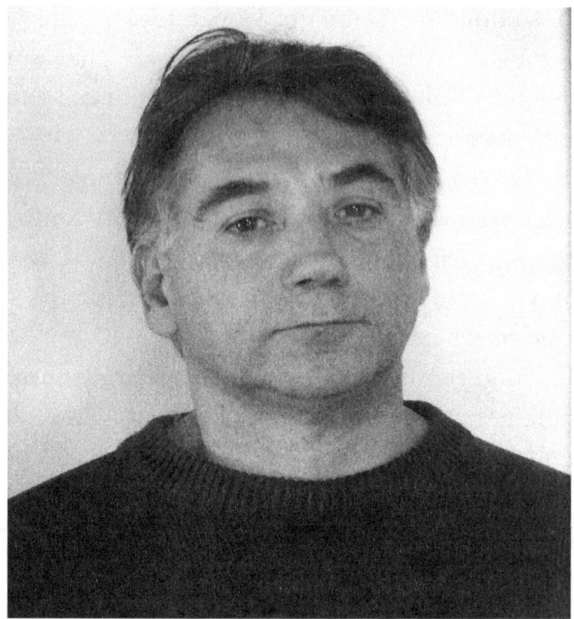

Vincent "Vinny Ocean" Palermo. *Department of Justice Trial Exhibit, US Attorney's Office, Southern District of New York / FBI*

of mob boss cooperators—and it was lonely at the bottom.* Vinny kept himself sane doing an insane number of push-ups and sit-ups.

Our challenge was to become Vinny's ally while still preserving the FBI agent at our core. It was a balancing act some agents in the Bureau's history hadn't properly managed; they'd let themselves get seduced into becoming "friends" with the very people they were sworn to investigate. Probably the most famous example is Special Agent John Connolly. In 1994, he tipped off Irish mob boss Whitey Bulger about Bulger's impending indictment for murder, extortion, and obstruction of justice, to name a few. I wasn't going to play the fool like Connolly. My suspicious nature went all the way back to Bainbridge Avenue. For me every mobster was a wolf in sheep's clothing.

* The only other mob boss to cooperate with the government before 2000 was Al D'Arco, acting boss of the Lucchese organized crime family. He flipped in 1991.

You're thinking, *But Séamus . . . Anthony Capo. Your relationship with him looks like a bond.*

It was. But it wasn't a bond between equals, not from my side and not from his. I needed Anthony to be a witness at future DeCavalcante trials. You can catch more flies with honey than with vinegar. That's all I was trying to do.

Anthony needed me right back. His goal was to get out of prison yesterday. Moreover, he had a wife and three children he couldn't provide for anymore. A happy witness makes a good witness, and for that practical reason, the government helped to the extent it could. Still, I wasn't going to let Capo or anyone else make me cross a line.

It's always a cat-and-mouse game between law enforcement and the mob.

John and George assigned Nora Conley—a venerable agent from Whitey Bulger's South Boston—the job of proffering and debriefing Vinny. But until Vinny signed a cooperation agreement, we couldn't talk to him about Fred Weiss and John D'Amato, at least not without Greg O'Connell, his lawyer, in the room.

"Vinny knows we know he killed those guys," Nora said in her trademark Boston accent. "Why else would he be the guest of honor at an FBI safe house?"

I got it. Until he was officially ours, we had to coddle him in those long hours when O'Connell wasn't available.

Vinny warmed up to us for his own strategic reasons. "I'm a pretty good cook," he said. "I'd be happy to make dinner."

I got that too. Vinny wanted us to see him as a human being, not a monster. All I was thinking was *He'll be in the kitchen . . . cooking. Is he going to bring a knife to a gun fight?*

Every so often before my shift, I'd stop off at Stew Leonard's to pick up a few filet mignons and a ball of mozzarella. I'd throw the groceries into a cooler and deliver them to Vinny.

"Thank you," he said. "That's some top-grade meat."

Turns out he was a damn good cook for a team of hungry agents. Plus he cleaned up after himself. A real "Employee of the Month."

"Mobster of the Month" too. In Capo's account, Vinny had driven John D'Amato's corpse up to Marlboro after the murder. Didn't leave an incriminating mess behind.

After Vinny finished feeding us, he watched TV. He sat with the remote in hand and channel-surfed the network and cable shows. He preferred the nightly news to *CSI*-type programs.

As a member of the security detail, I had to make sure everything in the safe house looked normal. The push-ups, the TV shows, the filet mignons.

Most normal of all: he didn't escape. And he was safe.

From Nora's debriefings, we learned Vinny became a made member of the DeCavalcante crime family in 1976 or 1977. He had plenty of street cred. He was a tough guy and a good earner, and it helped that his first wife was the niece of Sam "the Plumber" DeCavalcante, the Jersey family's founding father.

Everyone in C-10 took for granted that Fred Weiss's murder had predecessors. We were primed to hear about a trunkful of bodies.

There was only one.

We now knew how on a Sunday in summer 1978, Vinny's brother Patsy showed up at Vinny's house in Mill Basin, Brooklyn. Patsy said, "Vinny, I need to talk to you."

They went up to Vinny's bedroom and sat on the porch.

"Vinny, we need to kill Uncle John," Patsy said.

At first Vinny thought Patsy meant Johnny Riggi, the DeCavalcante boss. He asked, "Why? What'd he do?"

Patsy said he meant their actual uncle—their mom's brother. He said Uncle John drove by their mom's house and threw a bottle of acid on her niece and nephew. He drove by again and shot at her through a window. He missed.

Uncle John was pissed off about their brother dying and leaving Mrs. Palermo a trailer and a small sum of money. He accused her of getting hundreds of thousands of dollars and he wanted a hundred grand of it. If he didn't get it, he was going to kill her.

Patsy said, "I already took care of everything."

Vinny asked what he meant.

Patsy—a soldier in the Colombo family—had petitioned "Charlie Moose,"* his captain, for permission to kill Uncle John. Charlie gave his OK.

That wasn't going to be enough. Vinny still had to talk to *his* captain, Jimmy Rotondo.†

Vinny told Jimmy how Patsy came over and got approval to kill Uncle John, and Jimmy said OK.

But it still wasn't OK. An hour later, Jimmy Rotondo phoned Vinny. He said they had to take a ride to see John Riggi.

Vinny and Rotondo met the boss at a diner a block down from Riggi's house. Vinny explained the whole uncle problem to Riggi. He said Patsy had gotten permission from Charlie Moose to take care of everything.

Riggi asked Vinny, "Did you offer to go with him?"

Vinny said no.

"That's embarrassing to our family," Riggi said. He explicitly instructed Vinny to be part of the murder.

Jimmy Rotondo should have known to tell Vinny that. Now Rotondo had to do some CYA-ing. He told Riggi he'd ordered Vinny to go along on the killing. He hadn't.

It took a lot of work to kill Uncle John. The brothers still had to do surveillance to get a bead on the numbers route he ran for the Gambinos. They needed to pinpoint an advantageous place to whack him.

A couple days later, Vinny, Patsy and two other guys drove out to Bay Ridge. They met up with a carload of Colombos near Eighty-Fifth and Fourteenth Street.

Vinny spotted his uncle's car. He and Patsy in one car and the Colombos in the other pulled up on either side of Uncle John. The two brothers shot him dead.

The Palermo inheritance dispute made the McElearneys' look like a minor dustup.

* "Charlie Moose" was Charles Joseph Panarella (1925–2017).

† Jimmy "the Gent" Rotondo was the father of DeCavalcante captain Anthony Rotondo. The elder Rotondo was gunned down in his car in front of his Brooklyn house on January 4, 1988.

If I didn't know about the murders—if I'd only known about the hard-working son of an immigrant father and a chronically ill mother—I'd have thought highly of Vinny. He opened his first restaurant at sixteen, just after his father died. The place burned down a year later, and Vinny took a job at La Rocca Fish in the mob-controlled Fulton Fish Market. A year after that, he bought his own fish business and ran it for twenty-three years. Vinny was so much his work and his work was so much him that people nicknamed him "Vinny Ocean."

Vinny was destined for La Cosa Nostra. He had a Gambino uncle and a Colombo brother, and in due time, a slew of his wife's DeCavalcante relatives. In fact, from the very start of his married life, he was close to Robert Occhipinti, his father-in-law. The two of them spent Sundays at DeCavalcante coffee shops in Jersey, schmoozing, scheming, breaking balls.

Dealing with a perishable commodity like fish was a hard, dirty life. Vinny Ocean wanted easier money. Long afternoons spent drinking caffè cappuccinos with his father-in-law's *amici** introduced him to the lucrative world of construction kickbacks. Vinny learned fast. By the 1980s, he had traded up: he had a waterfront mansion in Island Park, Long Island, and a pretty new wife.

A week before his December 2 arrest, Vinny visited Anthony Capo at a Staten Island hospital, where Capo was under treatment for his diabetic condition and drug abuse problems. Vinny told Capo that they had a source in the Southern District, and suddenly time was of the essence: two bodies had to be moved from the "junkyard" upstate before the feds came calling. "John D'Amato," Vinny said. "And the fat kid Joey."

Vinny had been languishing in a cell at MCC since his arrest, wondering *Where the hell is Capo?* Vinny hadn't seen him in months. He had to be talking to the feds. What was Capo saying?

* Italian for "friends."

Within hours of the dig at his "junkyard," Philly LaMela got word out to the DeCavalcantes that, in fact, the FBI had come looking for bodies in Marlboro. The news reached the acting boss at MCC.

Bad enough Capo might have been talking to the FBI about Weiss and D'Amato. But why'd Vinny ever have to open his mouth to Capo about the fat kid Joey? Why'd he have to blab about their SDNY source? Vinny could've kicked himself.

I should never have taken that guy under my wing. Motherfucker.

Vinny was fifty-six years old. If he honored the Mafia code of silence, he was looking at LIFE. He weighed his options like a businessman. Five days before the arrest, his daughter had gotten married. Soon he'd be *Nonno* Vinny—Grandpa Vinny. Would he choose his crime family over his own blood?

We were debriefing up the wazoo. Now we had intel from Ralph Guarino and Anthony Capo that led us to Victor DiChiara, the DeCavalcante associate who had been part of the conspiracy to murder Charles Majuri. We had Anthony Capo to thank for telling us Victor was the driver in the John D'Amato murder. We'd corralled Capo, Vinny Palermo, and Anthony Rotondo. But Victor was a loose end.

He could move the bodies or go on the lam.

In April 2000, I swore out a complaint* in the Southern District against Victor DiChiara. I attested that Vinny Palermo had ordered the murder of Charles Majuri in April 1998, and Victor DiChiara was going to help carry it out.

We couldn't charge Victor yet for his role in John D'Amato's murder. The SDNY would value Capo's information, but it would need corroboration from another valid source. Nora had only just started debriefing Vinny, and we were waiting for Vinny to say, "Capo and Victor killed Johnny Boy on my orders." We weren't there yet.

---

* We were still investigating the leak in the Southern District of New York and didn't yet know the extent of it. That's why we decided on a complaint instead of an indictment. A complaint would simply involve a judge and government representatives, such as an FBI agent or an AUSA. No grand jury would be necessary.

We learned Victor was living in an apartment in Long Beach. I knew the area. My friends and I used to rent a summer home there near the boardwalk.

On a sunny Thursday, George Hanna, Stacy and I, and other C-10 agents, drove out to Long Island. We came armed with Glocks and so much dirt on Victor we could have planted rutabaga.

Thank you, Bainbridge Avenue! You taught me to trust my gut. As we headed for Victor's apartment, my gut was telling me he'd be looking for a way out of the life.

I trusted the facts too. Anthony was always dragging Victor into the crap. Like one time somebody picked on Capo's sister and it was "Victor, we got to go beat the shit out of this guy!" Then it was "Victor, we got to pull off this scam! Victor, we got to do this murder!" With Capo, it was always going to be "Victor, we got to do [fill in the blank]." Victor could take it to the bank: Anthony Capo was going to be his downfall.

Stacy and the others waited in Victor's living room. I didn't say a word while I watched Victor get dressed. When you're doing an arrest, you're presiding over one of the worst times in a person's life, and unless you have a reason to speak, you don't.

But I almost told him to hurry it up! We had to work fast. The last thing we needed was for the neighbors to see Victor get hauled off by the FBI. In the nick of time, Victor said, "Ready," and we were out the door.

Stacy and I guided Victor into the backseat of our FBI Pontiac. At thirty-six, the guy was looking ahead to twenty-five, thirty-five years of prison time. You didn't have to be a mind reader to know what Victor had to be thinking: *Why should I be loyal to the DeCavalcantes? I'm not even made.*

On the drive to 26 Federal, I said, "Victor, somebody very close to you has been talking, and you know who he is."

"Save yourself," Stacy told Victor. "Everyone else is."

Victor met Stacy's eye in the rearview mirror. I waited a beat and gave Victor the clue he didn't need. "You said, 'Hit him again!'"

Stacy and I went silent.

Victor bit his lower lip. Oh yeah. We'd read his mind.

"You're being charged with conspiracy to murder Charles Majuri," I said. "But you've got bigger things to think about now."

Like your role in the murder of John D'Amato.

I could only plant the seed and hope he saw no way out but cooperation.

Victor wasn't a dummy. With the conspiracy-to-murder complaint, he knew we were just showing him the whipped cream. Soon we'd ask him to show us the whole bowl of ice cream.

At 26 Federal, we got Victor fingerprinted and photographed. We filled out the never-ending paperwork for the marshals.

While Victor was getting his picture taken, Stacy passed a comment to me: *Séamus, did you notice Victor looks like you?*

Yeah, the strawberry blond hair. I remembered Capo saying Victor bore an eerie resemblance to me.

Trust me. Our coloring is where our similarity ended.

After he got processed, Victor wanted to know what cooperation was all about.

We got another live one, I thought.

He flipped. He hadn't even left the building.

The Southern District got Victor a court-appointed lawyer. All of us—the Southern District and the FBI—agreed to release him on bail. Maybe we'd use him to make consensual recordings for us, despite our squad being stretched thin. Had to think about that one. Victor said he'd be willing to make recordings. The only problem: he hadn't had much to do with the DeCavalcantes lately. It might look suspicious for him to show up at their usual haunts.

For now, he was going home a free man. Stacy would be his handler. She'd debrief him and write the 302s.

Back at our desks, Stacy said, "Séamus, I think George would be proud of us."

I heard about a female agent who marveled that I had been on the squad a year and I'd already flipped a made guy. In all her time on C-10, she had never flipped anybody.

Pride goeth before the fall, and I ragged on myself for gloating. Flipping somebody is not easy. I hadn't been able to flip Mike Massa, and he should have been a slam dunk. I came into C-10 when all the stars were aligned. I had two great supervisors in Jack and John. A brilliant mentor in George. An ideal partner in Stacy. And I had a Bronx IQ. How'd I get so lucky?

I couldn't help it! Flipping Capo, Palermo, and DiChiara was a thrill. But flipping them would be a hollow victory if it didn't lead us to a new round of DeCavalcante arrests.

A hundred years of nothing and suddenly four cooperators: two associates, a soldier, and an acting boss. Man, we were making history.

C-10 was a high-speed train about to run over the DeCavalcantes.

June 8, 2000

After six months of debriefing, Anthony Capo signed a cooperation agreement and pled guilty in the Southern District of New York before Judge Lawrence M. McKenna. Between 1980 and 1999, as either a DeCavalcante associate or a made member, Capo participated in dozens of unlawful activities. He pled guilty to:

- Two murders, namely Fred Weiss and John D'Amato.
- Eleven murder conspiracies. Yes. Eleven.
- Manifold extortions of local businesses.
- Two home invasions.
- Numerous assaults, countless conspiracies to commit robberies, stock fraud, labor racketeering, distribution of illegal drugs, illegal gambling, and possession of illegal firearms. Almost every imaginable crime you could think of.

Conspicuously missing from Capo's cooperation agreement were charges related to the Colts Neck murders. The DNA results confirmed the blood found in Albert Alain Chalem's home was not Anthony Capo's.* It was a glimmer of good news for Anthony Capo.

All in all, though, his guilty plea exposed him to a LIFE sentence.

---

* The murders remain unsolved to this day.

August 24, 2000

After four months of debriefing at the US Attorney's Office or various NYC hotels, Victor DiChiara was ready to sign a cooperation agreement and plead guilty in the Southern District of New York before Judge McKenna. A heavy dose of reality set in. Victor wasn't going home.

He pled guilty to a laundry list of crimes. As a DeCavalcante associate from 1988 to 2000, he participated in:

- One murder, specifically John D'Amato
- Four murder conspiracies
- Robberies, extortions, stock fraud, arson, possession of an illegal firearm, and assaults

Like Anthony, Victor was now exposed to a LIFE sentence, all because he had trusted us with his life.

After he pled, Victor voluntarily surrendered to the government.

The judge could have called the marshals in, but Stacy and I agreed to walk Victor over to their office.

"Stay strong, Victor," I said.

"You're doing the right thing," Stacy said. "We'll see you soon."

Our witnesses were never housed together. So whenever Stacy scheduled a debrief with Victor, she had to pack a suitcase. I'd accompany her on most flights.

Those were great trips. One time, after debriefing him, Stacy went back to the hotel and watched cable TV. I was a single guy in a hopping town. I ventured out for a cold beer and some nightlife.

Next morning, I greeted Stacy in the hotel lobby with a grin. "Oh, I can't join you for dinner tonight," I said.

She asked me why not.

"I met a lady last night. We have a date."

"We're not even here twenty-four hours and you have a date? What about Millie?"

"We broke up. She's a great girl, but things just didn't work out."

"McElearney, you're a piece of work!"

My FBI partner was like a third sister to me. She loved busting my stones.

On another trip, Stacy and I slept through our alarms. Total pandemonium to get to the airport in time to catch our flight back to New York. We arrived so close to departure time I had to drive our rental right up to the curb and leave it there. We flashed our FBI badges at the car rental kiosk, threw our keys on the counter, and took off to get our boarding passes.

We looked as if we'd run a marathon through a hailstorm. But hey. We made that flight.

October 18, 2000

After seven months of debriefing, Vinny Palermo signed a cooperation agreement and pled guilty in the Southern District of New York before Judge McKenna.* Between 1965 and 1999, he participated as a DeCavalcante associate or made member in:

- Four murders, including his uncle John Suarato, Fred Weiss, John D'Amato, and Louis LaRasso, a DeCavalcante captain who tried to take over the family
- Nine murder conspiracies
- Extortion, armed robbery, distribution of marijuana, obstruction of justice regarding the leak in the SDNY, and illegal gambling

* Vinny signed his cooperation agreement on October 18, 2000. Due to logistics—Vinny was in a safe house—he couldn't get to the SDNY to plead guilty before the hierarchy arrests. He pled guilty on October 20, 2000.

Vinny also had to forfeit $2 million. And he was exposed to a LIFE sentence.

Meanwhile, we were still negotiating with thirty-six defendants from the initial indictment to determine their disposition. Would they plead guilty, cooperate, or go to trial?

We used all the information we'd gotten from our four cooperators to secure a historic indictment against the DeCavalcante hierarchy, totaling thirteen family members and associates.

Our plate was full. But we were all set to add a heaping spoonful to it.

15

OUR BIG ARREST PROVOKES A BIG THREAT

WITH THE INDICTMENT IN HAND, FBI New York was all set to arrest the DeCavalcante hierarchy in New Jersey. We extended an olive branch to FBI Newark to work together, but Jersey didn't want to. We were going to enter their jurisdiction, though, so Newark sent agents to assist us in the arrest. Newark didn't say why they wanted to do their own investigation. Fine. C-10 had four cooperating witnesses. C-10 had information we could use at trial. C-10 had the SDNY. It was time to act.

I took another look at the Jersey organized crime family through Anthony's eyes. The DeCavalcante ship was about to be torpedoed. Named in our October 19, 2000, indictment were the last of the big guns. John Riggi, winding down a twelve-year sentence in a North Carolina prison, topped the list. Right below him were the remaining two panel bosses, the consigliere, three captains, three soldiers, and three associates. For Anthony, there was no going back. One day in the not-too-distant future he was going to look his former family in the eye and expose them as extortionists, fraudsters, and murderers.

I got the ticket to arrest Steve Vitabile, the DeCavalcante consigliere. I prodded Capo for intel on him.

Capo told me, "Steve wakes up every morning, gets dressed, and waits to be arrested." Don't worry, he added. "Steve isn't going to give you a problem. He's always a gentleman."

It was fitting that I got to arrest Vitabile. During my drudge initiation into the Bureau, I had transcribed a consensual recording in which Ralph and DeCavalcante soldier Joseph Sclafani analyzed the role of consigliere. "Tin Ear" Sclafani described the consigliere as part King Solomon, part Cesar Chavez:

> Sclafani: You got three guys and the consigliere. The consigliere picked them to be on the ruling panel.
> Ralph: Really?
> Sclafani: Steve Vitabile. He picked three guys to run the family. There's a boss, underboss, and consigliere. The consigliere is with us.
> Ralph: Right.
> Sclafani: I got a problem with my skipper,* I go to him.
> Ralph: Oh, is that how you work that out?
> Sclafani: Oh yeah. Like, say I got a beef with another wiseguy.
> Ralph: Oh, I know that. That's when the consigliere comes in.

To hear Sclafani tell it, Vitabile was something like your high school guidance counselor running interference between you and the geometry teacher who flunked you. But your high school guidance counselor doesn't counsel you about murdering your geometry teacher. And he doesn't direct you to another DeCavalcante who might let you use his property to blow your teacher's brains out, as Vitabile did after Vinny Palermo asked him to find "someone to dig a hole for me" to bury Tommy Salvata, a suspected rat and loyal employee of Palermo's strip club.

Stefano "Steve the Truck Driver" Vitabile had the luxury of keeping his hands clean while advising others to get theirs dirty. Somewhere along the line, he'd learned to approve the cold-blooded murder of a human being with a single word: "OK." For most people, actions speak

* A skipper is another name for a La Cosa Nostra captain.

louder than words. For the DeCavalcante consigliere, words spoke louder than actions.

Still, from what I saw at his arrest, Vitabile had the temperament of a low-key mediator, not a fork-in-the-face lunatic. The white-haired gentleman with the big black-rimmed eyeglasses was as different from Anthony Capo as osso buco is from spaghetti and meatballs. He didn't even look surprised when we showed up at his door in Millstone, New Jersey. He was all dressed up with somewhere to go.

Where he was going was straight to New York for his arraignment. He waived his legal right to be presented in New Jersey.

We had our work cut out for us. We were indicting the white-haired gentleman alone on two murders,* eight murder conspiracies,† and union extortion.‡

Our four government witnesses had led us to this new trove of mobsters and their crimes. They were teaching us about the DeCavalcante matrix—how it functioned as an independent entity and how it interlocked with New York's Five Families. But before we could delve more deeply into the Jersey organization, Frank Scarabino stepped out of the DeCavalcante lineup to save Anthony Capo's skin.

And his own.

By his own admission, Frankie "the Beast" Scarabino was good with his hands. In Bensonhurst, where he went to high school, the kids who got picked on paid Scarabino to fight off their bullies with his bare hands. As the Beast came to tell Anthony Zampogna, his FBI handler, thuggery was the way of the world in his Brooklyn neighborhood, where the Colombo, Gambino, and Genovese crime families ruled the streets.

* The two murders: Louis LaRasso and John D'Amato, both in 1991.

† The murder conspiracies targeted Frank Scarabino, Thomas Salvata, Frank D'Amato, Charles Majuri, Daniel Annunziata, Gaetano Vastola, Louis LaRasso, and John D'Amato.

‡ Vitabile and other October 19, 2000, defendants used threats of violence, work stoppages, and the DeCavalcante reputation to force construction contractors to pay them and others kickbacks to ensure labor peace and salaries for relatives, friends, and associates of the defendants.

Scarabino believed he had a good financial brain, and he was wasting it on a legitimate fish market salary.* He already had some shylocking money with the Gambinos, but in March 1987 he gave up his Gambino affiliation to be with Michael "Mickey" DiPietro and the DeCavalcantes. Now the bruiser with pterodactyl tattoos on his upper chest and arms was on the DeCavalcante "payroll" to commit extortion, loan-sharking, gambling, and murder.

Business as usual came to a standstill on October 19, when the FBI arrested the Beast for all of the above.

Five days into his imprisonment at the Metropolitan Correctional Center, Scarabino knocked on the door of his cell. His cellmate, a DeCavalcante soldier named Louis Consalvo, was due back soon from a meeting with his lawyer, and Scarabino had to act fast. He lifted the hinged flap on the iron door and got the attention of the guard outside.

"Officer Aquadino?" Scarabino whispered.

Yeah.

"Can you please crouch down."

OK.

"Officer, do you know who I am?" Scarabino asked.

Yeah.

"So you know what I'm about to tell you could get me killed."

"I won't do that to you," Aquadino said.

Scarabino said, "Well, you get in touch with the FBI and tell them Frank Scarabino wants to talk to them. Tell them I have information that somebody's wife and kids are in jeopardy."

Twenty minutes later, two corrections officers showed up at Scarabino's cell, clapped him into handcuffs, and brought him out to a telephone.

George Hanna was on the other end. He said he was with Special Agent Jay Kramer from the FBI's New York office. Jay was Nora Conley's partner and a lawyer by trade. He was a well-respected agent and had been on the squad for a while.

* For much of the twentieth century, the NYC fish industry had a reputation for being mobbed up, but I found no evidence that Scarabino's early work experience was connected with any of the city's Five Families.

Scarabino cut to the chase. He told them about a contract to kill Anthony Capo's wife and kids.

George asked Scarabino how he knew that.

Scarabino said he was the guy with the contract.

Retaliating against a La Cosa Nostra defector by killing his loved ones was a time-honored Sicilian custom. It was rarely done in the United States, the attack on Pete Chiodo's sister notwithstanding. Yet our counterparts in Italy were telling us they heard rumblings that mob elements there were coordinating with Italian OC families here to reinstitute the old ways. The Italians wanted to send a message: a snitch doesn't just walk away.

Was it coincidence that Frank Polizzi, Scarabino's captain, said he was going to start importing "ghost soldiers" from Sicily to do what the Italian Mafia had done to Judge Falcone? In Sicily, Polizzi said, people feared the Mafia, but in America, the Mafia was becoming a joke. The only way the DeCavalcantes could restore the family reputation and maintain order in the ranks was to target law enforcement agents, government prosecutors, local cops, informants, and rat families. The American Mafia's old code of honor—a social contract with a hands-off clause for family and law enforcement—had outlived its usefulness.

Frank Polizzi had cancer. It had spread into the bone and left him paralyzed from the waist down. Scarabino had been better than a son to Polizzi, even changing his captain's adult diapers. Shortly after Polizzi was discharged from a New Jersey rehabilitation facility, Scarabino paid him a visit, as he often did on Sunday afternoons. When he arrived, a team of DeCavalcantes, including Mimmo Marzullo, straight from Italy, and **Vic Moretti**, the son of a captain, were in the dining room.

"Vic and Mimmo came over to me and told me that Frank was very agitated," Scarabino said. "He had been on pins and needles waiting for me to get there. . . . He needed to speak to me. I wasn't really sure what the problem was."

Scarabino went into the den, where Polizzi had his bed, and bent down to kiss him. "Hey, Poppa, how are you?" he asked. There was no affection in Polizzi at that moment, Scarabino observed.

Francesco "Frank" Polizzi. *Department of Justice Trial Exhibit, US Attorney's Office, Southern District of New York / FBI*

Polizzi pulled Scarabino close to him and said, "You know this Anthony Capo? You know this Anthony Rotondo, this Vinny Ocean? I want you to understand this. They're not men. They're garbage. They're pieces of shit. You can't think of them as men. They're nothing. They're no good."*

Polizzi asked Scarabino if he knew where Anthony Capo's family was. Scarabino said yeah.

"'Kill Anthony Capo's wife and children. We'll make these people understand nobody is going to hurt us. You can't think of them as people. They're not people.'"

* In mid-October 2000, Anthony Rotondo had not yet begun cooperating with the government. Just like Vinny Palermo before the December 1999 arrests, Polizzi was infected by the paranoia running rampant through the DeCavalcante family.

Scarabino told George he went numb. Killing somebody's wife and kids was totally beyond what men of honor like him were capable of doing.

But there'd be a price for saying no to an order. That's why the Beast didn't say no. He just kept dragging his feet. When he wasn't moving fast enough for Polizzi, Scarabino also ended up on Polizzi's kill list. And if Polizzi couldn't get to him, he would try getting to Scarabino's wife and children. The thanks you get for changing Poppa's diapers.

We took the threat seriously. We had to get Scarabino out of MCC and protect two women and eight children. FBI NY notified headquarters to alert all field offices of the threat, and the news filtered out to the FBI agents and prosecutors in Lower Manhattan.

George told us about an AUSA waiting for him on the corner of Worth and Park Row. She was petrified. "She was screaming at me, 'I'm a target out here!'" George said. "I was running a little late, but I was on my way to pick her up."

In fact, George was still in the office when he took that call. I'm surprised he didn't tell her, "I'm coming over the bridge." George was always late and coming over the bridge!

C-10 was so maxed out I drove alone the next morning to see Anthony Capo. All the way up the Thruway, I wondered how to broach the threat with him. There was no sugarcoating this news.

Capo nearly collapsed in his chair when I told him about the death threat against his family. I hadn't seen this sensitive side of him. He tried to speak, but the words wouldn't come. I had to wonder, *Does Anthony regret flipping?* I mean, the guy was a psycho. He killed people. He could snap and blame *me* for putting his family at risk.

Two possibilities: he'd stop cooperating with us, or he'd become more determined to cooperate.

Inside prison, Anthony Capo was powerless. I was his only link to his wife, kids, mother, and sister. "Stacy and I'll drive out to Staten Island tonight," I reassured him. "We'll talk to your wife."

"As if she didn't hate me enough already," Capo said.

The Capos were getting divorced. Their marriage had been in the tank for years. His kids were his world, though. He needed to make sure they and their mother were safe. "You've got to move them," Anthony pleaded with me.

"The FBI will get them all resettled in a safe place," I promised.

That evening Stacy, George, and I drove out to Staten Island and told Mrs. Capo she had the resources of the federal government behind her. For her safety and the children's, she had to relocate.

She refused to move. She rejected our offer to go into Witness Security. My hands were tied. But I kept in touch with her to make sure she was safe.

We went back in early 2001 and pleaded with her again. She wasn't budging.

Stacy and I went to see her one more time on February 23. I showed her an envelope of cash. "The FBI will pay you to relocate," I said. To get the money, Mrs. Capo had to sign a liability release form. She signed the form and took the cash.

We made it clear that the farther away she moved the better.

She moved to another neighborhood on Staten Island. Whatever.

Scarabino told Agent Zampogna that Vic Moretti and Mimmo Marzullo were champing at the bit to kill Capo's family. I couldn't stop thinking about that.

I tried reason. "Mrs. Capo, there's a direct threat against you, Anthony, and the kids. These guys are not joking around. They want to kill you."

You couldn't separate her from Staten Island with a car jack.

Capo was beside himself.

To be fair, I wasn't moving my family either. But I had a gun. I could defend myself.

I did take precautions, though. I altered my route to and from 26 Federal, and to and from visiting Capo and Palermo. Life throws a lot of punches at you. You dust yourself off, you keep fighting, and you stay aware of your surroundings.

My saving grace: work was an F'ing joy. Flipping Capo, Palermo, and DiChiara had created a critical mass of witness cooperation that kept rippling through our December 1999 arrestees. In due time, all of them pled guilty, notably one of the co-conspirators in the unsolved murder of wheelchair-bound Joseph "Joe Pitts" Conigliaro.

Tommy DiTorra was one of the alleged DeCavalcantes listed in our initial indictment, but all we knew about the Shrek-sized associate was that he played a role as a lender and collector of loan-shark debts. We did know he was an associate in Joe Pitts's crew,* along with Mike Massa, the associate I'd tried, unsuccessfully, to flip. To our knowledge, however, DiTorra hadn't killed or conspired to kill anybody, and after his December 1999 arrest, he got out on bail.

Unbeknownst to us, DiTorra was becoming more and more unglued with each fall of a DeCavalcante domino. With our four cooperating witnesses, DiTorra figured it was only a matter of time before one of them incriminated him in the Joe Pitts murder.

Actually, DiTorra realized he'd already incriminated himself more than once. He remembered talking to Ralph Guarino about extorting a bus company. He'd talked to Vinny Ocean about the bus company too. Worst of all, he, Mike Massa, and a third associate, Joey Brideson, had spoken directly with Anthony Capo about getting permission to kill Joe Pitts.

DiTorra could feel the walls closing in on him. It was just a matter of time before the government put two and two together. He met with his attorney in March 2001 and said he wanted to cooperate. His attorney got the ball rolling by calling the AUSAs and the FBI.

In a series of debriefs, DiTorra told the FBI how he, Mike Massa, and four other co-conspirators planned out the murder of Joe Pitts on January 23, 1998. Just about the time I joined the Bureau.

---

* According to a *Daily News* reporter, the DeCavalcantes "treated Joe [Pitts] as a made guy. If it wasn't for the fact that he was confined to a wheelchair, [the DeCavalcantes] would have straightened him out a long time ago." Hence, Joe Pitts could run a crew of associates even though he was merely an associate himself, not a captain. See "Saga of Mob Ironside and Lead-Filled Demise" by Greg B. Smith, *Daily News*, April 9, 2018, https://www.nydailynews.com/2002/12/04/saga-of-mob-ironsides-and-lead-filled-demise/.

Joe Pitts used to report to Rudy Farone, a real old-time DeCavalcante, DiTorra told us. Joe Pitts was heavy into narcotics trafficking, construction extortions, and loan-sharking. He treated his crew like crap. He was super cruel to Mike Massa, and DiTorra confirmed that Pitts extorted Massa nonstop. When Vinny Ocean became acting boss, he began supervising Joe Pitts and his crew. Massa, Brideson, and DiTorra went to Vinny Ocean and asked him to kill Joe Pitts.

Vinny Palermo considered doing the job, but ultimately backed out. DiTorra and his fellow associates asked Palermo for permission to kill Joe Pitts themselves. If anyone was made for the job of whacking, it was DiTorra and Brideson. They were Goliaths. Capo called them the Twin Towers.

Vinny Ocean told the Twin Towers, "Do what you've got to do," DiTorra recalled.

Mike Massa hired a bus driver named Martin Lewis to shoot Joe Pitts. Lewis had never murdered anybody before, but he was game.

The co-conspirators waited for a day when Joe Pitts left his snarling German shepherd at home. The perfect day was dark and rainy. Joe Pitts didn't want his dog to get wet.

DiTorra told the FBI that on the day of the murder, he, Brideson, and Massa had Marty Lewis meet Joe Pitts at his social club on Court Street in Brooklyn. After a while, Marty and Massa hitched a ride home with Joe Pitts. Massa got dropped off first. Then Joe Pitts drove Marty to his home.

When Marty Lewis—a guy with *sad sack* written all over him—got out of the car, he pulled out a .25 caliber semiautomatic equipped with a silencer. It belonged to Joe Pitts, but Joey Brideson kept it, and all of Joe Pitts's guns, in his apartment. Marty shot Joe Pitts with his own weapon.

Six bullets and the old buzzard didn't die. Pitts drove himself back to his social club. By happenstance, Brideson lived in the same building on an upper floor. Pitts honked the car horn. Brideson came out. Pitts asked him for help. What could Brideson do but get into the passenger seat? Joe Pitts drove them both to Methodist Hospital in Brooklyn.

Brideson was shaking like a leaf. He called his cousin Michael Silvestri, a detective with the NYPD. He told Silvestri they had a situation. Meet me at Methodist Hospital, he told his cousin.

Detective Silvestri couldn't say no. He was a DeCavalcante mole inside the NYPD. Outside the hospital, he cleaned the shell casings out of Joe Pitts's car.

Marty Lewis radioed DiTorra and got him up to speed. I need my ten grand, Lewis demanded. I got to get the hell out of town.

Marty was in hot soup, DiTorra said. They all were. DiTorra went and got Massa, and the two of them drove out to Red Hook in Brooklyn to pick Marty up. He was waiting on the curb with his bags packed and holding the hands of his two young daughters. His second wife had died of a heroin overdose a few years earlier.

They stashed the little girls at the home of a DeCavalcante associate named Ruben Malave. All of them, Marty included, drove to Malave's social club. Pretty soon Marty was in high spirits. He acted out the murder for his pals. He said he was shocked that after the victim drove off wounded, he used his blinker to make a left at the corner.

"'When I seen that,' Marty said, 'I wanted to shit my pants. I shit my fuckin' pants.'"

DiTorra and Massa drove out to Methodist Hospital. Joey Brideson was still there.

Brideson explained how Joe Pitts had driven to his building with six bullets in his side, DiTorra continued. Joe Pitts kept saying, "I can't believe Marty shot me." He knew Mike Massa had something to do with this. Joe Pitts said he was going to take care of them.

Before he went into surgery, Joe Pitts ordered Brideson, "Tell the cops a Black guy was the shooter."

Shaking my head.

DiTorra and Massa drove to Brideson's apartment building to collect Joe Pitts's guns. They transported the cache to DiTorra's house in Brooklyn and dumped it into a garbage can.

Joseph "Joe Pitts" Conigliaro never made it out of surgery.

With Conigliaro out of the way, Vinny Palermo started taking Joe Pitts's cash cut of Mike Massa's construction company.

Poor Massa. He hadn't considered the inevitable. After Joe Pitts was dead, he'd have to kick up money to some other higher-up. Tommy DiTorra didn't have to say it: Massa was the perfect DeCavalcante victim you could fuck and fuck and fuck again.

My colleagues Eileen O'Rourke and Courtenae Druker got DiTorra wired up to make consensual recordings of his co-conspirators. Eileen was a part-time agent with five young kids. She did more than some full-time agents in the FBI. Courtenae was a former probation officer. She fit right in with the hard-charging women on C-10.

Wearing a wire was a big risk for DiTorra. If he could pull it off, though, it would be a feather in his cap. DiTorra was ready. He had an airtight pretext for getting together with Marty Lewis and Ruben Malave. "The FBI issued me a subpoena for fingerprints," DiTorra lied. "They called me into their office at 26 Federal Plaza. Before I know it, they're asking me about Joe Pitts."

The FBI monitored DiTorra's meeting via transmitter. Marty and Ruben didn't suspect a thing.

Marty, for one, didn't need prompting. Half the time he was laughing, half the time he was dramatizing how he pumped lead into Joe Pitts. "At some point, I took off one of my gloves," Marty recalled. "I probably left fingerprints behind, but I wasn't worried. I was in that car a lot of times."

Marty said some good had come out of doing bad: "I used the money to get a new apartment and furniture for my daughters."

Ruben Malave reminisced about hiding Marty Lewis in his club. He was relieved he hadn't made any phone calls the NYPD could trace.

The value of Tommy DiTorra's recording rose exponentially when Lewis and Malave praised Michael Silvestri for removing the shell casings from Joe Pitts's car. And how great was it when Detective Silvestri backed up his cousin Joey Brideson's story about a Black man shooting Joe Pitts—even though Silvestri thought the story was ridiculous?

It took DiTorra one day—March 27, 2001—to capture Marty Lewis's gleeful reenactment of the Joe Pitts murder on tape. Most FBI agents aren't lucky enough to experience that even once in their career.

On April 19, 2001, FBI agents swept up another round of DeCavalcantes in New Jersey and Brooklyn. The superseding indictment ran fifty-nine pages long and mapped out the murders, murder conspiracies, industry extortions, illegal gambling, and loan-sharking operations that knit the DeCavalcantes together into a social network that had infiltrated the construction industry, the securities markets, and unions in New Jersey and New York. Many of the DeCavalcantes named were directly involved in the murder of Joe Pitts. The rest were mobsters whose names came up in the course of debriefing our cooperators about the Fred Weiss, Joey Garofano, John D'Amato, and John Suarato murders.

We got several high-level DeCavalcantes on conspiracy to murder Danny Annunziata and Gaetano "Corky" Vastola, two DeCavalcante soldiers who balked at killing Fred Weiss in their homes.

We got others on conspiracies to murder their fellow DeCavalcantes.

We picked up a horde of DeCavalcantes for the murder of Louis "Fat Louie" LaRasso, the captain with ambitions for the top job. His qualifications: he helped strangle a Gambino associate, ran $20 million worth of illegal gambling, and oversaw operations at the Laborers' International Union of North America (LIUNA) Local 394. He disappeared in 1991 on his sixty-fifth birthday.

Frank Polizzi's name was sprinkled throughout the indictment, pointedly in "Racketeering Act Twelve: Conspiracy to Murder the Wife and Minor Children of an Individual Suspected of Cooperating with the Government."

The rest of the counts and charges encompassed:

- Construction industry extortion (January 1980–April 2001)
- Loan-sharking business (1990–October 2000)
- Illegal gambling (1990–October 2000)
- Conspiracy to commit securities fraud (January 1993–March 1999)
- Corruptly persuading another to destroy evidence (this count applied exclusively to Joey Brideson)
- Obstruction of justice and jury tampering (January 1990–July 1990)

The charges were so tight even Houdini couldn't have wriggled out of them.

Tommy DiTorra pled guilty on April 23, 2001. He'd have to sit in a WitSec facility at least until December 2, 2002—the first day of the Joe Pitts murder trial. He'd solved an unsolved murder for us, and I was confident his 5K letter would spare him a LIFE sentence.

I was just as confident Mike Massa was going to get fucked again.

You know who else stood to get F'd? Me.

By May 2001, debriefing Anthony Capo was one of my top priorities. No rush to turn my notes into finalized FD-302 reports, I was advised. But whoever said "Don't put off until tomorrow what you can do today," they were right.

I get word the Eastern District of New York wanted Anthony Capo to testify at the trial of a Gambino associate named Joe Watts who was currently facing money-laundering charges.

Now, I'd been getting Capo ready to be a witness in the Southern District of New York, and I wasn't eager to have him go testify in another court of law and potentially shit the bed. Meaning, if Capo went over to the EDNY and screwed up, he was going to be pretty useless for us at trial. And all the work I'd done to prepare him for trial would have gone up in smoke.

I might have been handling Capo, but I was still a grunt, and I didn't get to decide in which jurisdiction my cooperating witness would testify. Instead, I suddenly had a rush job: I had to hand over something like seventy-five individual accounts Capo gave me about every crime he could remember committing. It was already late on a Monday and the EDNY needed all of my Capo reports by Thursday morning for purposes of discovery. I had two days to compile almost a year and a half of handwritten debriefing notes.

Fortunately, Jack Stubing and I had just standardized organized crime source reporting. To this day, the source report looks like this:

FEDERAL BUREAU OF INVESTIGATION

Date of transcription________________

Source, who is in a position to testify, provided the following information:

Names in bold print are the names by which the individuals identified by the SOURCE are known to the Federal Bureau of Investigation (FBI) and are not necessarily the names by which the individuals are known by the SOURCE.

THIS INFORMATION DOES NOT NECESSARILY REPRESENT ALL THE SOURCE KNOWS ABOUT THIS TOPIC, OR ABOUT ORGANIZED CRIME IN GENERAL.

<u>TOPIC</u>

PARAGRAPH 1
PARAGRAPH 2

Now you know what kind of person comes up with the intake forms that are the backbone of a government bureaucracy. Hey, I never said every minute of my day was a thrill. But it is amazing, in a small, quiet, reassuring way, that Jack and I made a mark in FBI source reporting protocol.

I descended into my basement for forty-eight hours straight. Barely slept. Barely ate. Typed up reports and included an "administrative section" with dates, addresses, and other info that put Capo's reports into context. In the end, Capo's information about Joe Watts helped the EDNY prosecutors get him to enter into a plea agreement with the government.

I didn't get F'd. Instead, I walked away with a big lesson learned: anticipate the unexpected.

I rewarded myself by taking my annual cruise with my Bronx boys. Carlos'n Charlie's in Cozumel was the perfect place for letting off steam. After forty-eight hours of the most stressful task in my FBI career, I had plenty of steam to let off.

We made two more arrests after the April 19 indictment.

We arrested NYPD detective Michael Silvestri on May 10, 2001, for tampering with crime scene evidence. It was pathetic. Silvestri was a vertically challenged guy, and his being the cousin of a brawny mob associate wouldn't guarantee him—a short cop—protection in prison. I didn't even want to think how he was going to make it through.

We also closed the circle on the leak in the Southern District when we arrested Genovese crime family captain Federico "Fritzy" Giovanelli on August 1. Thanks to a contact of his in the SDNY, Fritzy broke the news in late 1999 about an impending indictment to arrest thirty-nine alleged members and associates of La Cosa Nostra, most of them with the DeCavalcante family. He had also alerted Vinny Palermo about a confidential informant working with the government. Vinny suspected Ralph Guarino. Sometimes when you're paranoid, you're right.

Fritzy was a seasoned organized crime survivor. In 1957, when he was twenty-five, he was listed by a congressional committee investigating "improper activities in the labor field" as the secretary-treasurer of corrupt Local 531 of the United Industrial Union. His qualifying experience for the job: robbery and assault. Killing an NYPD cop in January 1986 should have put Fritzy away a good long time, but he never got convicted on the murder.

By the time he'd stand trial for the grand jury leak, he'd be in his seventies. If he got convicted, Fritzy would spend his super old age in prison.

16

AFTER 9/11, JUSTICE GOES SILENT

Murder never got old at C-10. Every killing, every cold case, was an opportunity to breach the Cosa Nostra stronghold. My squad had become a battering ram, and not just because we had flipped four DeCavalcante murderers. We were also tunneling deeper into the Bonannos' underworld empire. For one, we were closing in on the killers of Gerlando Sciascia. His wake had been one of my earliest surveillances. Then, in January 2001, my squad mates arrested a Bonanno associate/extortion victim named Barry Weinberg and told him wearing a wire was preferable to going to prison for tax evasion. Weinberg, a much-married, chain-smoking father of four, had had a crush on the mob for decades. But with prison looming ahead, he flipped. C-10 got him wired up and put him back out on Mulberry Street in Little Italy to make consensual recordings of the men close to Bonanno boss Joe Massino.

Back in DeCavalcante world, we continued to reap a rich harvest of intel from Anthony Capo. Now we could charge Anthony Rotondo, out on bail since his arrest on December 2, 1999, with the murders of Fred Weiss and John D'Amato. In late February 2001, his bail was revoked and he was remanded into FBI custody.

We wuz sizzlin'.

Then the sizzle fizzled through no fault of our own.

Early on the morning of September 11, 2001, Liam and I were working out. We had turned our basement into a gym complete with free weights, strength-training equipment, and cardio machines. Staying fit at the FBI was as important as handling firearms and learning courtroom procedure. You didn't want to collapse on a park bench next to a senior citizen just as you were about to catch a thief. Great job! We got paid to work out. My brother and I planned on getting downtown by ten o'clock.

We were just wrapping up when our mom yelled down to us, "Boys! Turn on the TV! They say a plane just crashed into one of the Twin Towers!"

Every news program was broadcasting footage of the North Tower with smoke pouring out of the upper floors.

Liam got a page on his work beeper. My brother had left his FBI mechanic job and begun working as an FBI police officer. He was ordered to report immediately to 26 Federal Plaza—a half mile north of the World Trade Center.

We showered and changed into our work clothes just as the second plane flew into the South Tower. Neither Liam nor I had any doubt that our country was under attack.

"Two more planes!" my mom yelled up to us. "They got two more planes!" She also knew we were under attack.

We gathered up our work gear and ran out the door.

"Be safe!" our mother called after us.

"We'll be fine!"

"Call me!"

As usual, Liam and I got into our cars and went our separate ways. I was still mindful of the death threat against me and started out on the New York Thruway. As I switched to the FDR, a dispatcher on the Bureau radio ordered all FBI agents to Foley Square. It was right next to 26 Federal.

If you're a bad guy, wouldn't you love having three hundred FBI agents concentrated in the same public space? No way was I going to Foley Square to be a sitting duck.

Suddenly, around 10:00 AM, I heard a news flash on 1010 WINS that blew my mind: the South Tower of the World Trade Center had fallen in on itself. All I could think about was how many lives were going to be lost.

A new update on the FBI band directed us to congregate on Twelfth Avenue at the Starrett-Lehigh Building, or as we called it, the Twenty-Sixth Street Garage. It was the motor pool where agents brought their cars for repairs. It happened to be where Liam had worked as an FBI mechanic, and where Martha Stewart, the retail guru, had her Omnimedia headquarters in one of the upper stories.

The garage was a scene of mass confusion. Agents ran around like ants trying to figure out what the hell was going on. The place reeked of motor oil and brake fluid. Cars were up on lifts; tools lay scattered all over the place. Not exactly the sign of a high-functioning office. In the midst of the chaos I spotted George Hanna. As our new acting supervisor, he was taking a head count of C-10. We were intact.

Other squads weren't so lucky. An agent named Lenny Hatton from C-19's bank robbery squad was unaccounted for. We also heard that John O'Neill, head of World Trade Center security, had been in one of the towers at the time of the attacks. John was a recently retired FBI boss who had gotten wise to the al-Qaeda terror organization after the 1993 WTC bombing. Lenny and John lived and breathed law enforcement, and it wasn't like them to go AWOL. If anything, they ran toward danger. We feared the worst.

The wail of sirens from every direction told me stuff was going on I didn't know about. I heard an ASAC say we had flight manifests from the first two planes out of Logan International Airport in Boston.

The FBI was getting intel that Washington, DC—possibly the White House—had been an intended target.

Somebody called out, "North Tower down!" My watch showed 10:30.

And then: "FAA shut down all commercial air travel!" The situation—the crisis—was changing minute to minute. It hit me that Nora Conley and AUSA John Hillebrecht had flown to another state to debrief Vinny Palermo. They'd have to rent a car to get back to New York.

We agents milled around the garage for a couple of hours waiting to be dispatched wherever needed. We didn't have hard and fast numbers about casualties, but we heard St. Vincent's Hospital was standing by for an onslaught of wounded. It was sobering to consider that nobody had shown up yet.

Not sure how much time passed. An hour. Two. Three. Our supervisors sent us home. We were ordered back for a night shift at the Trade Center. How could we possibly sleep through the rest of the day?

I wanted to hang out until my shift. I loved coming into work every day, but from the moment I set foot in the garage—from the moment I saw the shock and grief on the faces around me—I felt such a bond with my fellow agents. I knew what everyone was thinking: *How did this happen? Could we have prevented it? What's coming next?*

Whatever crap I dealt with throughout my FBI career, this feeling of camaraderie never left me. All of us felt it.

I drove around the block to get onto the West Side Highway. Everywhere I looked, on the sidewalks and side streets, people were walking north: confirmation that Lower Manhattan had suffered a catastrophe. The Hudson River, usually busy with garbage barges, Circle Line tourist boats, and recreational skiffs, was devoid of traffic. Up until September 10, I had thought of September 11 as the day Fred Weiss was murdered. But now all New Yorkers were devastated by the scale of the disaster, and the attack on our hometown was going to supersede any other association I had with the day.

With my schedule turned upside down, with toxic smoke rising from Ground Zero behind me, with the radio playing "God Bless the USA," I felt like I was in a movie. I slowed down at the sound of a plane overhead. Up above the Hudson River in a perfect blue sky was a single fighter jet. I'd never seen one in flight before.

I tried to call Liam on his cell phone. No signal. Duh. The transmission antenna on top of the WTC's North Tower no longer existed. I'd been issued an FBI Nextel walkie-talkie, but I didn't know if Liam had one. I couldn't make contact with him, but I knew he was OK. Some of the agents had been down at 26 Federal and they'd seen him there.

It took me less than an hour to get home. I pulled into the driveway and saw my mom peering out the living room window. She didn't even wait until I got in the door. It was one of those rare New York September days and we stood outside in the sunshine for a few minutes just repeating everything we'd heard. My mom's big concern, of course, was Liam. I reassured her he was fine, but the truth is I was worried that Liam—and all law enforcement—might be a target.

If I was going to make it through my night shift, I had to nap. But I could not stop watching the local cable TV news coverage. Amateur videographers had caught the two planes plowing into the Twin Towers, and a loop of their video ran all day.* Professional news teams captured both towers pancaking—and now I understood what happened when two of the tallest buildings in the world fell in on themselves. It was a foregone conclusion that people still inside the buildings were buried underneath tons of rubble. On my way downtown, I'd heard the sirens of fire trucks. The FDNY knew their way around disaster. I wanted to believe the firefighters, who'd run toward the conflagration, were safe.

Around 9:00 PM I left home for the "pit," the deep gash that used to be the WTC footprint. At Christopher Street on the West Side Highway, I was forced to slow down. Dozens of people were standing on the median strip, waving American flags and holding up signs of gratitude. The citizens of New York City really energized us. They gave us the courage to descend into the pile.

Like my brother and sister agents, I was wearing an FBI raid jacket. The clothes really do make the man, because everyone outside the FBI assumed we knew what we were doing.

We didn't.

I was put on a team with Konrad Motyka, an agent on the Russian organized crime squad, and Dave Shafer, the agent who thought Capo could have been the triggerman in the Colts Neck murders. Facilities personnel had set up industrial floodlights, but it was still hard to make

* FBI supervisory surveillance specialist Rick Sutton took video of the towers from the twenty-fifth floor of the NYO. It wasn't shared with the public until 2021. See the opening minutes of *26th Street Garage: The FBI's Untold Story of 9/11*, directed by Judd Ehrlich and Shawn Efran, Paramount+, 2021.

out what we were seeing. I was stunned when Konrad and Dave identified part of an airplane wing. It made us feel even closer to the victims.

At some point that evening, Stacy and I ended up on patrol together. We wandered over to a triage area near Moran's bar,* where some organization, or maybe just an ad hoc health care team, was on hand to deal with the wounded, if any showed up. Volunteers were passing out bottled water, rain gear, masks, and blankets. I can't believe how lucky I was to be with Stacy. She insisted we pick up masks. I was too numb to fathom the dangers associated with breathing the toxic air. Boy, am I glad I listened to her.

Science 101 tells you your lungs are in danger if your living room sofa goes up in flames, let alone two tall buildings full of asbestos, gypsum, calcium carbonate, pulverized rock, carpet fibers, metal and glass particles, lead, and ninety-one thousand liters of jet fuel. No question about it, the air in Lower Manhattan was poisonous. Depending on which way the wind blew, you were smelling death.

We were tramping through a slurry of mud and detritus when Stacy spotted three men sitting in front of a Borders bookstore next to a Century 21—formerly the East River Savings Bank branch where I once worked. The entire area was lit up like a baseball stadium, and we saw clearly that those three people were firefighters. We now knew upward of three hundred of them had gone into the Towers. These men were sitting with their heads down, dazed, confused.

We ran over to them.

"Listen, guys," I said. "You're sitting underneath a dangling shard of glass. If it falls, it'll slice off your heads. Get up very slowly, but you've got to move ASAP."

They got up in a stupor and left. We didn't see them again.

Boy, did I need a breather. I ducked into a Borders bookstore. A wire display rack of postcards was still standing near the cash register as if tons of concrete hadn't just rained down a block away. I took one

* Moran's served its last Guinness in July 2011 after a twenty-five-year reign two blocks south of the old World Trade Center. St. Joseph's Chapel nearby became a place of refuge where nurses gave massages to first responders. It closed down in January 2018. Neither institution could afford the high rents that turned the neighborhood into an upscale district.

of the postcards. It was a photograph of the Twin Towers against a brilliant blue sky. That was the Manhattan skyline until 8:46 that morning. I have that postcard to this day.

My shift ended at 6:00 AM. Despite no traffic on the West Side Highway and the FDR, and no trouble getting home fast, I didn't expect to get much sleep between then and whenever I had to be back on duty. My next evening shift would begin on the USS *Intrepid*, the aircraft carrier museum at Pier 86 on the Hudson River. I was assigned security watch, and I'd be standing at the far end of the ship with a shotgun at the ready. For all we knew, an enemy was hatching an attack by water.

Whenever I closed my eyes, I saw the three firefighters beneath the jagged glass.

But I also kept seeing the New Yorkers on the West Side Highway and the love they gave us.* Every time I passed them, it seems, the radio played "God Bless the USA."

"And I won't forget the men who died . . . 'Cause there ain't no doubt I love this land . . . God bless the USA!"

I'm proud, and relieved, to say the FBI recognized the danger the air in Lower Manhattan posed to first responders. Ground Zero, and the concentric circles radiating out from it, was a serious pollution problem. All but essential workers, like Liam, were kept away from 26 Federal. I was glad when our base of operations moved from the *Intrepid* back to the Twenty-Sixth Street Garage, now an indoor command center that fit us into a matrix of federal and state law enforcement agencies. Martha Stewart on the ninth floor baked us a cake. It was a nice gesture on her part, but the entire thing was gone before I ever saw a slice.

You may think I'm idealizing, but the petty infighting typical among bureaucracies was nowhere to be found. The work we did with, say, the Secret Service, IRS, Drug Enforcement Administration, Department

* This citizen tribute takes place every September 11 on that West Side Highway median. Never forget!

of Labor, NYPD, and US Postal Service was collegial. The FBI participated in task forces with a mix of such groups—about two dozen of them—and began investigating "suspicious activity" called in by citizens. It didn't matter which agency employed us. We were all determined to help any way we could.

At the same time, you couldn't blame us for the three-ring circus that arose out of our partnerships. We weren't used to interlocking with other bureaucracies. They had their protocols. We had ours. Moreover, the FBI's computers in no way resembled the cutting-edge technology we carry around in our pockets now. Leads—many of them placed by concerned citizens and not closely vetted—were entered into a database we didn't update in a timely way, and quite often one team of investigators duplicated the efforts of another. Yet I'll vouch that we worked harmoniously. I never saw better teamwork between constituent groups than in the 9/11 period.

It was pouring out. Stacy got into my FBI car.

"Séamus, my socks are drenched," she said. "I know you have an extra pair. You're always prepared."

"It's wartime," I said.

"What's that supposed to mean?"

"It means I'm not giving up my socks."

"Are you serious?"

"Yep." I laughed.

"Séamus, I need some dry socks!"

"I'm not giving you my only pair of clean socks," I said.

"Stop being a jerk!"

It felt inappropriate to be laughing, but I couldn't stop.

"I gave you a mask!" Stacy said. "Someday you'll thank me!"

"I'm thanking you now."

Teasing Stacy was just what the doctor ordered. To this day we both get a lot of mileage out of those socks.

But you know, Stacy? You were right. I was a jerk.

And, damn, I swear the mask saved my life.

I want to think I made up for being such a jerk with Stacy by inadvertently arranging for Michael Rourke, a supervisory special agent, to be out of his WTC office on 9/11.

On Friday, September 7, I walked over to the Southern District with Pat Kern, a C-10 agent, to meet with a potential source who had some kind of information for us. After hearing the gentleman out, we decided his info was more relevant to money-laundering, not organized crime.

My supervisor contacted SSA Rourke and told him about the individual who had information that might help him.

On 9/11, Rourke went to the SDNY as opposed to his WTC office to meet the potential source. If Rourke had stayed in his WTC office that day . . . who knows what would have happened.

I ran into him later in the year. He thanked me for intervening in his fate. The truth is, I had forgotten all about his meeting. I had so many other things on my mind.

Like 9/11 giving La Cosa Nostra a free pass.

The 9/11 attacks gave New York's Five Families—plus whatever remained of the DeCavalcantes—a chance to get back to business as usual. Who was going to stop them? FBI resources were redirected to counterterrorism. We did what we could to protect the country.

I won't lie. I missed OC like crazy. In my two years at the Bureau, dismantling the Jersey mob had become my passion. But the DeCavalcantes would have to wait—in prison or out on bail—for C-10 to run them again.

Prosecutions were on hold. So was my relationship with Anthony. I didn't see him in person from September to December. We did speak by phone, and my fork-in-the-eye guy used to tell me to stay safe. It struck me as funny—strange funny, not *ha-ha* funny—that a mobster could be in a state of disbelief about the World Trade Center like everybody else. It's one thing for Ralph Guarino and his Three Stooges to rob a Bank of America branch office on the eleventh floor of 1 World Trade Center and walk off with a haul. It's quite another for a terrorist to destroy the buildings and not make a single dollar in the process.

I wasn't happy about not seeing Capo. When you run a made man, you want to be consistent. Anthony understood why I'd been redeployed. After all, he'd been redeployed in his line of work more than once too. But I was concerned that all the work he and I had done together—the debriefs, the kibitzing—all of it could atrophy over time, and I'd have to start from scratch preparing Anthony for trial.

I didn't have to worry. Capo called me every few weeks. Kind of crazy how he'd developed a bond with me. But he also had a practical reason for staying in touch: he needed to make sure no new threats against his kids and wife had surfaced.

"Hey Anthony. How're you holding up?"

"It's life in a box, you know," Capo said.

"Hang tight. The 9/11 investigations won't last forever."

"I hope you're staying safe."

"We're always on the lookout," I said. I never wanted to reveal too much.

"Tell me something new," Capo said. "You dating anybody?"

"You know me," I said.

"Who's the new babe?" he asked.

"Nice girl," I said. "Remember I went on a cruise to Cozumel?"

"Yeah. A while ago. Séamus, you holding out on me?"

"I met her on the ship. I'm flying out to Michigan to see her next week."

"Is it safe enough to fly?" he asked.

"I'm not worried." And I wasn't. As an FBI agent, I was authorized to travel armed. The weapon was coming on board with me.

"Have a real good time for me," Capo said.

"Anthony, I'll see you as soon as it's possible. I'll get you ready for trial."

"Steve Vitabile?"

"Actually, two trials," I said. "Joe Pitts and Wes Paloscio." Westley "the Kid" Paloscio was charged with conspiring in the murder of Joey O Masella, one of the associates on Capo's home invasion team.

Anthony didn't immediately say anything.

"You there?" I asked.

"Yeah, I'm nodding."

"Nod harder if you want me to hear the marbles rolling!"

Capo laughed. "Any chance they might plead?" he asked. I got it. He'd rather not testify.

"They haven't yet. They are entitled to their day in court."

"I should think of them as spring training," Capo said.

"Before the big season opener."

"I'll be glad to see you, Séamus."

"Same here."

"Take care of yourself."

"You too, Anthony."

Ten days or so after 9/11, I was on a plane to Michigan. As I'd told Capo, I wasn't afraid to fly. In fact, I appreciated the flight attendants hugging me. They knew I was an armed FBI agent, and it gave them peace of mind. I took a lot of pride in that.

When the plane took off, I remembered what Anthony said about passing his days "in a box," and here I was about to soar over the clouds. High above New York, I looked down at the awful smoking pit where the Twin Towers once stood. I thought about the 343 firefighters who ventured into the towers that day with such courage. I thought about the FBI's own Lenny Hatton and John O'Neill. It still hurts that they didn't make it out alive.*

When I got back to C-10, I went out on a personal mission to locate my friend Kevin Frawley's car. "Frawlguy" was my old college buddy who'd helped C-10 evaluate the foreign currency in Ralph Guarino's heist. He died in the Twin Towers on 9/11. Knowing Kevin, I wouldn't be surprised if he stayed on the eighty-fourth floor of the South Tower to help people get out. That's the type of person he was.

* Unfortunately, first responders at the World Trade Center on 9/11 are still dying from exposure to toxins.

Kevin's wife told me where her husband usually parked. They'd been married only one month to the day.

I found Frawlguy's car. Toxic air had gotten into the vents and the car was condemned. It had to be destroyed. I was able to retrieve Kevin's personal effects, though, and give them to his wife. All we could do in those days were small acts of kindness.

Not so kind was the rumor started by a friend of an old girlfriend of mine. Before long people in our common circle of friends were saying I'd gotten killed in one of the towers. Makes you wonder, *When are people ready to call a rumor fact?*

We'd never go to trial with something we couldn't prove.

17

I PREP CAPO FOR THE "WHEELCHAIR KILLER" TRIAL

PRISON IS A FUNNY THING. Some of the worst offenders find God—even though I didn't know God was missing. Some get civic minded and help fellow prisoners with legal appeals. Anthony Capo got composure. Nobody would have put money on that one.

The FBI and SDNY trusted the new and improved Anthony Capo to testify at the December 3, 2002, trial of *United States of America v. Martin Lewis et al.* The so-called Wheelchair Murder Trial would be a major test case for the DeCavalcante hierarchy trials we were gearing up for in the new year. We had Tommy DiTorra's jaw-dropping consensual recording in which Marty Lewis confessed to murdering wheelchair-bound Joseph "Joe Pitts" Conigliaro. But we still needed Anthony, because of his direct conversations with the defendants about their intention to kill Pitts.

Capo's transformation, if in fact that's what it was, didn't happen overnight. I credit myself for it, not because I remade Capo but because I remade myself.

During one of Capo's initial proffers, we were waiting for George Hanna at SDNY White Plains. AUSA Maria Barton grew restless. She decided she was going home. I was stuck in the middle of this mess. My blood was boiling. I left the room and went to check on Capo. He was sitting with his lawyer. Capo asked me some stupid shit.

I snapped at him. "Shut the fuck up!"

Capo learned I too had another side.

For the Wheelchair Murder Trial, I needed to exhibit as much self-control as George had with Ralph Guarino, an erratic character George chose not to showcase on any witness stand. If I didn't want Capo to get rattled, I couldn't get rattled either. I admit I have the Irish temperament, and when I have cause to vent my spleen, I don't hold back. So much was riding on Anthony testifying with a cool head. When prepping him for trial, I had to lead by example.

I headed out to Capo's WitSec facility in the spring of 2002. I worried that prison life and our long 9/11 hiatus had weakened his resolve to cooperate fully with us.

Anthony looked healthier and thinner since the day I arrested him. "Hey, Séamus," he greeted me in our usual visitors' room. "Are you still working at the pit? It's got to be tough seeing all that destruction."

Anthony was genuinely concerned about me. "You're a witness to history," he said.

I was a witness to history when I arrested him too, but I didn't want to give him a big head.

Before we sat down to work, Anthony told me the FBI had been right to focus its manpower on fighting al-Qaeda. Shades of Tony Soprano! He wouldn't be the only made man—real or fictional—to applaud the Bureau for prioritizing counterterrorism and taking its eye off organized crime. I reassured him C-10 was back to fighting the mob.

Anthony got comfortable on the couch and wisely maneuvered the conversation to a more immediate matter. "Séamus, I don't mean to bug you," he said. "Is my family safe?"

Anthony already knew his wife wouldn't leave Staten Island. The Bureau wasn't able to offer her round-the-clock security. And in any case, she didn't want it.

"You're not bugging me," I said. "All I can say is the people who threatened your family are in our custody. They can't get at your kids."

"Prison wouldn't stop them," Capo said.

"They've got a lot of heat on them now."

I couldn't say this aloud, but we were at our wit's end with his wife. We had to get on with problems we could solve.

Capo asked, "What about the Zips? In Italy?"

We couldn't control what the Italian hit squads might do. I said, "George Hanna says they've gone silent."

"They can fly in and out in twenty-four hours," Capo said.

"It's been a year since the death threat, Anthony. And you know Frank Polizzi died last Christmas Eve. Very fitting, if you ask me."

I was confident the DeCavalcante top dogs didn't pose a threat to Capo's family. They'd all been arrested. Moreover, we had no new intel from Italy or the United States. The chatter about hurting witnesses and law enforcement had ceased.

"You don't worry for yourself or your family?" Anthony asked.

"Honestly, I go hours at a stretch without thinking about it."

Anthony leaned back into the couch. Voicing his fear seemed to quell his anxiety. "All right," he said. "What's with the damn Yankees falling to Toronto?"

I couldn't control the uncontrollable and was glad to move on. "The Yanks get another chance in eight days," I said. "They'll be back."

I promised Anthony we'd talk baseball after we finished prepping for the Joe Pitts trial. And we'd share the Italian hero I'd bought at a Lucchese-controlled deli.

"The defense attorneys want to piss you off," I began. "If you can't be trusted to keep your composure, you can't be trusted to tell the truth either, right? They want to show the jury the old you. Don't let 'em."

"I'll do whatever you tell me to do, Séamus."

Man, who *was* this guy?

I said, "You're going to face guys you did crimes with, guys you hung out with, made guys you reported to."

"I'm going to face guys who'd have killed me and never looked back."

What a difference a few months in WitSec make.

"I understand your anger," I said. "But testifying isn't about retaliation. It's about telling the truth."

"I know that."

"I know you do, Anthony. Whatever you once thought about your 'friends,' whatever you think about them now, let it go. Make room for coolheaded testimony. No matter what crap their lawyers throw at you, answer like you're talking to your mom about the weather or a piece of toast, or I don't know what."

"Or I'll be toast!" Anthony said.

I told Capo he had a big advantage. "You're going to take the jury into the world of the 'real Sopranos.' You're going to take them in as a level-headed guide."

"Yeah, a level-headed killer," he said.

"A level-headed reformed killer. You're working with the government because you've changed. You want a second chance. You're not who you once were and you want the jury to know that."

"Right. I'm a Boy Scout. Séamus, they're going to think what everybody thinks: I'm pointing a finger instead of a gun 'cause I made a deal with the feds."

"That's exactly what you had the brains to do. But I like the way you're thinking. You're anticipating what the defense attorney's going to tell the jury."

Capo rested his elbows on his knees. He wasn't looking confident.

I said, "The defense attorney will basically accuse you of testifying to anything to get a reduced sentence. Think about what you'd say to that."

Anthony sat up straight. "I lead a different kind of life now," he said as if responding to a jab by the defense.

"Oh, have you seen the error of your ways, Mr. Capo?" I went on in the same vein.

"I have."

"How's the old Capo different from the new Capo?"

"The old Capo was all about himself," Anthony said. "The new Capo takes responsibility for the pain and suffering he caused."

"Mr. Capo, has the government promised you anything?"

"Promised? No."

I feigned irritation. "Are you saying you get nothing in return for testifying against Martin Lewis and Joseph Brideson?"

"I could get nothing, Mr. Defense Attorney."

"Mr. Capo, isn't it true you're getting a reduction in prison time?"

"That could happen, but's it's not a promise. It's up to my sentencing judge."

I said, "The defense will ask you the same question in slightly different ways. They want to trip you up. You didn't get ruffled. Anthony, you're hitting it out of the ballpark."

Capo was all into the role-playing. "Mr. Defense Attorney, can you restate your question?" he asked.

I laughed. "Good! You can ask the defense attorney to repeat a question. Then answer simply. Let the defense pry information out of you."

"You make it sound like a game."

"You got to play offense but make it look like defense. Don't let them yank your chain."

"I want to do a good job," Capo said.

Did he undergo a personality transplant when I wasn't looking?

"I'll be in the courtroom," I promised. "Answer the defense the way you talk to me. Never forget: I'm on your side."

"Séamus, how come you didn't become a lawyer?"

"I like the street better than the courtroom," I said.

"If I'd known that was the prerequisite for an FBI agent, I'd be an agent today!"

Oh boy, I thought to myself. *Anthony Capo: FBI agent.*

"At least I wouldn't have put my family in danger."

"Joining the Bureau wasn't the best way to protect my family either," I said.

"Well, Joey'd still be here," Anthony said.

Wow. Capo knew Joey Garofano would be alive now but for his talking to Anthony Rotondo about how Joey wouldn't take the heat for the Weiss murder. This was practically a confession. Not the legal kind, but the gut-wrenching kind you have to live with the rest of your life. That's what happens when you do time. Anthony had a lot of it to do, and thinking about the death threat to his family got him to thinking about the death threat he'd brought to his oldest friend.

Anthony no longer had Quaaludes and Special K to silence his conscience. I didn't want to rub salt in the wound. We'd talk about Joey another time. I circled back to our prep.

"When you're on the stand, be respectful to everybody, especially the defense attorney," I said. "But don't feel intimidated by them. Not by their education at Harvard or Yale or Brown. Not by their Armani suits. Some of them think they're holier than thou. And shit, maybe they are. But they don't have any life experience. They don't know the street."

"I never heard of Brown," Capo said.

"I'm not downplaying the shit you did, Anthony. But you know something about life they never will."

"Séamus, you like the bad guys, don't you?"

That was the furthest thing from the truth. I had to set the record straight: "I like realness," I said. "And I respect common sense."

"I'm real," Capo said. "But I don't have common sense."

I didn't want to leave him down in the dumps. "You're going to come through," I said. "You're going to have a better life."

"I appreciate the pep talk, Séamus. But in this world it's better to be a Brownie."

I'd never trade the street for Brown or Harvard or Yale. But if I were Anthony, maybe I would.

As promised, we talked baseball for a couple of minutes. Then I gave Capo half the Italian hero. He bit into it and then lifted the top half of the roll to examine the contents inside.

"Where'd you get this?" he asked.

"From a Lucchese deli."

"No wonder it tastes good."

Maybe you can get La Cosa Nostra out of your blood, but you can't get it out of your gut.

Capo debuted as a government witness in July 2002. I'd prepared him to testify in *United States of America v. Westley Paloscio*, in which the defendant was on trial for conspiring to murder DeCavalcante associate Joseph "Joey O" Masella. Besides taking part in some of Capo's home invasions, Masella had overseen a DeCavalcante gambling operation and was himself a profligate gambler who owed a lot of money to loan sharks and mobsters.

A *New York Post* reporter who attended the trial had nothing but contempt for us using government witnesses like Anthony Capo. You know how it is. People criticize what they don't know and come up with vague solutions: like "doing police work, which the NYPD does all the time."* Meanwhile, back in the real world, where the FBI and SDNY rely on cooperators as well as documents to build a case, the Paloscio trial let us see how Anthony would perform as a witness. We didn't know how Capo was going to hold up, and we were relieved he didn't shit the bed.

Lo and behold, the guy who once stuck a fork in a rival's face now conducted himself like a diplomat. Under direct examination by John Hillebrecht, the government prosecutor, Anthony was open about his life as a DeCavalcante associate and made man, just as I'd counseled him to be. He knew that he'd have to reveal the two murders, eleven murder conspiracies, and slew of home invasions and robberies he'd racked up in his adult life. He knew that he'd have to testify without rancor. Consequently, when the defense did its cross-examination, the whole truth about Anthony Capo would already be out. What worse crap could Joseph Tacopina, Paloscio's lawyer, throw at him?

It's not as if Tacopina didn't try.

"Mr. Capo, did you ever in the middle of the night say to yourself, 'What a bum I am?'" Tacopina asked Anthony.

Anthony was unflappable. "And much worse than that, Mr. Tacopina."

I think somebody in the courtroom laughed.

Tacopina was speechless.

---

* "It Gnaws at Me When the Feds Deal with Rats" by Steve Dunleavy, *New York Post*, July 26, 2002, https://nypost.com/2002/07/26/it-gnaws-at-me-when-the-feds-deal-with-rats/.

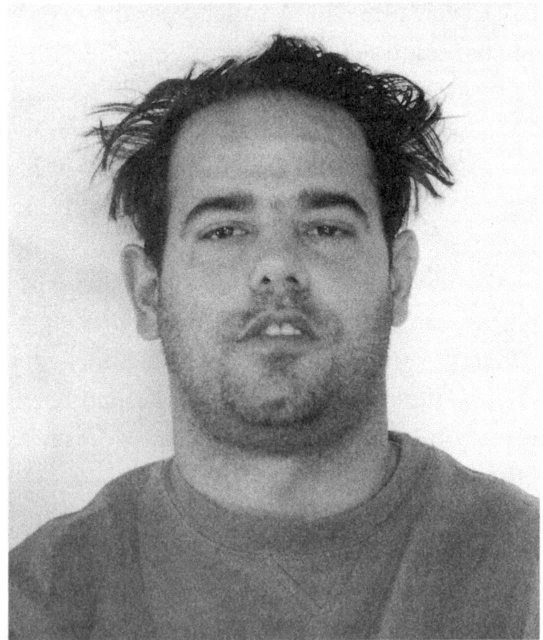

Westley "Wes" Paloscio. *Department of Justice Trial Exhibit, US Attorney's Office, Southern District of New York / FBI*

"I've tried to be a better man since I was incarcerated," Anthony said. "It's a work in progress."

You know the old joke about how the surgery was a success, but the patient died? Anthony's testimony was a success, but the trial ended in a hung jury. AUSA Hillebrecht hadn't convinced every member of the jury that Paloscio—touted in the press and the courtroom as a "degenerate gambler"—had the mental wherewithal to plan the murder of anybody, let alone Joey O Masella.

Paloscio was convicted on gambling charges. The government would get a second crack at trying him on the murder charge in August 2003.

Capo had another chance to gain more self-confidence as a witness. He appeared in October 2002 at the Newark trial of Jimmy Palermo, a member of the DeCavalcante ruling panel. Palermo was on trial for various racketeering charges, one of them involving the bribery of an Ocean County, New Jersey, housing inspector. Capo hadn't had any contact with Jimmy related to these charges. He took the witness stand only to educate the jury about the existence of La Cosa Nostra and to affirm that Palermo sat on the ruling panel. People no longer question the reality of Italian organized crime, but all the mob TV shows and movies notwithstanding, they usually don't know how the criminal syndicate works. Capo served as a de facto DeCavalcante historian/anthropologist.

No matter that the trial ended with a deadlocked jury. As far as Capo was concerned, he had done his duty: he had been willing to testify and he had told the truth. Jimmy Palermo's Jersey trial had gotten Capo in shape for the major league to come in 2003.

Nobody likes testifying, let alone testifying at three trials in one year. Whenever Anthony showed up in court, he knew he wasn't the most popular person in the room. He was a murderer. He took the witness stand to testify against fellow murderers. Anthony had plenty of sleepless nights in the days before his appearances. But testifying for the government sure beat going away to prison for life.

As for Jimmy Palermo, he could look forward to another Jersey trial and a trial in the Southern District of New York. He hadn't seen the last of Anthony Capo.

Next up: the Wheelchair Murder Trial. December 2002. The actors in *United States of America v. Martin Lewis et al.*:

- AUSA John M. Hillebrecht
- AUSA Michael G. McGovern
- AUSA Dani R. James
- FBI SA Nora Conley
- FBI SA Stacy Bowery

Despite me razzing Stacy over stuff like socks, I knew she was a one-of-a-kind agent. She was able to snap at witnesses, Capo included, and get them to focus on the matter at hand. Yet she could be compassionate with a witness's family. She'd help them get relocated and find a school for the kids. Trial is 24/7. It's stressful. Not to mention Stacy had gotten married and was in her first trimester of pregnancy. But sitting at the FBI table in court alongside Nora, she was a model of tranquility.

For newspaper reporters, the most sensational revelation in the Joseph "Joe Pitts" Conigliaro murder trial wasn't about caught-on-tape triggerman Lewis or his paraplegic victim. Reporters were most excited by the role played by NYPD detective Michael Silvestri. For better or worse, Capo didn't have anything to say about the diminutive cop who'd aided and abetted Silvestri's cousin Joey Brideson by removing the shell casings from Joe Pitts's car. Still, like the Westley Paloscio trial, the Wheelchair Murder Trial got Capo more comfortable with federal court procedure. By the time we began prosecuting the DeCavalcante head honchos, Capo would be a savvy witness.

In a "calm voice," as the newspapers put it, "mob rat" Anthony Capo testified that Joey Brideson told him about the conspiracy to murder Joe Pitts. As Capo recalled, Brideson and two other aggrieved associates in Joe Pitts's crew—Mike Massa and cooperating witness Tommy DiTorra—asked Vinny Palermo to whack Joe Pitts. After all, Brideson warned Vinny, Joe Pitts wanted to kill Vinny.

Ever suspicious, Vinny thought Brideson and his pals were setting him up to get killed. In the end, Vinny let them do whatever they decided. Never one to miss a moneymaking opportunity, though, Vinny took over Joe Pitts's cash cut from Massa's construction company.

Capo told me how AUSA Hillebrecht had prepared him for trial. "Mr. Hillebrecht went over the questions he wanted to ask me in court," Capo said. "Like 'Did Marty Lewis tell you about the hit?'"

"How'd you answer?" I asked.

"I said, 'No, sir.' Then he asked me if Joe Brideson told me about the hit. I said, 'No, sir. Joe only told me about the murder conspiracy.'"

"Of course John knew how you heard about the hit on Joe Pitts."

"We went over his line of questioning a lot," Capo said.

"And you said?"

"I said I heard about the hit on Joe Pitts from Imus."

"And John said, 'Imus who?'" I asked.

"He goes, 'I'm sorry. Is Imus a member of the DeCavalcante crime family?'"

"I said, 'No, sir. *Imus in the Morning*. The radio program. I listen to it all the time.' Mr. Hillebrecht goes, 'So you heard about the murder of Joe Pitts the same way any other New Yorker would have heard about it?' And I go, 'Yes, sir.'"

After the trial was over, Capo told me he'd been tempted to end with a quip about Imus. "I wanted to say, 'You should listen to him, sir. He's informative.' But I kept my mouth shut."

A+, Anthony.

Capo liked being part of a team.

Conspicuous by his absence during the three-week Wheelchair Murder Trial was Mike Massa. It finally dawned on him that he was likely to get a LIFE sentence if he went to trial, and just before *US v. Lewis et al.* began, Mike pled guilty. He was sentenced to thirty-five years.*

Numbers are better than letters.

Cooperating would have cut down Massa's prison time dramatically, possibly even to time served. Tommy DiTorra did two-plus years of prison time after getting the confession from his co-conspirators—one of the FBI's greatest-ever consensual recordings. It took him only a couple of hours to seal the fate of Marty Lewis and Joey Brideson. They both got sentenced to LIFE.†

NYPD detective Michael Silvestri was convicted as an accessory after the fact to murder, and ultimately was sentenced to twelve and a half years. The testimony that crushed him came from Michael Pierre, his former NYPD partner. In court, Pierre revealed that he lied when he originally told the NYPD that Silvestri hadn't removed spent shell

* On June 26, 2020, Massa's sentence was reduced from thirty-five to thirty years. According to the Bureau of Prisons, Massa's release date is scheduled for January 4, 2026.

† Joey Brideson passed away in prison on December 10, 2020. On July 31, 2021, Lewis's sentence was reduced from LIFE to thirty years. According to the Bureau of Prisons, Lewis's release date is November 11, 2026.

casings from Joe Pitts's car. He also confessed to filing a fake investigation report in which he said he and Silvestri interviewed Brideson's wife on the night of the shooting when, in fact, he and Silvestri were at Brooklyn's Seventy-Sixth Precinct station house. In exchange for Pierre cooperating, the government didn't prosecute him.

Reuben Malave, who hid Lewis in his club after the shooting, got sentenced to thirty-three months.

I got why these guys hated Joe Pitts. He was a killer and a tyrant. He made his own crew his victims. But once he was out of the way—then what? Kicking up to Vinny Palermo wasn't ever going to feel like making a deposit at Bank of America. Only Tommy DiTorra was smart enough to see that keeping quiet about the Joe Pitts murder was a risk in need of management. His consensual recording was a down payment on his future life. You couldn't say anything like that about the others and the choices they made.

LEFT: Michael "Mike" Silvestri. RIGHT: Joseph "Joey" Brideson. *Department of Justice Trial Exhibit, US Attorney's Office, Southern District of New York / FBI*

LEFT: Martin "Marty" Lewis. RIGHT: Americo "Mike" Massa.
Department of Justice Trial Exhibit, US Attorney's Office, Southern District of New York / FBI

Mike Massa pushing Joe Pitts in his wheelchair in May 1997—seven months before Pitts's murder on January 23, 1998. *Department of Justice Trial Exhibit, US Attorney's Office, Southern District of New York / FBI*

18

THUS BEGINS THE HIERARCHY TRIAL OF THE "REAL SOPRANOS"

JUDGE MICHAEL MUKASEY OWNED HIS COURTROOM. If he saw you flipping through a *Daily News* instead of paying attention to his instructions, he'd ream you out until you felt as if you'd committed a Class A federal felony. The man had covered the waterfront. He'd been in private practice and had served as an AUSA before rising to chief judge of the SDNY in 2000. He'd overseen the trial of Sheikh Omar Abdel Rahman, the blind Islamic cleric who planned a bombing rampage in NYC that would have targeted the United Nations, the Holland and Lincoln Tunnels, the George Washington Bridge, the United Nations, and our FBI building. *United States of America v. Stefano Vitabile et al.* wasn't going to ruffle one closely cropped white hair on Judge Mukasey's head.

"The lawyers wanted me to ask specifically about a television program called *The Sopranos* and the jurors' acquaintance with it," Judge Mukasey told the assembled attorneys before the jury filed in. He said he could read off the statement to the jurors he'd used in the Joe Pitts trial:

"Many, or perhaps all of you, may have heard of a television program called *The Sopranos*. First, has anyone watched *The Sopranos*?

"And we will get hands on that," he said.

"And then," he continued, "Is there any juror who believes that if he or she saw any evidence presented in this case that reminded that juror of an episode or a conversation portrayed on *The Sopranos*, that that juror would have difficulty separating the evidence presented in this case from the portrayal in the program?"

Judge Mukasey stopped reading and looked up over his eyeglasses. "Does anybody have strong feelings one way or the other about those questions?" he asked.

The defense attorneys asked the judge to mention the show in his instructions to prospective jurors.

Indeed, Judge Mukasey asked scores of prospective jurors if they had seen *The Sopranos*, and if they had, whether they believed they could distinguish between the evidence in the case and the drama they'd witnessed on the TV show.

No juror said they had a problem distinguishing between the fictional story and the real one about to unfold before their eyes. Of course, C-10 was discovering similarities between the "real" and fictional Sopranos that seemed more than coincidental.

Jury selection was under way on April 21, 2003, when Louis "Louie Eggs" Consalvo and Greg Rago—two of our "*et al.*" defendants in the case—pled guilty. Consalvo pled to securities fraud and conspiracy to murder Louis "Fat Lou" LaRasso. He got thirteen years. Rago pled to a firearms charge and conspiracy to murder LaRasso. He got fifteen years. We'd already negotiated a plea deal with Charlie "the Hat" Stango, a DeCavalcante associate. He pled in March to securities fraud and construction industry extortion, as well as conspiracy to murder fellow defendant Pino Schifilliti. He got thirteen years. Now we could look forward to a shorter trial.

Our SDNY courtroom was about as big as the old mom-and-pop Italian restaurants my friends and I ate at in Little Italy downtown. When you enter, you see the jury panel, two rows deep to your left. The judge is straight ahead on an elevated platform in the middle of the room. Directly in front of the judge is the government's long wooden table. Behind the government at another long wooden table are the defense attorneys and their clients. The public and media, including a court sketch artist, are up in the galley.

Government and defense attorneys began making their opening statements on April 28, 2003. The government actors in *US v. Vitabile et al.*, our first hierarchy trial:

- AUSA John Hillebrecht
- AUSA Michael McGovern
- AUSA Miriam "Mimi" Rocah
- FBI SA Jay Kramer
- FBI SA Séamus McElearney

You cannot go into trial cocky. It's hard to get twelve people to agree on what they're having for lunch, let alone agree on the fate of a defendant. The unexpected happens plenty of times in everyday life, and it happens in a courtroom too, when you least expect it. I will say, however, that when AUSA Mimi Rocah gave the government's opening statement to the jury, I thought, *We're off to the races.*

The DeCavalcantes were complicated, and Mimi had her work cut out for her. Sure, you could reduce their motivation to greed and their goal to making money, but you'd still have to explain bid-rigging, loan-sharking, extortion, bookmaking, securities fraud, and the narcotics trade. Mimi knew she couldn't get super granular with a panel of jurors, none of whom were familiar with courtroom procedure beyond what they'd seen on *Law & Order*. She made it easy for them. Mimi framed her remarks against Steve Vitabile, Philip Abramo, and Pino Schifilliti as a case hinging on the "cold-blooded murder" of Fred Weiss. The "shocking testimony" she would elicit from our government witnesses would show that Weiss, a Staten Island newspaper editor turned waste dump mob associate, was murdered as a favor to the Gambino crime family.

Gambino boss John Gotti had concluded, with no more evidence than his own paranoia, that Weiss was ratting him out to the FBI, and he wanted him dead. Gotti made a game out of killing Weiss by challenging the DeCavalcantes to whack him before his own Gambino thugs got to him.

Mimi didn't have to spend a lot of time explaining Gotti to this New York jury panel. The majority of jurors were in their thirties and forties, and if you asked them to name only one mobster other than Tony Soprano, Vito Corleone, or Al Capone, they'd say John Gotti, the dapper boss famous for strolling around Little Italy in Manhattan with his entourage of grifters. They might even have known that Gotti died of throat cancer in 2002, less than a year earlier, and that he'd spent the last ten years of his life in prison because government witness Sammy "the Bull" Gravano had testified against him in the Eastern District of New York. Among Gotti's most sensational crimes was the execution of Paul Castellano—a necessity, in Gotti's view, so he could usurp the top Gambino job. Gravano was an expert on the hit, because he was in on it too.

"Now, the evidence will show that the Gambinos, the family headed by John Gotti, turned to another organized crime family to help in the murder of Weiss," Mimi told the twelve jurors and six alternates.

This trial featured three big mahoffs from "another organized crime family," Mimi said. They, like every member or associate of the DeCavalcantes, were eager to do Gotti's bidding. Ingratiating themselves to Gotti would enhance the family's standing. Murdering might even return them to their glory days of the 1920s–1950s. "We have whisky, women, wine, and slot machines," once trumpeted a South Jersey power broker who controlled government and organized crime in Atlantic City from 1913 to 1941. "I won't deny it and I won't apologize for it."*

The DeCavalcantes gave it their best shot—no pun intended—to win Gotti's praise. In our fifty-odd debriefs, Capo recounted scenario upon scenario in which consigliere Vitabile and captains Abramo and Schifilliti approved of murders or participated in murder conspiracies. Now the DeCavalcantes could be more like the tough guys in Ozone Park.

As bad as the murders were, prosecuting them was just a beginning. The killings served as a portal into the unlawful moneymaking universe

---

* See *Garden State Gangland: The Rise of the Mob in New Jersey* by Scott M. Deitche (Rowman & Littlefield, 2019), 15. "Atlantic City was viewed as such a friendly place for gangsters that a large meeting was called there in 1929, a meeting that has gained mythical status in Mafia lore." Some of the attendees: Lucky Luciano, Frank Costello, Meyer Lansky, Dutch Schultz, and Al Capone.

of the Jersey crime family. As John Riggi, the imprisoned DeCavalcante boss, once boasted, "Not a nail doesn't go through a wall that we don't get a piece of."* You couldn't blame anybody who watched *US v. Vitabile et al.* from beginning to end if they concluded everyone in New Jersey, New York, Connecticut, and Florida was six degrees of separation away from a construction contractor, union member, small business owner, or loan shark debtor who'd been shaken down by the DeCavalcante mob.

Lest any juror be inclined to exonerate the threesome on the grounds that none of them had actually fired a shot at Fred Weiss—or Joey Garofano, Fat Louie LaRasso, or Johnny Boy D'Amato—Mimi introduced the panel to the RICO Act.†

RICO was brilliant. It said the leaders of a criminal organization are just as liable as the lower-level member who pulls the trigger. Indeed, as Anthony Capo testified again and again, he himself—a violent personality all his adult life—never initiated a kill on his own. "I needed to hear the order from my captain," he told me in our debriefings.

Mimi called out the defendants for who they were. "Ladies and gentlemen," she said. "We will prove to you through overwhelming evidence that these three men—Stefano Vitabile, Philip Abramo, and Pino Schifilliti—are all high-ranking members of the DeCavalcante organized crime family. We will prove to you that each one of them has sworn a blood oath to live by the rules of that society: To murder when ordered to do so, and . . . to choose La Cosa Nostra above all else."

Mimi reassured the jury they'd have no trouble finding the defendants guilty. "This is not the type of case you will have to piece together from fragmentary evidence," she said. "We will rely on direct testimony from people who will give you unequivocal evidence that these three men were top members of the Mafia, and that they committed the crimes with which they are charged."

* United States of America v. Girolamo Palermo, a.k.a. "Jimmy Palermo," trial vol. 5, September 29, 2003, 678.

† The Racketeer Influenced and Corrupt Organizations Act, Title IX of the Organized Crime Control Act of 1970, was drafted by attorney G. Robert Blakey. Blakey became interested in organized crime as a law student when he read about the unsuccessful prosecution of attendees at the Mafia's 1957 Apalachin Meeting.

She summarized the DeCavalcante org chart in a couple of sentences. The DeCavalcante family was an "organized hierarchical group of thugs." At the bottom of the chart were associates. They reported to soldiers, the lowest rank of made men. Soldiers in turn reported to captains. The associates and soldiers made up a captain's crew, or regime. Above the captains lay the upper echelon of the family. Although he was only third in line after the boss and underboss, consigliere Steve Vitabile played a highly influential role as the organization's general counsel.

"You are not going to hear that Stefano Vitabile took a gun and shot any of his victims," Mimi said. "Vitabile didn't get involved in the day-to-day dirty work of the family. That was a luxury of being consigliere. What you will hear is Vitabile was one of the people who sanctioned the murders, the murder plots, and the beatings, that the people under him carried out."

The jury was rapt as each member listened to Mimi explain how Vitabile cascaded his orders out to his fellow defendants. "Philip Abramo and Pino Schifilliti, they were also high-ranking members of the family," she said. They made the tactical decisions, "such as recruiting and assigning soldiers and associates for the murders and the beatings. And they also directly supervised the extortions, the loan-sharking, and crimes that brought money into the family."

Within ten minutes, Mimi had made a connection between the DeCavalcantes' murders and their moneymaking businesses: the Jersey crime family would go to any lengths to protect schemes that enriched them and impoverished the saps they exploited, mostly in industries from Cape May, New Jersey, to Buffalo, New York.

From our two previous DeCavalcante trials, we knew Mimi still had to persuade the jurors on a key point: that the government had a legitimate—and moral—right to enter into an arrangement with the cooperating witnesses who would take the stand against their former overlords. In exchange for their testimony, a government witness could hope for a reduced sentence. The defense attorneys in those earlier trials had homed in on this premise as an example of corrupt quid pro quo: How trustworthy is a witness "bought" by the government? The lawyers for Vitabile et al. would certainly do the same.

Mimi didn't sugarcoat our strategy. "Let's be clear, ladies and gentlemen," she said. "Palermo, Rotondo, Capo, and DiChiara are not coming to testify out of the goodness of their heart or because they are upstanding, solid citizens. No. They are all cooperating with the government and each hopes that in exchange for that cooperation and exchange for their testimony, the judge will give them a break at sentencing. For this reason, you should scrutinize their testimony closely. And we urge you to do so. . . . You are not being asked to evaluate them as people, but as witnesses. . . . We submit to you, ladies and gentlemen, that everything these witnesses tell you will be corroborated by other evidence."

Mimi went on to summarize the ground we would cover:

- The murder of Fred Weiss
- The add-on murder of Joseph Garofano to keep him from talking to the Feds about Weiss
- The conspiracy to murder Danny Annunziata and Corky Vastola, the two DeCavalcantes who refused to murder Weiss in their homes
- The murder of Louis LaRasso, who had ambitions to take the reins from John Riggi
- The murder of John D'Amato for refusing to pay back gambling debts and for engaging in hookups with men
- The conspiracy to murder Frank D'Amato, a DeCavalcante hell-bent on avenging his brother John's murder
- Steve Vitabile's role in the conspiracy to murder Tommy Salvata, Vinny Palermo's strip club employee, falsely suspected of talking to the FBI
- The conspiracy to murder Frank Scarabino, also mistakenly thought to be a government witness
- The control by the DeCavalcantes—primarily Pino Schifilliti—of Laborers' International Union Local 394 in New Jersey
- A lucrative but fraudulent stock scheme perpetrated by Philip Abramo and soldier Louis Consalvo
- The dissemination of the leak by Fritzy Giovanelli about the government's planned arrest of thirty-nine alleged members and

associates of La Cosa Nostra, most of them connected with the DeCavalcante crime family

The corroborating evidence would come from hundreds of consensual recordings made by Ralph Guarino.

"Again, ask yourself whether those tapes support the witnesses' testimony," Mimi said, to conclude her opening statement. "Ladies and gentlemen, when you take these tapes and you put them together with all of the other proof in the trial, the evidence in this case will leave no doubt in your mind that the DeCavalcante family is exactly what the government alleges: a longtime Mafia family involved in murders, robberies, and beatings, and a whole gamut of criminal activity. And these three defendants were all involved and participated in these crimes."

If none of Mimi Rocah's opening statement sounds completely new to you, it's because it essentially came from our debriefings with Anthony Capo.

LEFT: Giuseppe "Pino" Schifilliti. RIGHT: Philip "Phil" Abramo. *Department of Justice Trial Exhibit, US Attorney's Office, Southern District of New York / FBI*

Stefano "Steve" Vitabile.
Department of Justice Trial Exhibit, US Attorney's Office, Southern District of New York / FBI

"The government concedes that they cannot say that Steve ever shot or physically harmed anyone," said Stefano Vitabile's defense attorney Michael Santangelo in his initial shot across the bow. "No, [their witnesses] did all the shooting and harming you are going to hear about. But they will try to tell you that despite the fact that one of them hatched the murder conspiracy, or one of them carried out the killings for purely personal reasons, Steve nevertheless approved it or said they could do it. That, members of the jury, we allege, is a total falsehood. . . . The government's case rises and falls and is totally dependent on the unholy three. . . . No, ladies and gentlemen, it's Capo, Palermo, and Rotondo, who no longer work for the Mafia. They now work for the government."

It was Santangelo's job to make the jury think a low-level DeCavalcante could decide on a course of action and execute it without the go-ahead or even the knowledge of the higher-ups.

Vitabile's flinty-eyed lawyer skirted any mention of RICO, the hammer the government would bring down on his client to put him away long enough to get one of those HAPPY 100TH BIRTHDAY cards from some future US president. Vitabile didn't have to "hatch" any of the DeCavalcantes' murder conspiracies to share in the responsibility for them. As for not approving any of them, Capo—as well as Vinny Palermo and Anthony Rotondo—would testify under oath that a Mafia subordinate cannot murder a foe without the permission of his superior. Just think of all the round-robins Vinny had to do so he could kill Uncle John. Everyone on the jury, from project manager to NYC Housing Authority employee, from telecom field technician to USPS clerk, could relate. They took their marching orders from their executives too.

The only problem was Santangelo's attack on the government MO of using cooperating witnesses. The jury might have the mistaken idea that serving as a CW would assure Capo, Palermo, Rotondo, and DiChiara of a luxurious old age on the Riviera. It would be Mimi and John Hillebrecht's job to explain that our four cooperating witnesses would have to find a legitimate source of income for the rest of their working lives, the same as everybody else.

Martin Klotz, Philip Abramo's attorney, performed a high-wire act when he asserted in his opening statement that his client was merely "present at some meetings" where others were actively planning the murders of Weiss, Garofano, and LaRasso. That's like saying Brutus was merely "present at some meetings" when Cassius and his allies conspired to murder Julius Caesar. Another absurdity in Klotz's argument involved a charge of loan-sharking as a predicate act supporting a charge of racketeering. "But again," Klotz said, "[Abramo] is not going to be charged with lending out any money. You are not going to hear any evidence about him doing any acts of violence or threatening somebody. It is simply that he is going to be somewhere in the background of those charges."

I don't know about you, but I'm *never* "present at some meetings" or "somewhere in the background" where people are planning murders or reviewing loan-sharking debts. In fact, it would take a complete overhaul of my life to be present at even one such meeting.

Abramo's lawyer argued further that Abramo simply knew John D'Amato as a friend and driver—as if every normal citizen had their own driver. I looked forward to hearing Anthony talk about "Philly's" reaction to the news that John D'Amato had "poor relationships with men," as Mr. Klotz delicately termed D'Amato's same-sex encounters. Despite Abramo knowing all the principals involved in D'Amato's murder, Klotz said that after the government witnesses killed him, "there was a division between various people under which they had almost nothing to do with each other." Once D'Amato was dead, there was "almost no contact between the government's witnesses—Capo, Palermo, DiChiara, Rotondo—and Mr. Abramo, or anybody associated with him. That's important, because much of the government's case has to do with what was Mr. Abramo doing since 1991 when Mr. D'Amato was killed by the government witnesses." Klotz said Capo et al. had "almost no direct knowledge of that." Indeed, anything the witnesses learned about Philip Abramo after John D'Amato disappeared from the face of the Earth was hearsay—and inadmissible as evidence in court.

How to explain, then, that one of our cooperating witnesses had worked as a stockbroker for Abramo's fraudulent Sovereign Equity Management Corporation in the 1990s?

The crazy thing was that, by law, the prosecution had to provide the defense with information about our witnesses as part of the discovery process.* Klotz would know in advance who among the government witnesses had had regular interactions with his client. I didn't understand why he'd offer a defense he couldn't support.

Here too, though, I could foresee where we had a concern. Klotz said the "guts of the government's argument" lay in the integrity of the witness testimony. "You should believe these four witnesses," Klotz said in real or feigned disbelief, "not because they are good people, not because they are honest people, but because the four witnesses tell the same story, and they couldn't get together and make up a story like that if it weren't true." In Klotz's view, our four witnesses had "advance notice" by dint of the leak that they would be arrested, and they had plenty of time to get their stories about the Fred Weiss murder straight.

---

* The term "3500 material" is associated with the Jencks Act (18 U.S.C. § 3500). It requires the government to produce statements and reports of its witnesses to the defense. By now, Capo had testified at several trials, and his 3500 material was voluminous.

The jury would have to decide if the four cooperating witnesses were telling the same story because they had colluded with each other or because, well, they had committed these crimes with each other.

I could almost pity Robert Schwartz, Pino Schifilliti's lawyer. His strongest defense of Pino Schifilliti rested on an assertion that Pino made frequent two-hour round trips between his suburban home in Toms River, New Jersey, and Elizabeth, New Jersey, to meet with fellow immigrant Italians to "sip espresso, play games, associate together, and reminisce." The rest of his defense was a rehash of his fellow defense attorneys. The government's chief witnesses—"self-confessed con men, thieves, burglars, robbers, arsonists, gun men, and murderers"—had one "overriding goal" in testifying against Schifilliti. "That goal is freedom," Schwartz said. "The freedom to get back to what they know best, being professional criminals."

Schwartz was not unfamiliar with the government's cooperating witness system. Our witnesses were, indisputably, "as unsavory a group of gangsters" as you would ever see "assembled outside the walls of a prison," as Schwartz put it. But according to the terms of their cooperation, they were never going back to a life of crime. If they did, they were going back to prison. Need I say more than "Sammy Gravano"? Less than a decade after he testified against John Gotti, Gravano was arrested in connection with an Ecstasy drug trafficking ring that netted him about $500,000 a week.* Gravano was sentenced to twenty years in an Arizona state prison for that. His past testimony against Gotti was not a get-out-of-jail-free card. It was go-to-jail, do-not-pass-go.

The government would not help our newly reformed "Boy Scouts" get "back to the street" to commit more crimes any more than it had helped the Bull get "back to the street" to peddle Ecstasy.

It's kind of funny. As Schwartz saw it, the defendants in this trial were innocent until proven guilty, while the government witnesses were guilty until proven innocent.

* Gravano was arrested in February 2000, along with his wife, daughter, and son.

19

OUR FLIPPED WITNESSES ASCEND TO THE STAND

ANTHONY CAPO NEVER COMPLAINED about wearing prison garb, but whenever he appeared in court, he took pains to make his fashion statement. Before trials, I always coordinated with Capo's family to pick up his clothing—anything to tone down his criminal vibe. On his first day testifying in *US v. Vitabile et al.*, he appeared in dress pants and long-sleeved button-down shirt. He came across as a confident cooperating witness and instantly set the tone for the case. The government came out swinging.

The jurors were riveted as they watched the first episode of the "real Sopranos." John Hillebrecht, the government attorney who opened direct examination, asked Capo where he lived.

"I live in jail," Capo said.

"How long have you been incarcerated?" Hillebrecht asked.

"Since December 2, 1999."

In the first thirty seconds of the trial, Hillebrecht challenged the defense's allegation that the life of a cooperating witness was all sunshine and blue horizons. We had promised the jury transparency into the lives of our witnesses. Capo was all set to deliver.

"Is it fair to say, sir, that for most of your adult life you have participated in organized crime?" Hillebrecht asked Capo.

"Yes."

Capo went on to assert the existence of the DeCavalcantes as the "Jersey crew" and the "sixth family"—a constituent member of seven OC families that also encompassed the Gambinos, Colombos, Genovese, Luccheses, and Bonannos of New York, plus Philadelphia's Angelo Bruno family. The Philly mob had a faction in Newark.

Capo was imperturbable in his role as DeCavalcante historian. Hillebrecht asked where, other than Elizabeth, New Jersey, the DeCavalcantes conducted its criminal operations.

"Everywhere, wherever it took us," Capo said. "It took me to Atlanta, it took me to Florida. But predominantly New Jersey, New York, all the five boroughs, Connecticut, Upstate New York."

Hillebrecht jolted the jury into an awareness of Anthony Capo's essential nature. "Who were you charged with conspiring to murder?" he asked Capo.

"Charlie Majuri."

Capo added that Majuri was on the DeCavalcante ruling panel at the time of his arrest. For conspiracy to murder alone, he could get a ten-year sentence. If convicted on all crimes charged in 1999, he could face thirty-seven years in prison.

Hillebrecht asked Capo if he had been charged with loan-sharking, illegal bookmaking, gambling, extortion, labor racketeering, or armed robberies—all of which Capo had admitted to us from his earliest debriefings. Hillebrecht would show the jury that Capo had volunteered every last bit of dirt about himself to the government. If Capo could tell the complete truth about himself, he could tell the complete truth about the DeCavalcantes.

"When you entered your plea of guilty in June of 2000, did you plead guilty to the charges, just to the charges that were contained in your original indictment on which you were arrested?" Hillebrecht asked.

"No, many more," Capo said.

"When you went to court in June of 2000 and you entered a plea of guilty, did you plead guilty to any actual murders?"

"Yes."

"How many?"

"Two."

"Did you personally commit any of those murders, Mr. Capo, by which I mean with your own hands?"

"Yes, I did."

"Who did you kill personally?"

"I killed John D'Amato."

At the time of "his demise," Capo explained, D'Amato was the acting boss of the DeCavalcante family and its official underboss.

Hillebrecht asked, "Was murdering John D'Amato something you did on your own authority?" There was much to admire in John Hillebrecht's reiteration that a soldier, like Capo, did not kill on his own volition.

"No, sir," Capo replied.

"You mentioned two murders," Hillebrecht continued. "Who was the other victim of the murders to which you pled guilty?"

"Frederick Weiss."

"Were you a shooter in that one?"

"No, I was not."

"What was your role?"

"Driver."

"Who were the shooters of Fred Weiss?"

"Vincent Palermo and James Gallo."*

It may take a village to raise a child, but in La Cosa Nostra, it takes a village to plan and carry out an individual murder.

Before delving into the Weiss and D'Amato murders—and Capo's eleven murder conspiracies—Hillebrecht let Capo inform the jury about his illicit drug use.

"Marijuana, cocaine, heroin on two different occasions, prescription pills, GHV, Special K," Capo offered up. He explained that Special K was a cat tranquilizer. "Amazingly so," he added.

"How many times did you take Special K?" Hillebrecht asked.

"Too many times," Capo replied.

* James Gallo had pled guilty on January 18, 2002, to predicate acts of conspiracy to murder Fred Weiss, Charles Majuri, Vincent Ensulo, and Dennis Moglienicki. He also pled to the use of an illegal firearm. On April 29, 2002, Gallo was sentenced to twenty-five years in prison. He died behind bars on September 30, 2019.

"You also mentioned that you used heroin. Did you inject that heroin?"

"No, I did not."

"How did you take it?"

"I snorted it."

Capo's former drug abuse contrasted with the insulin he now took to manage his diabetes, and the amitriptyline to counteract the nerve damage in his legs. Our prep sessions really paid off. Capo gave honest answers to painful questions.

Hillebrecht introduced the jury to a smattering of the beatings and extortions Capo relayed to us during his debriefings. He asked him to say what qualified an associate to become a made man.

"He would have to show loyalty, be stand up, have a propensity for violence, be at your beck and call, always willing to kill for you or do anything for you or the family," Capo said. "And he would have to be Italian on his father's side also."

Capo said an associate could be proposed for twenty years but might never get "straightened out," or made. "His name would be taken around to the bosses of the five families on a list and it would have to be approved by each of the individual families, the five families in New York, the names that I had mentioned earlier," Capo said.

Further evidence that broad consensus was the rule when it came to major decisions in La Cosa Nostra. For Capo, doing as he was told was a chief component of LCN doctrine.

"During your time as a soldier in the DeCavalcante organized crime family, do you have an understanding of what would happen to you if you refused to obey an order from a superior in your family?" Hillebrecht asked.

"I would get killed."

"And the boss of the family. What are the duties of the boss?"

"That's the ultimate ruler," Capo said. "To take care of the family, sit down with other bosses, decide disputes. . . . He has the ultimate say who dies and who lives and who gets killed."

When Anthony Capo got the order from his captain, Anthony Rotondo, to drive Vinny Palermo and James Gallo to Fred Weiss's home on Staten Island, he didn't even consider saying no.

Capo never heard the name "Fred Weiss" until John D'Amato mentioned it at John Gotti's Mulberry Street club in Little Italy. He used to go there to see Johnny Boy when he was the DeCavalcante underboss. "John and Phil Abramo used to go see John Gotti at the Ravenite on Tuesday," Capo testified his second day on the stand.

Capo said D'Amato needed to get hold of Rudy Farone and Anthony Rotondo. The two of them would handle tactical matters.

"John Gotti needed us to do a piece of work for him with some guy in Staten Island he was having [a] problem with," Capo said. "A fellow in Staten Island that he was under suspicion of cooperating . . . against Joe Watts, who is a close personal friend of John. Needed our help to kill him."

Joe Watts was the gangster whose money-laundering trial in the EDNY forced me to type up seventy-five of Capo's witness accounts in forty-eight hours.*

"You referred to 'a piece of work,'" Hillebrecht said. "What does that mean?"

"Killing somebody," Capo replied. ". . . Hurting somebody."

"And did D'Amato tell you anything else about what he intended to do, other than say that he needed to get in touch with Rotondo or Farone?"

"He said he wanted to get it done," Capo said. "This was very important for our family. It would give us some credence or make us look good with the other five families. Important that John Gotti was willing to use us in something as serious a matter as this."

Hillebrecht asked why D'Amato would disclose "a serious matter as this" to a low-level associate like Capo.

Capo said he was very close to John D'Amato. He was sure D'Amato wanted to involve Capo in the murder as a way of getting him "straightened out with the DeCavalcante family."

---

* Watts did not face consequences for his role in the Weiss murder until he pled guilty in 2011. He served a thirteen-year sentence at a federal correctional institution in Cumberland, Maryland. Watts was released from prison on January 14, 2022. He was eighty years old.

The next day, Anthony Rotondo met with Capo on Bay Street, just north of the Verrazzano-Narrows Bridge, where Fred Weiss had an office. Rotondo talked to Capo about killing Weiss. Also in attendance were John D'Amato and DeCavalcante soldier Danny Annunziata, Capo testified. He wasn't sure, but he thought Vinny Palermo might have been part of the talks too.

"He planned to use me in the murder," Capo testified about Rotondo. "[It would] give me a better opportunity to get straightened out with the family. Also we needed Danny Annunziata. That was one [of] the reasons John Gotti came to us, because Danny Annunziata was very close friends with Fred Weiss. Was in some type of business with him, and we needed him [Annunziata] to lure him [Weiss] to his house."

But luring Weiss into his house was out of the question for Annunziata. "He said, 'Fuck John Gotti and the Gambino family,'" Capo testified. "'Why should I put my life on the street like that?'"

The DeCavalcantes pursued an alternate plan. Joey Garofano surveilled Fred Weiss's movements in the morning when Weiss left for work and followed him at five o'clock to see where he went. Joey shared Weiss's daily habits with his co-conspirators. Capo and his gang used Joey's intel to drive around Weiss's neighborhood in two cars. They all kept in touch with each other via high-end walkie-talkies.

Capo picked up on Mimi Rocah's observation that the Gambinos and DeCavalcantes were in a race to shoot Fred Weiss. "As we were doing surveillance, we passed a Gambino squad while they were doing the same thing," Capo said. "I saw Fat Dom, Frankie Fappiano, Mikey Scars, another guy I couldn't make out."

Fat Dom, Fappiano, and Mikey Scars were Gambino soldiers.

"Strange," Capo observed. "I mean . . . two different sets of guys trying to kill one guy. But I knew we had to get it done right away. We knew the sense of urgency was there. Time was of the essence."

The first in-depth planning session was at Anthony Rotondo's four-column colonial house on Staten Island. As an associate, Capo was not invited into the "Florida room," where D'Amato, Rotondo, Annunziata, Farone, Michael DiPietro, and Phil Abramo had congregated.

"I was at the kitchen table having a sandwich, so I could see them," Capo said.

Capo saw Danny Annunziata getting "pretty animated." Soon Annunziata got up and left. Luring Weiss into an ambush through a friend and business partner was too perfect to quash. D'Amato had been insistent.

"Guys were pretty pissed off," Capo said. "Danny refused to do it . . . He would not set the guy up in his own house."

"During this conversation, where was Phil Abramo?" Hillebrecht asked.

"He was right there. He was always with John, John D'Amato."

The next planning session was in the home of Rudy Farone's girlfriend near the Staten Island Expressway. It was one day before the target date.

"And what was the subject matter of this meeting, Mr. Capo?" Hillebrecht asked.

"It was discussing how we were going to go about killing Fred Weiss," Capo said. "Who the players were going to be and what their jobs would be. Also we had a discussion about the meeting that Phil Abramo and John D'Amato were going to have with Corky Vastola and Danny Annunziata at Danny's house."

Gaetano "Corky" Vastola was a DeCavalcante soldier and Annunziata's brother-in-law. D'Amato and Abramo were "hot," Capo said, over Annunziata's refusal to do as he was told.

"And was there any conversation about what was going to be done if Annunziata or Vastola refused to follow instructions?" Hillebrecht asked.

"Yes."

"What was discussed?"

"Myself and Vincent Palermo was going to kill them."

Hillebrecht asked, "Who was in the room when those instructions were given?"

"Philip Abramo, Rudy Farone, Michael DiPietro, Anthony Rotondo, Vincent Palermo, John D'Amato."

At Danny's house, Abramo and D'Amato tried one last time to enlist Corky and Danny's cooperation. No dice. "Corky told them I don't give a fuck what John Gotti wants or the Gambino family," Capo said. "We ain't doing it. And if you want, we'll go to war. I got my own guys you don't even know about."

Abramo and D'Amato said they did hear noises upstairs. They were worried they had walked into a trap. They were "smokin'" hot, but they left.

The DeCavalcantes came back to their senses. "It was decided . . . the most important thing to do was to kill Frederick Weiss," Capo testified. "That's the job at hand and to beat the Gambino squad to it. And that we could kill Corky and Danny at any time we wanted. It was a luxury. So it was more important to take care of that for John Gotti."

Hillebrecht: "Do you recall who it was that said the most important thing was to focus on Fred Weiss?"

"Philip Abramo."

Capo's answer was a quick jab. Abramo was stunned. I didn't understand why he didn't leap out of his chair and plead with the government to cooperate.

But the question remained: Would the jury believe Capo's testimony?

Fred Weiss. *Department of Justice Trial Exhibit, US Attorney's Office, Southern District of New York / FBI*

He who hesitates is lost, and with Joey Garofano's surveillance intel in hand, the DeCavalcante conspirators were primed. They would kill Fred Weiss on the morning of September 11, 1989, as he got into his SUV for work.

"We would meet early in the morning, at a preassigned spot," Capo said. "By the mall. A parking lot. And we put the plan into action."

Hillebrecht asked Capo to describe the day of Weiss's murder.

"We met at Anthony Rotondo's house," Capo began. "From there we went to this parking lot that we said we would meet by the Staten Island Mall."

Joey Garofano would stand watch near Weiss's apartment building and keep in touch with his fellow killers via walkie-talkie.

"They were very expensive," Capo recalled. "Nobody else could pick up on the conversation. We also had what we called a mouse, which is a police scanner that would pick up any police car calls in the area. Just in case, maybe if the police would come, someone who would see us sitting there, and we would have been able to know about it and leave or do what we had to do."

Once again, Hillebrecht asked Capo for a head count. At the mall parking lot were Capo, James Gallo, Vincent Palermo, Michael DiPietro, Philip Abramo, John D'Amato, and Frank Scarabino.

Capo, Vinny Palermo, and James Gallo headed off to a car parked on Forest Hill Road more or less equidistant from the Staten Island Mall and the La Tourette Golf Course. Victor DiChiara, a professional car thief, had stolen it a few days earlier. Inside the car was the equipment necessary to commit the murder: hats, glasses, radio, and revolvers.

"Always use revolvers," Capo emphasized in present tense. "You don't want them to jam."

The three killers donned gloves to avoid leaving fingerprints on the car. They got inside.

Anthony Rotondo and Michael DiPietro were on the scene in another car. John D'Amato and Philip Abramo occupied yet another car.

"We knew they wanted to be there," Capo said. "It was told to me because they wanted to be able to tell John Gotti that they were in the area, that they were part of it."

Garofano and Scarabino were in separate cars.

Capo got behind the wheel of the stolen car. James Gallo rode shotgun—again, no pun intended. Vinny Palermo sat behind Gallo. They headed to Wellington Court, where Weiss lived with his girlfriend.

"I drove up, not speeding," Capo said. "Quick enough to catch him when he was just getting into his car—into his truck. So I pulled up a little bit."

Hillebrecht asked what happened next.

"I stopped the car. Vincent Palermo and James Gallo jumped out and shot Fred Weiss numerous times."

"Did you shoot Fred Weiss?"

"No, I did not."

"What happened after you heard the shots?"

"James Gallo and Vincent Palermo jumped back in the car. James said, 'Go, go, go!' So I pulled away, not too fast, not too slow. When I got to the corner of the block, Joseph Garofano was on the other side of the street pointing back to where we were sitting. Mistakenly, Joey came around and made like a U-turn, backed up and followed us. That's how the people on the block picked up my license plate, my wife's license plate."

Joey Garofano had been tasked with stealing a license plate the killers could use on their stolen car. He was supposed to steal some plates off a car in a bowling alley parking lot. Instead, Joey stole the plate off Mrs. Capo's car.

What can I say. Common sense is not so common.

Capo drove back to Forest Hill Road near the golf course and parked. Joey followed in his car. Frank Scarabino arrived in the crash car.

"We got out of the car, making sure not to touch anything with our hands, with the gloves on," Capo said. "When I got out of the car, I grabbed the handle, but I wanted to make sure that I didn't touch the handle with my hand, so I rubbed it down with the glove. . . . Joey pulled up, put everything in the bag. We gave him the guns, everything—the hats, the glasses. He took them to dispose of them. And we got into Anthony Rotondo's car with Michael DiPietro, myself, Vincent Palermo, and James Gallo."

Rotondo drove the kill crew back to his sedate colonial house. "Anthony Rotondo and Michael DiPietro was happy," Capo said. "Happy that the work was done correctly, and congratulated us, kissed us both, once on each cheek."

Hillebrecht asked, "What did Jimmy Gallo do after that?"

"Jimmy Gallo said, 'Have a good day, I'm out of here, have to get back to work.'" Gallo needed an alibi to account for his whereabouts.

As planned, Capo, DiPietro, and Palermo headed off to Nathan's on Eighty-Sixth Street in Brooklyn. For years the Jersey and New York

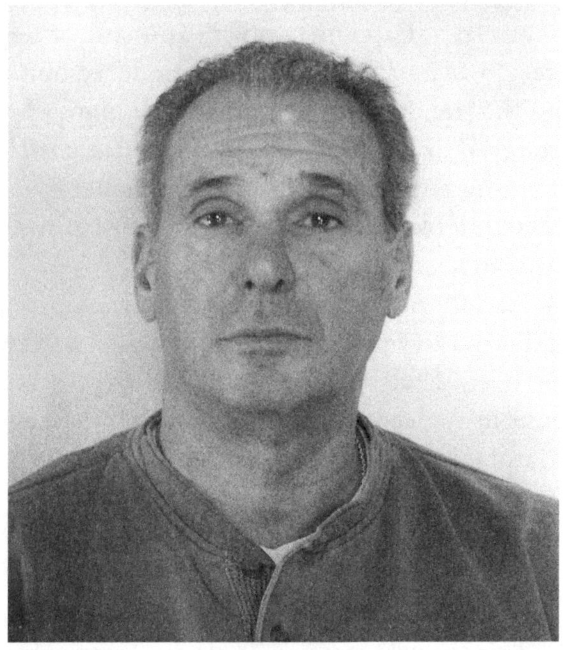

James Gallo. *Department of Justice Trial Exhibit, US Attorney's Office, Southern District of New York / FBI*

DeCavalcantes had made the hot dog joint an ad hoc office, sort of a mob WeWork.* Waiting there were John D'Amato and Philip Abramo.

"We sat down, told them everything was done, it went perfect," Capo said. "They kissed us and congratulated us."

All was sweet relish and honey mustard until D'Amato instructed Palermo and Rotondo to go meet Sammy Gravano, Gotti's right-hand man. They had to tell Sammy the job was done and it was done correctly. Neither Palermo nor Rotondo wanted to follow D'Amato's order. They'd been around the Mafia since childhood and they knew the culture: whatever you eat for breakfast, you digest it. You don't talk about it at lunch.

"They said, 'John, let them read about it in the paper,'" Capo said. "'Let them hear it on the radio. Why do we need to let them know that?'"

D'Amato said Gotti should know right away what a great hit team he had in the DeCavalcantes. Yeah, and Gotti would know Johnny Boy D'Amato had come through for him.

Several months later, Capo met up with D'Amato at Regine's on East Fifty-Ninth Street in Manhattan. D'Amato introduced him to John Gotti, who frequented the trendy disco along with the luminaries of the day.†

"I got introduced as a friend of ours, or *amico nostro*," Capo said, using La Cosa Nostra terminology to indicate his status as a made man. "We sat down. John looked over at me and winked at me, I guess to let me know I did a good job."

Maybe it was just a matter of time before law enforcement put two and two together—and Capo's days of partying with New York's glitterati would be over. That business with Mrs. Capo's license plate on a stolen car used in the commission of a crime? The beginning of the end for Joey Garofano.

---

* Nathan's Famous, at 650 Eighty-Sixth Street, shut down its grill on January 6, 2019. The red-and-green diner-like building sat idle for several years before being sold by Allied Properties to the NYC School Construction Authority for $25 million. The SCA had the building demolished in 2021.

† The ritzy New York club closed in 1991, a victim of economic recession and changing tastes in nightlife.

Crime scene photo from the murder of Fred Weiss, September 11, 1989. *Department of Justice Trial Exhibit, US Attorney's Office, Southern District of New York / FBI*

"Joey Garofano was very upset, scared," Capo testified. "The FBI was all over him, by his mother's house, his father's house. His father was giving him a hard time."

Capo told Joey to go over to Capo's house, get a gun and some marijuana Capo had stashed in an upstairs closet, and get rid of them.

"He says, 'Anthony, I'm not going down for nobody,'" Capo said. "'I'm not going away for this.' I said, 'Don't talk like that, Joey. Somebody's going to hear you. Don't talk about it. If anything, they are coming for me. I'll take the weight. Don't worry about it.'"

Capo said he felt cornered. He didn't want to get pinched in front of his wife and their newborn child, so he called his haircutter for an immediate appointment. He got in his car and rode off to the salon.

"I went around the block and four, six cars surrounded me," he said. "Police cars, detectives."

They arrested him for driving without a license and for concealing a blackjack.

Before taking Capo into custody, the police asked him about the Fred Weiss murder. "Did you tell them the truth?" Hillebrecht asked.

"No."

The FBI was on Capo's street all day. "As night came, you could see the van that they had," Capo said. "They had all these little lights and you could even see people in the van. And they were just walking up and down the block. And I knew that I was going to get arrested. I felt it."

"So what did you do?" Hillebrecht asked.

"I called an ambulance."

Capo needed back surgery. If he was arrested, he worried about the surgery available to him as a prisoner. At Richmond Memorial Hospital, Capo requested that he speak to a doctor friend of his chiropractor. "I told him I had to get operated on right away, that the FBI was after me," Capo said. "I grabbed him by his shirt—"

Hillebrecht said, "Slow down."

"Grabbed him by his shirt. Pulled him close. Said the FBI is outside. They're going to arrest me. I need to get operated as soon as possible."

Capo told the doctor he was a good friend of Johnny Pate, a captain in the Colombo crime family. Pate and the doctor were partners in a real estate deal. The doctor put Capo at the top of his surgery schedule.

After the surgery, Anthony Rotondo came by to visit. The two Anthonys took a walk in the hospital hallways and talked about the Weiss homicide. They also assessed the risk Joey Garofano posed. "Because he sounded like he was going to cooperate," Capo said about Joey.

"After you got out of the hospital, when was the next time you saw Joey Garofano?" Hillebrecht asked.

"I never saw Joey Garofano again," Capo said.

In fact, Capo wouldn't hear Joey's name mentioned again until his induction ceremony into the DeCavalcante crime family, when John D'Amato brought up the "fat kid." D'Amato asked what Capo would do if he knew the fat kid was in the house across the street.

"I said I would go in and take care of him to protect our family *borgata*," Capo told Hillebrecht. That's when Capo was sure Joey Garofano—his friend since the age of fourteen—was gone for good.

Nighttime. Winter 1989. Capo arrived at a house in New Jersey for the induction into the DeCavalcante family. He didn't remember the name of the town. He didn't know who owned the house.

"What I'd like you to do is take us through the day of the induction ceremony, beginning with how you got to wherever you were going to," Hillebrecht said.

"I was at home. . . . I was under heavy surveillance for the murder of Fred Weiss, and there were—FBI and government enforcement were following me everywhere," Capo recalled for the court. "So I had Victor DiChiara pick me up early in the day. We drove around for a while. I went to the hospital and through the loading dock and came out another few blocks away, through my mother's house, the basement. So I just kept on parking and stopping for maybe three, four hours. To make sure that nobody would follow me."

Anthony Rotondo had sponsored Capo for membership in the crime family. Only the day before, he'd told Capo to meet at a certain hour with some DeCavalcantes near Bradley Avenue off the Staten Island Expressway. The assembly point was familiar to Capo from previous rendezvous with the Brooklyn DeCavalcante faction on their way to Elizabeth to meet with the Jersey faction.

Capo was met by John D'Amato, Anthony Rotondo, Vincent Palermo, Joseph Sclafani, and Philip Abramo. He got into the car with them. DiChiara, an associate, could go home.

At the house in Jersey, Capo was eventually led downstairs. "I saw John Riggi at the head of the table," Capo testified. "Steve Vitabile, John D'Amato, Jake Amari, Philip Abramo, Vinny Palermo, and Anthony Rotondo were also seated."

"How did the meeting begin?" Hillebrecht asked.

"The meeting begins by everybody in the room, the captain and administration of the family, locking up, holding hands to say something in . . . Italian to keep the secret of Cosa Nostra in the room." Capo demonstrated what *locking up* meant by raising his hands.

"When that meeting began and people locked up, did you lock up with them?" Hillebrecht asked.

"Not initially, no," Capo said.

"Was there anybody else in the room who did not lock up?"

"Yes. Frank Guarraci. He was also to be inducted to the DeCavalcante family at that time."

"What's the next thing that happened?"

"We sat down. I sat down next to Anthony Rotondo. Vincent Palermo is to the right of me. And John Riggi asked if we knew why we're here. I said no."

Hillebrecht: "Why did you say no?"

"Because I wasn't supposed to know."

"Did you know?"

"Yes."

"And what did Frank Guarraci say?"

"He said no too."

Capo was asked how he felt about everyone in the room. He said he loved everybody. He agreed that he would kill for everybody in the room.

"Steve Vitabile said, 'Who is going to be your godfather?'" Capo recounted. "And Vincent Palermo said he would. He sat behind my chair. I don't know what the significance of that was at the time. I never even thought to ask. And then they told me to come to the front of the table. By Steve."

On the long rectangular table lay a gun, a knife, and a picture of a saint.

"Steve told me to hold my hand out," Capo continued. "First he told me to prick my finger. Then he held the saint and he let blood drip on the saint, crumbled the saint and he put it in my hand. He lit it on fire and spoke some words in Italian."

"Did you understand the significance of those words in Italian?" Hillebrecht asked.

"Yes."

"What?"

"That I would burn like the saint if I divulge the secret of Cosa Nostra," Capo said.

"And after Vitabile lit the saint on fire, what happened?" Hillebrecht asked.

"I just held it in my hand. It was burning. I let it burn out. After it got down, [I] dropped it. Everybody congratulated me. I was introduced to everybody around the room, kissed on both cheeks."

"Did Phil Abramo participate in that?"

"Yes, Phil Abramo was there."

"Kiss you on both cheeks?" Hillebrecht was trying hard not to enjoy himself too much.

"Yes, he did congratulate me," Capo said.

"And that warning you were given with that saint in your hand about not divulging the secrets, is that what you are doing here today?"

"Yes."

If Capo felt bad about breaking DeCavalcante rules, he didn't show it. Why would he? Rules, he learned that very day, were made to be broken.

Hillebrecht: "Can you tell us first who was telling you about the rules?"

"I believe it was Steve was telling me," Capo said. "That no bank robbery, no pornography, not to assault another made member of the family. No drug dealing. Don't go to another member's wife. Or no pornography or counterfeiting."

"And were any other rules mentioned?"

Capo could let Jimmy Sarullo, a Gambino soldier and his wife's godfather, and Johnny Pate, the Colombo captain, know about his induction, but otherwise he had to keep his new DeCavalcante status under wraps, at least for six months. Secrecy was a precautionary measure. Induction could signal that Capo had been rewarded for a murder. Why take a chance that the feds hear about it?

To conclude the ceremony, Capo and Guarraci "locked up" with the other made men.

John D'Amato took Capo aside. He said pornography was in.

"In your experience as a soldier in the DeCavalcante family, were all the rules always adhered to?" Hillebrecht asked.

"Never."

"When you say 'never,' what do you mean?"

"We broke rules," Capo said. "First rule I was given, not to be introduced to anybody, they brought me over to Philly Dogs who was, at the time, was a soldier in the Gambino family and introduced me to him. So as soon as we left there [the induction], a half hour later, we broke a rule."

Not to mention that a couple months later, Gotti winked.

Capo ended his second day of witness testimony by talking about something that always made him squirm: the fat kid.

Hillebrecht drew on our debriefings to ask Capo to recall a conversation he had in the mid-1990s with Michael DiPietro about Joey Garofano.

"We were discussing Bernard NiCastro," Capo said. "He was a proposed associate of Anthony Rotondo."

Hillebrecht asked Capo what specifically DiPietro said about NiCastro.

"What a coward he was," Capo answered. "He said he would never forget the face on Joey Garofano after Virgil shot him and that Bernard NiCastro ran out of the room. He was supposed to clean up, but he ran out of the room scared."

Hillebrecht: "Who did you understand Virgil to be?"

"Virgil Alessi. Soldier in the DeCavalcante family."

John Hillebrecht knew he couldn't drive Capo hard about Joey Garofano. In our debriefings, Capo's voice would shake when he talked about his friend.

"You got your best friend killed," I'd said to Capo. "It's a fact."

"Some nights I can't sleep," he'd said. "I dream about Joey."

Defense attorneys would have a field day if Capo broke down on the witness stand. Better for Capo stick to the facts, like telling Hillebrecht about the plans John D'Amato and Anthony Rotondo were making to kill Danny Annunziata and Corky Vastola.

"John D'Amato wanted to kill the two of them," Capo testified. "But what he wanted to do was learn what businesses they had. They had big money. Danny and Corky had a lot of money, a lot of different kinds of businesses. John wanted to learn what they had, get close to them, and kill the two of them. And we would take over their businesses."

And here we'd thought killing Annunziata and Vastola was all about their failure to follow orders.

20

UNION TAMPERING IS THEIR CASH COW

Capo's extortions, beatings, and scams were like the opening act for his ultimate headliner performance. In and of themselves, they were awful, but they foretold much worse to come. I never had a chance to ask the jurors what they made of Anthony Capo's crime résumé, but the expressions on their faces told me Capo was one of the most depraved monstrosities they'd ever met. Judge Mukasey never had to reprimand a single juror for not paying attention. Each one of them was spellbound by Capo's exposure of his misdeeds, from sticking a fork in a rival's face to shooting an acting boss in the head.

Before getting to the main act—that acting boss's murder—Hillebrecht asked Capo to talk about the union corruption that was his entrée into the DeCavalcante family. He had to continue putting all of Capo's illegal activities on the record lest the defense accuse us of withholding information.

Capo said he'd just graduated from high school and was working on Wall Street as a back-office clerk when he met Anthony Rotondo. Capo said Rotondo took a liking to him and asked him if he wanted to make $500 a week at the Laborers' International Union Local 394 in New Jersey. You won't have to do any work, Rotondo promised.

A no-show job was right up Capo's alley.

He drove out to Elizabeth, New Jersey, and met DeCavalcante boss John Riggi. Riggi arranged a job for Capo at the Exxon power plant in Linden five miles south on Route 9. When Capo got there, the foreman asked, "Who sent you?" Capo said John Riggi. Apparently, that was the wrong answer. Instead of doing nothing for the day, the foreman ordered Capo to get into a hole as high as his nose and dig.

When the work day ended, Capo called up Anthony Rotondo. "What's the story over here?" he demanded to know. "You said we weren't going to do no work."

Rotondo said all you had to do was say Jimmy Rotondo sent you—Capo wasn't supposed to use the boss's name. The next day Capo went back to Linden and used Jimmy Rotondo's name. It was like magic. The foreman transferred Capo to a work gang and made him a crew foreman. Capo spent the day driving around in a van doing nothing.

Easiest $500 a week he ever made.

In all his time with the DeCavalcantes, Capo found similar "jobs" at Merck, FedEx, Chevron, and the Newark Mall. He kept riding the DeCavalcante gravy train even after John Riggi got arrested in late 1990; Pino Schifilliti handled all such job assignments. Capo couldn't get fired even if he tried.

In fact, a construction site foreman in Carteret, New Jersey, tried to fire Capo after Capo attacked him. "They had a foreman there that was from where I grew up on Bath Avenue in Brooklyn," Capo testified. "Very nasty, cursing everybody on the job, and called them MFs and cursing everybody out. . . . One day he screamed and cursed at me when we were pouring concrete and he cursed me out. I didn't like that."

"What did you do?" Hillebrecht asked.

"I chased him with a shovel."

"Did you hit him with that shovel?"

"I think I caught him in the back with it. Flung it at him."

"After that what happened to you?"

"I got fired."

Capo reported the incident and his firing to John Riggi.

"And what happened?" Hillebrecht asked.

"He shut down that job and all of Carteret. Nobody worked for three days until they put me back on."

Hillebrecht asked Capo to explain what he meant by shutting down all of Carteret.

"No trades could work," Capo said. "Nobody could work. The laborers, carpenters, nobody. He had that kind of control over the unions then."

Hillebrecht asked what happened next.

"Oh, I went back to work in three days," Capo said.

"And after you returned to that job in Carteret, did you do any work?"

"Of course not. There was nobody was going to fire me then."

"Did you get paid?"

"All the time. Overtime too."

Hillebrecht asked Capo how it was possible for the DeCavalcantes to have such an airtight lock on the local union. Capo said the union had gotten started when the Italians emigrated from Ribera, Sicily, to the neighborhood of Peterstown, near Third Avenue in Elizabeth.

"The union goes way back to Manny Riggi, which was John Riggi's father," Capo explained. "He was the business agent, and when he retired, he installed his son."

The shovel incident was not a one-off. At Chevron in Perth Amboy, Capo was part of a team that built pipe scaffolding. A "little guy" from Perth Amboy walked up to Capo and said he had to get the fuck out of the union. "'We don't want no New York guys here,'" Capo quoted him. "'My father and I are going to take the union back.'"

Capo swung a scaffold pipe at him. He got fired.

But when he went to the office to complain, the site foreman was ecstatic. "'I can't believe you did that,'" Capo quoted the foreman. "'That's great. It's going to scare them.'"

Capo held on to one Laborers' Union job or another up until a few months before he got arrested on December 2, 1999.

"We always got the best jobs," Capo testified. "It was our union."

In September 1986, when Capo finished serving a sentence in Danbury for extorting small businessmen, he got involved with **Tremont**, a construction company. Prison hadn't brought out Capo's innate entrepreneurial spirit. He was on probation until September 1991 and had to show his probation officer a paycheck. Indeed, Capo actually served as a liaison for a guy named **Sheldon** who wanted to hire nonunion contractors for Tremont. "I would take care of the union end, the nonunion, make sure he [Sheldon] got paid," Capo testified. Capo's "value-add" was his access to contractors through his ties with organized crime.

One such contact was Anthony Scotto, a Gambino soldier who was vice president of a company called Herbert Construction.

"Anthony Rotondo knew him well," Capo told Hillebrecht. "[Scotto] put me on the bidding list. If I am bidding for drywall contracts, knowing that I can go nonunion . . . I can keep the bid close to the vest and beat anybody else out. And that's what I was able to do."

Illegal bid-rigging accounted for only half of Capo's "service offerings." In one instance, Capo used **Min-gi**, one of Vinny Palermo's associates, to con another Korean businessman.

"Min-gi had a friend of his, a Korean fellow, that had a construction company," Capo testified. "He was building a supermarket on Eighty-Sixth Street in Brooklyn, in Bensonhurst."

Capo and Palermo decided to extort Min-gi's friend. "So what I did was, I went, I met the guy, told him if he had any problems to give me a call," Capo said. "I got three or four guys that were around me, big guys. I sent them to the job. They told the Korean fellow to stop the job, that he can't work there no more unless he has union men. . . . They didn't touch him or nothing, but they let him know that he wasn't going to work no more."

A short time later, Capo drove up and listened to the businessman's tale of woe. He pretended not to know the supposed union thugs and assured the businessman he could handle the problem. The businessman showed his appreciation for Capo's "help" by giving him around $15,000.

About a week later, some guys from the local union showed up and told the businessman he had to stop using nonunion workers. Once again Capo represented himself as reliable help.

"I reached out to Frankie Fappiano," Capo said. Fappiano was the Gambino soldier he'd spotted doing surveillance on Fred Weiss.

"I told Frankie the situation," Capo continued. "He said that he would take care of the situation, and I gave him about $1,500, $2,000, although he didn't want it."

Capo and Fappiano had grown up in the same neighborhood. Fappiano really was ready to do Capo a favor, but Capo knew some day he'd be calling on his old friend again. "I just paid him," Capo said.

Fappiano made sure no one from the local bothered the Korean businessman anymore.

So Capo made money. Fappiano made money. The businessman was out $15,000. The nonunion laborers got paid something. And the union members, who paid their union dues to a mob-infested union, didn't get a cent.*

John Riggi created a second Laborers' Union local targeted at workers in the asbestos removal industry. He located Local 1030 about a block away from Local 394 in Elizabeth. Because members of the asbestos union had to be licensed, they needed to enroll in a program where they'd learn how to detect and remove asbestos. Riggi, who arguably knew nothing about asbestos remediation, created an "asbestos school" in the early 1980s.

He hired his son Manny to run it. Manny Riggi was a DeCavalcante soldier, but he'd been "put on the shelf," or temporarily banished from the organization, after committing an infraction of the rules.

The asbestos local wanted Anthony Capo to get an asbestos remediation license.

"And did you go to class?" Hillebrecht asked.

"Couple classes."

"What did you do when you went to class?"

"Went to sleep."

Pretty soon Capo stopped going to class altogether. Manny asked to speak with him.

* Later Frank Fappiano cooperated with the government and pled guilty to the conspiracy to murder Fred Weiss.

"'What's going on, you don't want to come to class,'" Capo quoted Manny.

Capo told Manny he was busy.

"'Maybe you want me to take the test for you and pass,'" Capo quoted Manny again. "I said, yeah, can you do that? He said OK." Capo got a license to remove or detect asbestos.

"And when you received your license to remove asbestos, did you know the first thing about how to remove asbestos?" Hillebrecht asked.

Capo said, "No, I wouldn't know it if I was sitting on it."

The jurors couldn't help but chuckle.

21

CAPO WHACKS THE ACTING BOSS

As *US v. Vitabile et al.* headed toward the murder of John D'Amato, Anthony Capo testified that D'Amato himself had participated in his fair share of murder conspiracies. The conspiracy to murder Louis LaRasso was only one of at least ten examples. When LaRasso was sneaking around behind Johnny Boy's back, trying to take the family away from him, D'Amato decided LaRasso had to die. At a meeting that included Pino Schifilliti, Philip Abramo, and Steve Vitabile, D'Amato said he would set LaRasso up by luring him to the site of a supposed administration meeting. Then Schifilliti, feigning concern about security, would drive LaRasso to another house. Abramo volunteered Louis Consalvo's house. Virgil Alessi would shoot LaRasso there. Capo and Greg Rago would be on hand to help.

As a DeCavalcante soldier, Virgil Alessi pulled the trigger in the rubout of Joey Garofano—and suffered a heart attack moments afterward. He survived, and his bona fides as a longtime heroin peddler qualified him to captain a crew. Don't go thinking Alessi's heart gave out because he had qualms about killing Joey, though. When given the assignment to kill LaRasso, Alessi boasted he would shoot him "here, here, and here"—his head, his heart, and his belly. Seeing as Alessi had already given the matter some thought, D'Amato left the tactical details up to him. Alessi figured that because Consalvo was having some work done on his house, it made sense to use the plastic sheeting on the floor to contain LaRasso's blood. Capo, Rago, and Consalvo would wrap LaRasso up in the plastic, heave him into the trunk of his car, and transport his hefty bullet-riddled corpse to a parking lot at Newark Airport.

Capo and Rago would do a couple of dry runs to the airport to make sure they had the route down pat.

Just like that, everyone had committed conspiracy to murder. All the attendees locked up.

In the end, Capo was pulled from the job. The Jersey guys—led by Pino Schifilliti—would handle the hit.

Everyone knew why Pino volunteered for the job. Pino had to redeem himself. He'd bailed on his crew during an attack on a physically large Italian guy. In that episode, Pino sped off in his van instead of defending his crew with his gun. Vinny Palermo said Pino should have been killed for stranding his crew. But Jake Amari said the LaRasso murder would give Pino a second chance to prove his loyalty.

D'Amato would be dead two weeks after Mrs. LaRasso last saw her husband alive.*

Hillebrecht showed Capo Government Exhibit 152, my chart reflecting the hierarchy of the DeCavalcante crime family in 1991. John D'Amato appeared on it as the acting boss and official underboss. He asked Capo where D'Amato was in the days before he killed him.

"In Florida," Capo replied. "John D'Amato had gone on the lam. He had taken off. He was running away from law enforcement to avoid capture, arrest."

Did Capo speak to D'Amato about his reason for going on the lam?

Yes, Capo said. He recounted a conversation he, Vinny Palermo, and Anthony Rotondo had with D'Amato. D'Amato was almost certain

* LaRasso was last seen on November 11, 1991. His car was found at JFK Airport on November 18, 1991. The plan to dispose of LaRasso in Newark evidently changed.

that his earlier conversations with John Gotti and Sammy Gravano had been wiretapped in an apartment upstairs from the Ravenite on Mulberry Street. D'Amato assumed the government had caught him on tape talking about the Fred Weiss murder.

While D'Amato was in Florida, Capo talked to Palermo, Rotondo, and Rudy Farone about D'Amato's fitness as acting boss. None of them were happy about D'Amato's performance.

"What were some of the complaints or concerns?" Hillebrecht asked.

Capo spoke for Palermo, Rotondo, and Farone when he said nobody liked the promotions of Charlie Majuri and Jo Jo Ferrara to captain, both of which D'Amato had green-lighted. They didn't like D'Amato borrowing money from the other *borgatas* either. D'Amato had even asked Vinny Palermo to borrow money from Wild Bill Cutolo, underboss of the Colombo family.

"He would borrow money from other families and say that the DeCavalcante[s] was responsible for that money, which he had no business ever doing," Capo told Hillebrecht. "He wasn't using the money for us, he was using it for himself. Gambling debts. Things such as that."

Capo didn't mind when D'Amato decided to lay low in Florida. In fact, he and Victor DiChiara drove him in D'Amato's rental car to the airport. For the fun of it, the two held on to the rental for a couple of days. On November 2, 1991, when they drove from Brooklyn back to Staten Island, they smoked some pot. Victor was so high he kept weaving in and out of his lane. The Port Authority Police pulled him over. Victor and Capo both got tickets to appear in court.

The traffic tickets were a lucky break. Detective John DiCaprio did a great job tracking them down. Capo identified them in court as evidence that he was where he said he was. He wasn't making stuff up.

"Now, sir," Hillebrecht said. "At the point in time at which we are talking about when Mr. D'Amato went on the lam, was he married?"

"Yes, he was," Capo said.

"To your knowledge, did he also have a girlfriend or girlfriends on the side?"

"Girlfriends."

"Did you know any of these girlfriends particularly well?"

"I met both of them," Capo said. "I knew them pretty well."

Kelly, one of D'Amato's girlfriends, told Capo how she and D'Amato were going to sex clubs in the city and swapping partners. She was "hysterical, crying," as she revealed that D'Amato was engaging in "homosexual activity."

"It shocked me," Capo testified. "I knew John for a long time. He was the boss of an organized crime family. He couldn't be acting that way. He was a leader of men. I was taken aback. I was in shock. I questioned her over and over again on the matter."

Capo was worried that if Kelly was talking to him about her boyfriend's sexual preferences, she might tell her girlfriends. She might tell other organized crime figures. "Nobody is going to respect us if we have a gay homosexual boss sitting down and discussing Cosa Nostra business with other families," Capo said.

Capo blabbed, exactly as he had blabbed about Joey Garofano. "I told Anthony Rotondo," he testified. Then he told Vinny Palermo and Rudy Farone.

All four DeCavalcantes talked about the inevitable: they had to kill the acting boss. Moreover, they were going to "sneak" D'Amato rather than get permission from the Commission, the ruling council anchored by New York's Five Families, as required by Cosa Nostra rules. The three DeCavalcante captains, however, would approach consigliere Steve Vitabile and acting underboss Jake Amari to get their permission. Just in case the Commission was upset, D'Amato's killers could say they got their orders from their superiors.

Within days of Kelly's allegation, Steve and Jake gave the go-ahead.

"Just so it's clear," Hillebrecht said. "Did you have any face-to-face conversation with Steve Vitabile in which he told you to kill John D'Amato?"

"No, I did not," Capo said.

Point taken. A soldier didn't need face-to-face conversation with the consigliere to act on his order.

Not long after the murder plan was in place, D'Amato called Capo and told him he was ready to come back to New York. He mentioned having had some problems with Kelly when he talked to her by phone. Nothing he couldn't straighten out once he was home.

D'Amato told Capo he and Victor DiChiara should come pick him up at a hotel near the airport. "Don't let anybody know I'm coming in," he said.

Perfect. D'Amato made it easy for Capo and DiChiara to eradicate him.

With John D'Amato in the DeCavalcante crosshairs, the family hierarchy needed a few good men. Anthony Capo and Victor DiChiara looked like the right fit for the job. The two of them already had history together. One time, for example, DiChiara told Capo about a scheme he'd concocted to steal money, jewelry, and a couple of Rolex watches from one of Philip Abramo's Sovereign Equity business partners. Capo arranged for two of his associates to assist in the theft. The robbery went off without a hitch.

In the aftermath of the robbery, though, Abramo asked Capo who the fuck robbed his partner. Capo said he didn't know, but he and Victor would find out.

They knew, of course, but didn't tell Abramo. Abramo's partner was out the money, the jewelry, and the Rolex watches. The worst loss was the watches. They were diamond encrusted.

Capo and DiChiara made some money on the heist. More important, they'd basically scammed another DeCavalcante, and each trusted the other to keep his secrets.

On or about Monday, November 25, 1991, Anthony and Victor headed out to the airport in Victor's car to pick up D'Amato and drive him to Kelly's house in Mill Basin on Jamaica Bay. They didn't immediately recognize the guy waving at them near the taxi stand. It was Johnny Boy decked out in a wig-and-baseball-cap disguise. An acting boss couldn't take too many precautions when law enforcement or other mob families came looking for you.

As the car approached Kelly's street, D'Amato said he'd beep Anthony and Victor when he needed to be picked up. He'd wait for them down the block.

After dropping off D'Amato, DiChiara drove Capo to meet up with Vinny Palermo, Anthony Rotondo, and Rudy Farone at a bus company between Avenues U and V on Sixty-Ninth Street. Because DiChiara was only an associate, he stayed behind in the car.

"At that meeting, were you given any instructions?" Hillebrecht asked.

"Yes."

"What were you told about what to do?"

"I was told, I was asked if I would be willing to kill John D'Amato when he got back in the car, and I said yes."

Vinny expressly said he had run the murder plan past Vitabile and Amari. It was full steam ahead.

But Capo had to dot one more *i* and cross one more *t*. Anthony has to give me the order, Capo told Vinny within earshot of Rotondo. "Anthony says, 'You heard him,'" Capo testified. "And I said, 'No, I didn't. You're my captain. You give me the order.'"

Capo meant no disrespect to Palermo or Farone. "I love them, I like them," he told Rotondo. "But you have to give me the order."

Hillebrecht: "What did Anthony Rotondo do?"

"'Kill him.' He said 'kill him.'"

Hillebrecht had Anthony explain why he insisted on hearing the order from Rotondo. "In the event that I had a problem later on or if anybody found out, I could just say I took my orders from Anthony Rotondo, as a soldier's supposed to take orders from his captain," Capo said. "Vincent Palermo and Rudy Farone, who I was very close to, I loved them both. But I was under Anthony Rotondo's regime."

Capo rarely showed feeling, but he was so emotional that he stumbled over "regime."

Capo testified that when he went to pick D'Amato up at the airport hotel, he, Capo, hadn't been armed. Before setting out to kill the acting boss, Farone gave him an automatic .22 caliber pistol with a silencer. The silencer added six to eight inches onto the weapon and made it too difficult to conceal.

"I told Rudy, 'This is too big. I'll do it without the silencer.' I screwed the silencer off and I gave it back to him."

Before long, D'Amato beeped Capo. Victor drove Capo to the appointed spot one block from Kelly's house.

D'Amato arrived at the car and sat down in the back. "He said, 'Let's go eat,'" Capo told Hillebrecht. "And as we pulled away, I turned and shot John D'Amato."

"How many times did you shoot John D'Amato initially, Mr. Capo?" Hillebrecht asked.

"Twice."

"Did he say anything?"

"'Oh, shit.'"

"What happened after you shot him twice?"

"Victor DiChiara said, 'He's still moving. Hit him again.'"

Capo shot D'Amato twice more.

I stole a glance at the jurors. They looked as if they'd heard all four gunshots.

As instructed, Capo had Victor drive on to Rudy Farone's home garage in Brooklyn.

"We got out of the car," Capo said. "Anthony Rotondo and Vincent Palermo came into the house, the garage. Rudy Farone was already in the garage to let us in, and we got kissed twice and congratulated."

The ad hoc kill team lugged John D'Amato's body out of the car. The weather was ridiculously cold. They hurried to place the body on top of some plastic tarps—the corpse bled "profusely" from the head—and then went through D'Amato's pockets.

Hillebrecht: "What did you find in his pockets?"

"Five thousand dollars in his wallet. Not in his wallet, but five thousand dollars and his wallet." The money would compensate Victor DiChiara for the loss of his blood-soaked car. It had to be destroyed.

Before heading off to the Kings Plaza mall, the killers wrapped up D'Amato's body in plastic tarp and secured it with rope. They stowed the body in the trunk of Victor's car.

The jurors looked as if they'd heard the thud of D'Amato's body.

Judge Mukasey checked his watch.

I was just as mortified as everybody else. I glanced down at my notes to avoid making eye contact with anyone.

At the mall, Capo said, DiChiara went inside to buy two sets of clothing, sneakers, socks, and underwear. "Any time we do a piece of work like that, you have to get rid of everything that you have on," Capo explained. "Burn it and get rid of it. This way there's no evidence, no DNA, no blood, no gunpowder."

Capo and DiChiara drove west on Shore Parkway to Rudy Farone's apartment in Bay Ridge to shower and change.

As for John D'Amato's body, Rudy Farone would call Phil LaMela up in Marlboro to let him know—in code—about its imminent arrival. LaMela could expect Farone, Palermo, and Rotondo within the next few hours.

"Anthony Rotondo said, 'I can't go,'" Capo said as he reenacted the scene. "'I got to take my wife food shopping, or shopping. I promised her. Take Anthony and Victor.'"

Farone was irked. "'What do you mean Anthony and Victor?'" Capo said, assuming Uncle Rudy's voice. "'They did their jobs. We need you to come with us.'"

Capo assumed Rotondo's voice. "'I can't,'" he said. "'I got to go home.'" Rotondo always managed to wriggle out of doing the nitty-gritty.

Rudy Farone and Vinny Palermo drove the corpse upstate.

The next morning, around ten, Capo and DiChiara came back to Farone's garage to clean up DiChiara's car as best they could. Rotondo was supposed to help, but he didn't show up.

DiChiara had the car crushed.

It went without saying that nobody was supposed to mention the D'Amato murder ever again. And yet when Rudy Farone ran into a Genovese captain who called the Jersey family's acting boss a "fag," Farone confirmed that the DeCavalcantes had dealt with the problem.

Don't worry about it, Farone told him. We clean our own house.

Farone shared the conversation with Capo. Capo blabbed to Rotondo and Palermo. "We were sick," Capo told Hillebrecht.

"Why?"

"We didn't want any of the other bosses or the other families to know that we snuck this guy.... They could have killed us. All of us."

Now Rotondo and Palermo had to let Steve Vitabile and Jake Amari know they might get approached by the Five Families Commission.

"Did Mr. Palermo describe to you what happened in his conversation with Steve Vitabile and Jake Amari?" Hillebrecht asked Capo.

"Yes."

"What did he tell you?"

"He said Steve and Jake, especially Steve, was trying to say we never, you know, we never said that, gave the order. Vinny goes, 'Listen, Steve. Don't pull that shit with me. You know you gave the order.' And then he [Steve] relented. He didn't want to argue with Vinny on something like that. And then he agreed. That he did give the order. And if he had to, he would relay that on to any other bosses of the other families."

The murder of John D'Amato was nonetheless an unsanctioned hit, and even other high-ranking DeCavalcantes hadn't known about it. They called a meeting in New Jersey to find out who had commissioned the hit—and who had carried it out.

Anthony Rotondo had coached Capo to say he last saw D'Amato when he dropped him off at Kelly's house. By no means was Capo to admit he'd shot D'Amato. "'Make believe you're upset about it,'" Capo quoted Rotondo. "'Say that you saw him leave and you dropped him off, and that was the last you saw him.'"

Several people at the administration meeting—Palermo, Rotondo, and Vitabile among them—knew beyond a shadow of a doubt that Capo was lying, but they kept mum.

"I explained the story to the administration of the family," Capo testified. "Philip Abramo was sitting next to me. When I mentioned about that Kelly had brought the story about his homosexual activity, Philly just leaned down and put his hands in his face and just shook his head. He was very upset."

"Did anybody ask you anything about like when was the last time you saw John D'Amato?" Hillebrecht asked.

"There was other captains that asked me that," Capo said. "Philip Abramo looked at me and he turned to me and he said, 'You believe that story? You saw him last, you're the one, that you're the one? You dropped him off last at Kelly's house?' You know, it was questions about what she said and if I believed it was true or not."

Even though half of the administration members at the meeting had planned, authorized, or executed the murder, nobody that day admitted to murdering John D'Amato. John D'Amato was history.

If anyone was capable of probing too deeply, though, it was D'Amato's brother Frank. Capo argued that once Frank got out of the federal pen at Danbury, Frank would exact revenge on John's killer. Capo conferred with Anthony Rotondo, Rudy Farone, and Vinny Palermo about killing Frank.

Capo recalled that when he and Joey Garofano drove up in the mid-1980s to visit Frank at Danbury, Frank brought up the subject of Jimmy Rotondo and how he had been murdered in front of his own house.

"'I tell you what,'" Capo quoted Frank D'Amato. "'I'm really not too crazy about my brother, [but] if they ever killed my brother, they better kill me the day I walk out. Otherwise, I'll be insulted.'"

Hillebrecht wanted to know specifically what Frank D'Amato meant.

Capo explained, "'If it was my brother or my father . . . I'm going to kill you.' He would take it as a slap in the face that nobody had the respect or respected him that he wouldn't seek revenge for his brother's murder."

Capo testified that he conveyed Frank's intentions to Rotondo, Farone, and Palermo. "I told them . . . 'I love Frank, I like Frank a lot,' but he was going to come after us," Capo testified. "Or certainly me. . . . We have to kill him."

I couldn't figure out how Frank D'Amato heard about his brother's purported killer, but as you've seen, the DeCavalcantes were a chatty bunch. Capo, too, worried that Frank knew whodunit.

After Frank got out of prison, he invited Capo to have dinner with him at Ballato's on Houston Street in Manhattan. Capo demurred. It's not just that Capo didn't trust Frank. He also didn't trust Phil Abramo, Greg Rago, and Louis Consalvo,* all of whom owned a social club together and were close to Ballato's owners.

---

* Consalvo and Abramo were brothers-in-law.

I don't really care for the food at Ballato's, Capo told Frank.

Hillebrecht asked, "Did you not like the food or was there some other reason you didn't want to go there?"

"They got great food there," Capo said. "There is only one way in and no way out. I didn't feel comfortable in there. I could have went to eat there and not left. So I wasn't going to go there, not to some place that they had."

Hillebrecht asked Capo to explain "that they had."

"Philip Abramo and the guys around him. John D'Amato used to go there all the time too. They were—that restaurant was associated with them."

Capo suggested going to SPQR on Mulberry Street. "The tourists go there all the time," Capo told the AUSA. "It's always crowded. It was on an afternoon for lunch, so it was jam packed. So I thought this was an ideal place to eat. . . . They ain't going to try to kill me there, Mr. Hillebrecht. Too many people around."

But what evidence was there that Frank D'Amato suspected Capo?

Capo explained: "He said he would bring Phil Abramo. I told him I would bring Victor DiChiara with me."

Capo and DiChiara came to SPQR armed. Capo asked Victor to watch Frank closely. "If he doesn't ask me about his brother, what happened to him, where is he, where did he go, then that means it's on," Capo testified.

Hillebrecht: "When you say 'that means it's on,' what does that mean?"

"They're going to try to come after us, try to kill us," Capo said.

From *antipasto* to *dolce*, Frank never mentioned his brother once.

Jimmy Gallo—one of the DeCavalcantes who shot Fred Weiss—solved the mystery about Frank D'Amato for Capo.

Hillebrecht asked what Capo had learned from Gallo.

Gallo was close with Philly Abramo's crew, Capo said. On a car ride down to the Jersey Shore with Abramo, Louis Consalvo, and Greg Rago, Consalvo told Gallo that Rudy Farone and Anthony Capo killed John D'Amato.

Gallo reported his intel to Capo and Vinny Palermo. But Gallo had even more intel. He'd learned that Charlie Majuri wanted Vinny

Palermo dead. "And Charlie was going to be in charge of cleaning up after they killed Vincent Palermo," Capo said.

Now Palermo had to off Majuri. Capo detailed the murder conspirators. "Myself, Jimmy Gallo, Victor DiChiara, and Joseph Masella," Capo told Hillebrecht.

After a bathroom break, Capo painted a picture of DeCavalcante members wildly pointing guns at each other.

Palermo and Capo had gotten permission from Steve Vitabile to kill Frank D'Amato. ("Do what you got to do.")

Charlie Majuri was rounding up a team of hit men to kill Vinny Palermo.

Vinny had put together a team of killers to whack Majuri.

Frank D'Amato and his allies, including Phil Abramo, would retaliate against Capo. Apparently, not every DeCavalcante cared very much that John D'Amato was—as the *New York Post* front-page headline blasted in towering type after Capo's testimony—their

FAIRY GODFATHER

Indeed, they were distraught that, as another *Post* headline unabashedly announced:*

MOBSTER SLEEPS WITH THE SWISHES

It wasn't for nuthin' that the Newark, New Jersey–based *Star-Ledger* called the DeCavalcantes a "virtual viper pit."† The DeCavalcantes were the gang that *could* shoot straight. But mostly at each other.

The subject of John D'Amato came up one last time before the December 2, 1999, arrest of thirty-nine alleged LCN members and associates.

* Both headlines are from the May 1, 2003, edition of the *New York Post*.

† "How a Crime Family Turned Dysfunctional" by Robert Rudolph, Newark *Star-Ledger*, May 9, 2023.

Anthony Capo was in the hospital to ameliorate his diabetic condition. On the evening of Monday, November 29, Vinny Palermo and Victor DiChiara came to visit him. The three of them found an on-call room nobody was using so they could speak without fear of being wiretapped.

Vinny told Anthony about the leak in the US Attorney's Office. He said the government had information about "that thing in Staten Island," Capo testified.

"And before Palermo left, did he bring up in the conversation any other homicides other than Fred Weiss?" Hillebrecht asked.

"Yes, he did," Capo said.

"What did he tell you about that?"

"He told me where—he told me that where Joseph Garofano and John D'Amato were buried." Palermo touched his nose when he said D'Amato's name.

"John D'Amato, he got a big nose," Capo explained.

That was the last time Capo heard John D'Amato's name until we arrested him.

Vinny also told Capo of another murder he planned to squeeze in before the presumed arrests. A DeCavalcante associate.

"He [Palermo] was going to get together with James Gallo, find Frank Poplizzi [*sic*], and kill Frank Scarabino," Capo testified. Scarabino was the DeCavalcante associate who loan-sharked money for Frank Polizzi. "Poppa" Frank turned on Scarabino after Scarabino didn't follow through on murdering Anthony Capo's wife and kids.

Hillebrecht's direct examination was winding down. Capo had been doing a great job. Throughout the trial, I didn't take anything for granted, though. Every day after testimony, I used positive reinforcement on Capo to keep his spirits up.

"Séamus, how do you think I did today?" Capo asked me.

"You're absolutely credible," I said. "That's what happens when you tell the truth."

"You'll keep me on track when I'm on cross-examination."

"Remember, Anthony, once cross begins, I can't talk to you."

"Right, right. I forgot."

"I can say hi. We can't discuss the case at all. It's the law."

"Understood."

“The defense is going to come after you,” I said. “Don’t get cute. Just answer the question. As you’ve always done.”

“They’re going to make me look like a horrible human being.”

“Anthony, you were. But who cares? You’re never going to see these people again.”

“You’re right. Never thought of it that way.”

“You got this!”

Capo was optimistic again. It was my rule of thumb: a happy witness is a good witness.

So far, so good.

22

HE'S SO BAD HE'S GOOD

The only thing that mattered in Judge Mukasey's courtroom was how credible the jury found Anthony's testimony. I'm guessing the forty-eight-year-old postal clerk and the forty-three-year-old schoolteacher on the jury panel had never come face to face with the kind of degeneracy that Capo, Palermo, Rotondo, and the other DeCavalcantes represented, and they had never been asked to trust anything a hardened killer had to say to them. Now that Capo was about to face three attorneys for the defense in a make-it-or-break-it trial, we had to deal with at least two unknowns. First, would Capo hold up under cross-examination? Second, would the defense persuade the jury that the government was offering Capo and his mob family a quid pro quo: your coerced testimony in exchange for our get-out-of-jail-free card?

Anthony Servino, one of Steve Vitabile's lawyers, began his cross-examination of Capo with a series of questions about the nature of truth that appeared to entertain and annoy the jury in equal measure.

"How many meetings would you have had with government representatives between the day of your arrest and June of 2000?" Servino began.

Capo had had at least twenty meetings with us.

"You were told you had to tell the truth at each meeting, right?"

"Repeatedly," Capo said.

Servino was barely three minutes into cross and he went down a kind of *Merriam-Webster* rabbit hole. "What's your understanding of the word or term *truth*?" he asked.

"It would be the opposite of not telling the truth," Capo replied. "Lying."

"Lying. So, the truth is just not lying, according to you?"

Well, also according to any number of English-language dictionaries.

"The truth would be telling the facts of what happened," Capo said.

"Would that include telling all the facts of what happened?" Servino asked.

"I don't follow what you're saying," Capo answered. "You tell the truth, you tell whatever happened, yes."

"OK. But generally speaking, it's your understanding of the term is the opposite of lying or not telling the truth," Servino re-summarized.

I couldn't blame Capo for adjusting his eyeglasses as a pretext for gauging the jury's reaction. Maybe Juror Number 6, a book author, could wax philosophical about the meaning of *truth*, but the jury overall was divided between stupefaction and amusement. To my mind, Servino's questions bordered on harassment.

Servino asked Capo if he had ever lied in 1991.

"The whole year, sir?" Capo asked.

"Yeah."

"I'm sure I lied."

After several minutes of this semiotics lesson, Servino arrived at his reason for discoursing about the truth. "Did you understand that being accepted as a cooperating witness and signing that cooperation agreement was the one way you could possibly escape the thirty-seven-year sentence that you were exposed to under your original indictment?" he asked Capo.

"The only way to do that was to tell the truth," Capo maintained. Not a strand of Capo's perfectly moussed quiff was out of place.

Servino drove Capo hard. "Well, isn't it a fact that the only way to do that, to be accepted as a cooperating witness, is sign the cooperation agreement, live up to the terms of the agreement, and hope for a 5K letter?" he asked.

"Yes."

"OK. Did you understand that every time you had one of those sessions with the government that you were in a struggle for your life?"

"If you could define 'struggle for my life,'" Capo said.

Two could play this game.

"If you didn't participate in those sessions, there was a possibility you would be doing thirty-seven years in jail."

"If I didn't tell the truth, I would be doing life," Capo said.

"I asked you if you understood that at every one of these meetings you were in a struggle for your life. Do you have an answer to that question?"

Finally! Judge Mukasey had had enough. "He's already given you an answer," he said, with no effort to hide his pique. "Will you please move on to something else?"

Thank you, Judge. We were all thinking, *Defense, is this the best you got?*

But Anthony Servino had brought his point home: that Anthony Capo, like any cooperating witness, would say anything the government wanted him to say in return for a lighter prison sentence. Or—to get philosophical myself—that anything the government wanted Capo to say would *become* the truth, whether it was really true or not. That the government decided what was the truth, not Anthony Capo.

I couldn't swear to what the jury was thinking, but I believed John Hillebrecht had done a yeoman's job in explaining the relationship between the government and a cooperating witness. The jury seemed to understand that without a quid pro quo with an unsavory character like Capo, the government might never penetrate an organized crime family and ultimately dismantle it.

Goading Capo into a gnarly conversation about a layman's definition was only part one of Servino's argument. In part two, Vitabile's attorney insisted that Anthony Capo would say or do anything to get what he wanted. Like the time Capo posed as a policeman to enter an elderly couple's home.

"OK," Servino said. "Is it fair to say that in your life of crime you found it necessary on occasion to play a role to get what you want?"

At times, Capo said.

"You wouldn't be pretending anything in this courtroom, are you?"

"That would be stupid."

"Why would it be stupid?"

"All I have to do is tell the truth to get a 5K1, so why would I pretend?"

"Only you know if you're telling the truth, right?"

Now it was Capo's turn to philosophize. "Only I know?" he echoed. "I don't know if only I know. I know I'm telling the truth. I couldn't speak for everybody else what they know."

Servino knew better than to irk Judge Mukasey again. He ended his linguistics lecture and focused on the inarguably disgusting activities Capo had engaged in his entire adult life, especially the murders and murder conspiracies. But Capo had already come clean about all the dirt in his life, and the jury couldn't be hounded into shock over the same revelations twice.

I looked over at John Hillebrecht every so often to see what he made of Servino's cross-examination and of Capo's response to it. He knew better than to roll his eyes at Servino or shake his head in wonderment at Capo's composure on the stand. He furrowed his brow, a tactic he'd used before to mask his sense that things were going very well.

Occasionally, Servino did nettle Capo. Early in his cross-examination, Servino asked Capo to recall how angry Anthony Rotondo, Vinny Palermo, and Rudy Farone were after John D'Amato made Charles Majuri and Jo Jo Ferrara captains.

"Would you say that the angriest of all of them, or the most pissed off, were Rotondo and Palermo?" Servino asked.

"No."

"You wouldn't say they were the angriest?"

"No."

Servino persisted. "Do you recall telling the FBI there, Agent McElearney, that they were the angriest?"

"They were all angry," Capo said. "How would I know who's the angriest?"

Judge Mukasey was an equal opportunity rebuker. He wasted no time in chiding the witness. "Mr. Capo," he said. "He asks the questions. You give the answers."

Ever respectful of the "boss," Capo apologized. "Excuse me, Your Honor," he said.

At least in this instance, I sensed the jury sympathized with Capo. If Servino had to resort to petty niggling, how strong could his case against our witness be?

After a polite "good morning," Robert Schwartz, Pino Schifilliti's attorney, picked up on Anthony Servino's line of attack by grinding away at three points. First, Capo was an inveterate liar. Second, the government coerced Capo into admitting to crimes he hadn't committed. Third, the government paid for Capo's testimony.

Schwartz brought up September 12, 1989, the day after Fred Weiss's murder, when Capo asked his chiropractor to backdate an appointment. The implication was, if Capo could lie to save his skin in 1989, he could lie to save his skin in 2003 too. Once a liar, always a liar.

The fact is, Capo had been disingenuous in the past. As far back as 1985, he had watched his lawyer stand up in court and proclaim that he, Capo, had learned his lesson and would never commit a crime again.

"And you told Judge [Leonard] Sand during that sentencing proceeding in June of 1985 that you were totally ashamed of what you had done that resulted in your indictment, isn't that so?" Schwartz alleged.

"Very well, I may have said that, yes," Capo said.

Schwartz told the jury that Capo—a convicted felon—had flouted the terms of his probation by visiting Frank D'Amato in prison many times. Indeed, Capo had lied routinely to his probation officer.

Capo admitted he had lied to her about everything: he said he hadn't consorted with known felons, hadn't possessed firearms, hadn't used illegal drugs, hadn't engaged in home invasions, hadn't participated in a murder. All lies.

With Capo's track record as a liar, why should the jury believe him now?

Schwartz had a fair point—but lying in the past doesn't necessarily mean you are lying in the present. And Capo's present circumstances were quite different from the ones in the past: in 1985, Capo's maximum sentence was five years. He did four months. Now, in 2003, without adhering to the letter of his cooperation agreement, Capo would face LIFE. Would *you* risk lying if you knew you'd be looking at four prison walls until the day you died?

Schwartz went on to argue that the government had compelled Capo to admit to crimes he hadn't done. "I think you told us—correct me if I'm wrong—you never refused to plead guilty to anything the government asked you to plead guilty to, right?" Schwartz asked.

"Only the crimes that I thought [I] was guilty of I pleaded to," Capo said.

"But the government presented you with a list of crimes that they wanted you to plead guilty to, right?"

"And I was guilty of those crimes."

"You didn't say, 'I'm not going to plead guilty to any of those,' right?"

"Why would I do that? I would only plead guilty to the crimes I committed."

I wished Capo had said he'd been suspected of murdering the two stockbrokers in Colts Neck but refused to take the blame for because it was something he hadn't done.

Schwartz insisted that Capo didn't mind pleading to any crime the government wanted to lay on him. "If you were getting life for the murders, you could have pleaded to a whole string of crimes," he said. "You couldn't get more than life, could you . . . ?"

"You get life, you get life," Capo said. "How many more lives could I get? I only got one life to give."

I wasn't sure Capo understood Schwartz was accusing the government of adding false crimes to his plea agreement. The government didn't make shit up. Capo pled guilty to all the crimes he told *us* about. We didn't know the half of it. Hello? The John D'Amato murder itself wasn't even on our radar.

In my view, Schwartz made a misstep when he stated that a cooperating witness benefits financially by cooperating with the government. "Has the federal government paid you any money in the last couple or three years?" Schwartz asked Capo.

"I've gotten money, but I don't know about—yeah, I've gotten money for my family," Capo said.

"Is your wife separated from you?"

"Yes, she is."

An implication that Capo was taking money he didn't pass on to his ex?

"Since June of 2000 when you signed this cooperation agreement, how much money did you get out of the federal government to you and on your behalf?" Schwartz asked.

"I don't recall the total," Capo replied.

"Over $70,000. Would that refresh your recollection?"

"I don't know exactly how much."

Schwartz showed Capo a financial statement. It documented how much money Capo "got out of the federal government."

When Robert Schwartz had no further questions for Capo, I was stumped. Seventy thousand dollars prorated over three and a half years was not a vast sum. It amounted to $20,000 a year. In his pre-prison life, Capo could have gotten his hands on seventy grand in a short time, especially if he'd applied his strong-arming tactics. All the government's "bribe" did was keep a roof over his family's head and pay for basic necessities over the course of four years. If the jurors did the math, I didn't think they'd begrudge Capo's kids some financial stability any more than they'd begrudge them protection from Frank Polizzi's death threat.

Laila Abou-Rahme, one of Philip Abramo's attorneys, was the weakest of the three defense attorneys to cross-examine Capo. She argued that he was so enmeshed in a life of crime that he didn't have the attention left over to notice what Abramo was up to. She made much of Capo's testimony that Abramo always wore a scarf.

"But in the pictures and videos we saw, Mr. Abramo wasn't wearing a scarf in any of those," she said in a gotcha moment.

"I don't recall the date of those pictures, but it did look like it was very warm out, because a lot of guys had short-sleeved shirts on," Capo said.

Anthony, don't interpret! Just ask the lawyer if she has a question for him!

"There were people in the pictures that were wearing sweaters, including Mr. Abramo, and he wasn't wearing a scarf. But your testimony is that he usually wore a scarf."

So if Abramo didn't wear a scarf one particular day, he couldn't possibly be the captain who conspired to murder several DeCavalcante members or associates? Lawyers. When they don't have much to go on, they go on about nothing much.

Abou-Rahme's coup de grâce was comparing Anthony Capo with Sammy Gravano. Abramo's attorney suggested Capo cooperated with the government because Gravano had. Frankly, that's not such a wrongheaded argument. We want cooperating witnesses to serve as role models for future OC criminals.

"And you knew that in exchange for his testimony, Mr. Gravano was sentenced to five years in prison," she said.

"I heard it," Capo said. "I read it on the paper when I was on the street."

"You also knew that the five years was retroactive and started running from the time Mr. Gravano was first arrested. Isn't that right?"

"I don't know. I wasn't part of his sentencing or how much time he did. I couldn't say for sure."

"But did you know that by the time Mr. Gravano helped convict John Gotti, he was pretty much done with his five-year sentence?"

"I didn't really pay attention to how much he had left or not," Capo said.

By early May 2003, when he testified in *Vitabile et al.*, Capo would have had three and a half years of prison time under his belt. As Abou-Rahme intimated, all Capo had to do was sit in prison another eighteen months—and then he was free as a bird.

Abou-Rahme pressed her argument. "Mr. Capo, you knew that Mr. Gravano, when he was done with his five years, he was in a witness relocation program somewhere in Phoenix, Arizona?" she asked.

Capo said he didn't know where Gravano had ended up.

"And were you aware that he actually went on to commit more crimes?" she asked.

Capo said he'd heard about that.

"And renouncing crime in order to get yourself out of a jam but then reverting back to a life of crime after promising to change your ways is what you did also the last time you were arrested in 1985. Isn't that right?"

Capo couldn't argue with that.

"Isn't it the case, Mr. Capo, that after hearing about Mr. Gravano, you made up your mind that if you were ever arrested, you would cooperate also?"

No, not at all, Capo said.

Abou-Rahme's point wasn't only that if someone like Gravano could become a government cooperator, then so could Anthony Capo. She was also underscoring Anthony Servino's point that government's witnesses ultimately returned to a life of lucrative crime.

Abou-Rahme conveniently didn't mention that the authorities nabbed Sammy Gravano again when he returned to his old ways and sentenced him to another twenty years.

Look, the Anthony Capo of 1985—the Anthony Capo who violated his probation and returned to a life of scams, ripoffs, beatings, mayhem, forks, and murder—was not the Anthony Capo facing prison and chronic ill health. This guy was never going to make it through thirty-seven years of prison time.

On redirect examination, John Hillebrecht asked Capo why the jury should believe anything he said. After all, he did lie to his probation officer about his commitment to leave his life of crime behind.

"When I was on probation, I lied to stay out of jail," Capo told Hillebrecht. Capo reiterated that all he had to do to get the 5K1 letter was to tell the truth.

"Do you think you could lie from that stand and get away with it?" Hillebrecht asked.

Capo said lying to the jury would be "asinine."

Anthony Capo had to be one of the most ethically and morally compromised witnesses ever to take the stand in the Southern District of New York. And yet when the SDNY trained a light on every despicable aspect of his character, he displayed some integrity. He never lost his temper. He didn't hurl insults at his adversaries. He exhibited respect to everyone from the judge to the defense attorneys. For somebody so bad, his performance on the stand was good. I told him it was superior.

As for the prosecutors and agents, our behavior was strategic. We were careful to display no emotion. We made virtually no eye contact with each other. The last thing we wanted was for a defense attorney to use a glance or an eyeroll as a weapon against our witness. Capo was the first cooperator in the ring, and the defense was going to use everything they could think of, including Capo's previous trial testimony, to trip him up. It was their tough luck the government, Capo included, had trained like boxers. We'd practiced sparring and feinting. We'd executed uppercuts when least expected. We survived our first round. We were going into round two without a single bruise.

Of course we still had to hear from Anthony Rotondo, Victor DiChiara, and Vinny Palermo before the jurors could decide if Anthony Capo had landed a crushing blow.

23

TWO MORE COOPERATING WITNESSES BLOW THE JURY AWAY

I SAY THIS HUMBLY: once AUSA Michael McGovern began his direct examination of Anthony Rotondo, the brilliance of the government's trial strategy was unmistakable. As a DeCavalcante captain—and the son of a DeCavalcante captain—Rotondo had spent his whole life around mobsters, and he knew the organized crime world the way my theology teacher at Cardinal Spellman knew Church doctrine. Until his arrest, Rotondo had spent three decades loan-sharking, illegally gambling, extorting, threatening violence, invading homes, committing arson, and dabbling in cocaine and Quaaludes. He had an insider's knowledge of La Cosa Nostra. And now, with his criminal shenanigans behind him, Rotondo made a frank—and, I believe, rueful—witness to the murder and mayhem he'd embraced in a misguided show of devotion to his father. Now stabilized by blood pressure medication and antidepressants, a bald, middle-aged Rotondo made a poignant presence in Judge Mukasey's courtroom.

Mike's deportment was striking too. He was forty-one, but I swear he could have passed for a seventeen-year-old altar boy. Here he was probing into the darkest corners of the New Jersey Mafia. The jurors loved him.

Early in Rotondo's testimony, the jury learned that even four years at St. Francis College in Brooklyn hadn't led Rotondo to a different kind of life. Indeed, Rotondo's induction at age twenty-four into the DeCavalcante family had been a more meaningful rite of passage than collecting his bachelor's degree in business administration. The ceremony took place in June 1982 in the Brooklyn home of Rudy Farone, Rotondo's baptismal godfather. In Farone's basement, Rotondo testified, Steve Vitabile conducted an initiation that, it turned out, was not quite "orthodox" enough to satisfy John Gotti. In 1988, Rotondo and several other "illegitimately" made DeCavalcantes—including Vinny Palermo—had to undergo a "legitimate" induction ceremony, complete with gun and knife on the table, a burning saint card in their hands, and a pinprick of blood taken from the trigger finger.

It seems during the original induction, the DeCavalcantes had skipped over these essential runes "because of the closeness and just informality that we felt," Rotondo testified.

How did Gotti even find out the DeCavalcantes were flouting La Cosa Nostra rules? The tale-bearing snitch was almost certainly John D'Amato. On paper, John Riggi was D'Amato's boss. For all intents and purposes, though, it was Gotti. D'Amato was enamored with the "boss of bosses," and he made a stealth report to him twice a week at the Ravenite.

Rotondo testified that DeCavalcante autonomy took another hit when Gotti declared the Jersey family could not make anybody from Brooklyn or Manhattan. From now on, aspiring DeCavalcantes could only be New Jersey residents.

Gotti had another punishment for his errant stepchildren: the DeCavalcantes now had to attend every Gambino wedding and wake. The Gambinos had scores of them. You had to wonder how anybody in these two OC families had a spare hour for any serious criminal activity.

"At that time," Rotondo testified about summer 1988, "we were answering to the Gambino family. We were subservient, for lack of a better word."

The murder of Fred Weiss a year later was supposed to change all that.

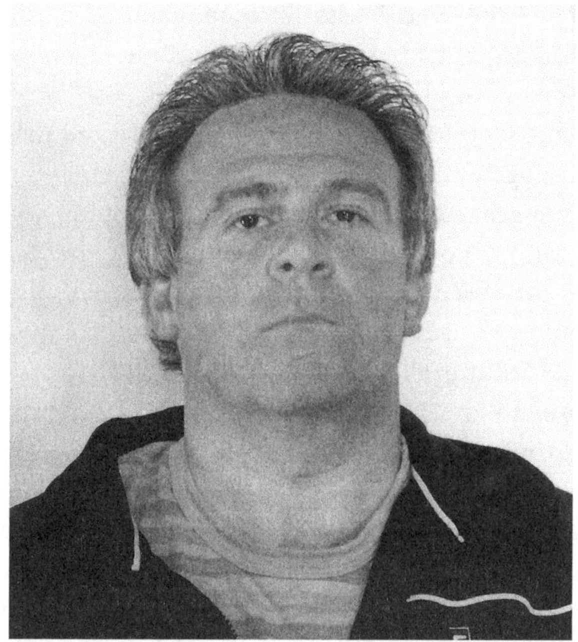

Anthony Rotondo. *Department of Justice Trial Exhibit, US Attorney's Office, Southern District of New York / FBI*

In no essential point did Anthony Rotondo deviate from Capo's testimony. His status as a Mafia captain, however, provided a "value add." He could reveal situations that Capo, as associate and soldier, couldn't have known about. Foremost was Rotondo's front-row seat on the scramble for power among the top-level DeCavalcantes.

Rotondo took the jury back to late 1990, when John Riggi got arrested. Before he was sentenced, Riggi appointed his son, Manny, whom he'd promoted to captain and put in charge of his asbestos union, to sit with underboss John D'Amato and soldier Paul Farina on a three-man panel. Steve Vitabile would continue to serve as consigliere.

That solution lasted a New Jersey minute.

Soon after the tripartite panel met, John D'Amato announced he'd uncovered a plot on his life. His nemesis was Manny Riggi.

Jimmy Gallo, the Fred Weiss hit man, exposed Manny's plot. He said Manny had recruited him to kill Johnny Boy. Manny was pissed off at D'Amato for touting himself as the DeCavalcantes' sole acting boss.

According to Rotondo, Jimmy Gallo had observed that Manny had been acting strangely the last couple of months. Manny had asked him for a gun with a silencer. Jimmy said Manny had complained that "this Johnny wants to take over the outfit, wants to take my father down."

D'Amato proposed a solution. Out of respect for John Riggi, D'Amato wouldn't kill his son. He'd simply put Manny on the shelf where he could rot, for all Johnny Boy cared.

Then D'Amato anointed himself acting boss.

A more prudent DeCavalcante would have thought twice, but D'Amato had the support of a very important person: John Gotti.

Good for D'Amato. Bad for the DeCavalcantes, who were now back at square one as the Gambino "farm team."

To add insult to injury, D'Amato wholeheartedly embraced Gotti's directive to disempower the DeCavalcantes' Brooklyn faction—Vinny Palermo, Rudy Farone, and Anthony Rotondo—and shift the power to New Jersey. To that end, D'Amato unilaterally appointed a team of captains loyal to him. The D'Amato regime would consist of Phil Abramo, Pino Schifilliti, Lou LaRasso, Charles Majuri, and several other DeCavalcantes. John D'Amato broke John Riggi's administration.

What did Johnny Boy think? That the Brooklyn faction would fold its hands and have some cookies and milk?

Brooklyn was disgruntled. For Anthony Rotondo especially, La Cosa Nostra rules were sacrosanct. D'Amato's *faccia tosta*—his chutzpah—was no more acceptable to him than John Gotti's was when Gotti had Paul Castellano whacked. Gotti hadn't gotten permission to kill Castellano and make himself Gambino boss either. As Rotondo saw it, D'Amato had chosen the wrong mobster as his role model.

Within weeks of installing himself as DeCavalcante acting boss, D'Amato detected a threat to his dominance from Lou LaRasso. "Louie knew the rules and he knew Johnny virtually took over the family without anybody's consent," Rotondo testified.

But D'Amato wasn't going to let anybody stand in his way.

At an administration meeting, Steve Vitabile, Phil Abramo, Pino Schifilliti, and Jake Amari voted to kill Lou LaRasso. Rotondo caved. He voted with the majority. No doubt he understood that if he didn't, he'd be next on D'Amato's dance card.

The LaRasso hit team would be Anthony Capo, Louis Consalvo, and Virgil Alessi—Joey Garofano's killer. Without explanation, Capo was pulled from the job. His was not to reason why. His was but to do and die.

LaRasso was out of the picture. The threat was neutralized.

D'Amato had redirected the heat on him onto LaRasso, but his gambling habits weren't exactly winning him any friends either. As Rotondo testified, D'Amato owed loan sharks from various mob families as much as $750,000. The DeCavalcantes were expected to pay it all back. How were they going to do that? D'Amato had bankrupted the DeCavalcante treasury, money set aside, at least theoretically, for the wives and children of imprisoned mobsters.

As Capo had already testified, Johnny Boy said he would go on the lam to escape a possible arrest after the FBI bugged John Gotti's Ravenite Club. According to Rotondo, just about everyone in La Cosa Nostra was abuzz with an explanation for D'Amato's sudden disappearance. "Bosses of other families approached us and said did we think Johnny took this money and just skipped, just robbed everybody," Rotondo said.

Rotondo confirmed Capo's testimony that John D'Amato wanted to come back to New York. By that point, D'Amato's same-sex activities were known to the DeCavalcantes, and the decision to murder D'Amato was a done deal. Rotondo admitted he gave Capo the go-ahead to be the shooter.

Like Capo, Rotondo recounted the administration meeting in which the DeCavalcante leadership went through the motions of "investigating" Anthony Capo after D'Amato vanished, because, as they maintained, Capo was the last person to see D'Amato alive. Rotondo affirmed Capo's assertion that the DeCavalcante bigs knew D'Amato was dead. If, impossibly, D'Amato ever turned up, the DeCavalcantes would have to kill him for having brought shame and bankruptcy upon them. In short, they would have approved killing D'Amato as soon as possible. As did a major money-making captain who hadn't immediately signed on to the murder conspiracy.

"Philly Abramo really wasn't for it at first," Rotondo testified. "But he did say that if the rules of Cosa Nostra were broken, then of course he [D'Amato] would have to go."

Phil Abramo was probably the only DeCavalcante at the administration meeting who didn't know beyond a shadow of a doubt that John D'Amato was already dead. It was a sign that the top DeCavalcantes weren't always kept in the loop about major hierarchy decisions.

Rotondo could also report on another facet of mob life he had observed since childhood: like the Five Families, the DeCavalcantes were committed to preserving the Mafia way of life no matter the cost. As Rotondo testified, a case in point was the murder of associate Joey Garofano.

Rotondo reiterated Capo's testimony that Garofano had played a strong support role in the murder of Fred Weiss. Joey's job was to steal some license plates off a car in a parking lot, affix them to his car with rubber bands, and take them off after the murder was done. Instead, he pulled license plates off the car belonging to Capo's wife. In the Mafia world, bungling a job was enough to get you killed. And Joey only made matters worse by throwing the murder weapons into a nearby creek instead of the ocean, as Vinny Palermo had ordered he do. Then, when things couldn't possibly go more wrong, a passerby stopped to copy down the license plate number on Joey's car. Soon law enforcement was in the neighborhood asking questions—and Joey freaked out. He all but signed his own death warrant when he told Capo, "I'm not going down for nobody. I'm not going away for this."

Rotondo learned about the Joey Garofano problem when he visited Capo at the hospital where Capo was having back surgery. No two ways about it: Joey was going to turn rat. He had to go.

Joey's murder wouldn't be anything like the sensational slaying of Fred Weiss in broad daylight. It would be one of the mob's "white deaths"—the old Sicilian way of disappearing a body. "It's a clean death," Rotondo explained to AUSA Mike McGovern. "There is no crime scene."

Rotondo testified that his next step was to see Rudy Farone, the man who had stood up for him at his baptism.

In an emotional delivery, Rotondo said, "I told him [Farone] I had saw Johnny and Philly Abramo the day before. I told him that we were going to supply Virgil Alessi to do the shooting, and I told him that I had spoken to Mickey DiPietro and Louis Telese and that they would also assist."

"Just if you could, just speak a little more slowly for the reporter," McGovern requested.

Rotondo took a breath. "OK," he said.

McGovern: Did Rudy Farone offer any suggestions about the killing of Joseph Garofano at that point?

Rotondo: Yes, he did.

McGovern: What did he suggest?

Rotondo: He said that the following week he was going to be out of town, and he offered his garage where the killing could happen there.

Now Rotondo testified how the DeCavalcante team of killers would entrap an unsuspecting Joey by pretending to sympathize with his anxiety. Uncle Rudy told Rotondo to tell Joey that "he would have a car and some money, and he [Farone] would supply a place for Joey to stay a little while." Rotondo would assure Joey that he would merely go on the lam for a "little while until things died down."

It takes a lot of manpower to eliminate a human being, and Farone recommended drafting DeCavalcante associate and loan shark Bernard NiCastro into the kill. Within a couple of days, Rotondo asked John D'Amato, Philip Abramo, and Virgil Alessi to get on board as well.

"I told them that I was in touch with Rudy and that Rudy was going to supply Philip LaMela to take Joey's body away," Rotondo testified about the additional plotters. "I also told them that we were going to use Rudy's garage and that Rudy had left a .22 caliber pistol with a silencer, some tarp, and some rope."

McGovern: Did you mention what role DiPietro and Telese were going to play?

Rotondo: Just that they were going to assist Virgil in wrapping up the body.

McGovern: What was Virgil's response to the information that the gun and silencer would be ready, waiting for him?

Rotondo: He said fine.

McGovern: Was Philip Abramo present for the entire conversation?

Rotondo: Yes, he was.

For Abramo, Rotondo's response had to be an uppercut punch.

D-day. Some of the team gathered at the Kings Plaza mall; some, including Farone, who, it seems, wanted in on the action, drove out to meet Bernard NiCastro at the construction site where he was working. NiCastro's role: he'd be on hand to let Louie, Mickey, and Virgil into Farone's home garage. Rotondo told his men that LaMela would show up at night to transport the "package" upstate.

Where was Joey all this time? He'd been afraid to stay in his childhood home lest law enforcement grab him there, and he'd been sleeping at Victor DiChiara's house. On a weekday, Rotondo enlisted an unwitting Victor to drive Joey to the Kings Plaza Diner on Avenue U in Brooklyn. From there, Rotondo and NiCastro would ferry Joey and his suitcase to Farone's house.

It was dark when NiCastro pulled up to Farone's garage. He let Rotondo out to open the wide automatic door. NiCastro drove inside with an anxious Garofano in the backseat. Rotondo pressed a button to shut the door behind them.

Rotondo: "After a few minutes, I heard a couple of muffled shots go off, and Bernard NiCastro came out of the back of the garage and walked up to the front with me."

Four shots in all. It was over.

Well, almost over. NiCastro, Telese, and Alessi labored to tie up the body. It was heavy.

Rotondo testified that Joey had made the journey upstate in LaMela's trunk and was buried the same night "without a problem."

In matters of self-preservation, time is of the essence. Making sure Joey Garofano didn't bring the whole house down required that this unscrupulous gang display trust, fortitude, speed. But why not say the obvious? Anthony Capo and Anthony Rotondo—the first to worry about Joey breaking ranks—were also among the first made men to flip.

In his cross-examination of Anthony Rotondo, Phil Abramo's attorney Marty Klotz crafted his questions to argue that Abramo had nothing to do with the "bad people" who had murdered Fred Weiss and John D'Amato. Klotz wanted to convince the jury that neither Anthony Capo nor Anthony Rotondo could possibly have known anything about Abramo's affairs.

Up next: AUSA Mimi Rocah. She announced, "The government calls Victor DiChiara," or, as the *New York Post* called him, "a marijuana-addled college dropout who began his life of crime as a teenager stealing cars in Canarsie."* With his fresh haircut and his stockbroker business suit, Victor was a far cry from the thug he used to be. DiChiara's testimony was about to contradict Marty Klotz's line of questioning. Klotz wanted the jury to believe that "after the government witnesses killed John D'Amato, there was a division between various people under which they had almost nothing to do with each other."

It didn't take DiChiara long to pitch that hogwash out the window. He testified that he and Abramo had enacted dozens of financial scams together—and if Abramo ever needed to strong-arm his stockbrokers into selling phony stock, he readily called on people like Anthony Capo and Jimmy Gallo to let 'em know who was boss.

Victor DiChiara was living proof that you're only as safe as the company you keep. Had Victor been off in the Bahamas, say, where he had some spurious investment accounts, he wouldn't have driven with Capo in November 1991 to pick up John D'Amato—camouflaged in wig and baseball cap—at a New York airport. Instead, he unwittingly waited

* "Wall St. Wiseguys—Mob Witness Tells of Brokers Packing Heat" by John Lehmann, *New York Post*, May 14, 2003, https://nypost.com/2003/05/14/wall-st-wiseguys-mob-witness-tells-of-brokers-packing-heat/.

in his car while Capo got hold of a .22 caliber pistol from Anthony Rotondo, Vinny Palermo, and Rudy Farone, and then watched Capo shoot John D'Amato seconds after D'Amato said, "Let's go eat."

Victor also wouldn't have urged Capo to "hit him again" when D'Amato took too long to die. Just like that, Victor DiChiara was a participant in a murder he'd otherwise have had nothing to do with.

Victor testified that he himself was lucky to get out of that murder alive. "As I was taking the body out of my backseat, I thought that—Vinny was hovering behind me," Victor said. "I thought that Vinny was going to shoot me next and push me in my car."

I don't want to mislead you into thinking DiChiara at thirty-eight was a babe in the woods. He was seventeen when he and his pals operated their stolen car ring in the Canarsie section of Brooklyn. "We would take orders from body shops and chop shops in the neighborhood and sell the parts to those establishments," Victor testified. "They'd primarily be either Genovese crime family or Gambino crime family [shops]."

By the time Victor started working stock scams with Phil Abramo, he had stolen credit cards, run a loan-sharking business from inside a carpentry company, operated a check-cashing scheme, illegally sold fireworks, scored some no-show jobs, attempted to rob a funeral home, and conspired to murder Charles Majuri. He testified further that he had even crossed paths with Joey Testa and Anthony Senter, Gambino soldiers who told him they had participated in the murder of Jimmy Rotondo.*

Capo didn't lead Victor down the garden path. Victor happily found his own way onto it.

At trial, Victor identified Phil Abramo at the defense's table as the gentleman "with the glasses on." He went on to offer a mind-numbing litany of securities frauds that he, as a licensed Series 7 stockbroker, had helped the so-called mob mastermind of Wall Street perpetrate, mostly over wealthy dupes.

Victor was working at Phil Abramo's Sovereign Equity Management Corporation when Abramo conspired with other mob-dominated

* Testa and Senter were convicted of multiple murders. They were never charged in the murder of Jimmy Rotondo. See "The Gemini Twins Implicated in Mysterious Unsolved Killing of Capo Jimmy Rotondo" in This Week in Gang Land by Jerry Capeci, *Gang Land News*, May 29, 2025, https://www.ganglandnews.com.

trading firms to issue stock for a company called SC&T. Even though SC&T was intended to be Sovereign's flagship initial public offering (IPO), Victor couldn't say what the initials stood for. He didn't even know that the company marketed stuff like keyboards and now-obsolete CD-ROM holders until the SC&T founders came by for a due diligence meeting that Victor wrote off as an empty dog and pony show. Abramo's goal was to announce the IPO at six dollars a share and manipulate the price up by two dollars. Then Abramo, DiChiara, and the other Sovereign brokers would buy up all the stock. At this point they and a handful of other brokers would be permitted to sell some or all of their shares to clients—or, rather, victims. Once official sales began a day or so later, the brokers would allow the clients to buy more but would use various tactics to keep them from selling.

Mimi Rocah continued, "When you would call up a customer to get them to buy SCTI [the company's stock ticker symbol], what did you say to them about the company, SC&T?"

"I fabricated the entire story about SC&T," Victor said.

When Victor began reciting his counterfeit sales pitch, Judge Mukasey had to remind him to slow down. I thought Victor was doing great. The court couldn't have had a more authentic display of flimflam. Victor reeled off his spiel with the skill of a carnival barker. The jurors would have had to pay a hundred bucks for this show on Broadway.

"Basically, we would call them up," Victor explained. "We would tell them the company had an innovative technology that was coming out that was going to shock the entire computer industry, that Dell was bidding for the technology, Apple Computer, Hewlett-Packard, and several other companies. If just one of the contracts were hit, the stock would be no less than twenty to thirty dollars. God forbid all four contracts get signed."

"And was any of this pitch accurate?" Mimi asked.

"Besides the company being called SC&T, no."

I had to suppress a laugh.

During his time with Sovereign, Victor expressed admiration for SC&T. "Phil," he told Abramo, "these guys, basically, they're bigger scam artists than we are."

Victor testified that a client could purchase the IPO only by being an existing client. "And to be an existing client, they would have to have some type of equity position either through a money market account or some other type of stock of their choosing," Victor told Mimi. If they agreed to buy in, he would sell their other stock holdings or dip into their money market account to pay for it.

The clients/victims had no idea that their investment—typically $250,000—was being held hostage until the stock price tanked. The client inevitably got shellacked, and the Sovereign brokers, who had knowingly bet that the stock price would plummet, walked off with the client's money.

"If I received a phone call for a client who wanted to sell stock," Victor testified, "I would try to convince him not only to keep the stock but to buy more. And if that didn't work, I would have to try to sell it to another client."

Mimi wanted to know what happened if that didn't work.

"I would sell out of Client A and convince Client B to buy it, and then that would be the other side of the transaction," Victor said.

"And what if that didn't work?" Mimi persisted. "What if you didn't have another client to buy it?"

"Then I would park the stock in an account who had cash."

Victor explained that stock parking was an illegal practice of shifting money from one account to another without the recipient's knowledge. "If I had a client who had X amount of dollars that would be enough to cover the purchase, I would park the stock in that account," he said.

One time a client discovered the unwarranted purchase of SC&T stock in his account. Victor told him he would investigate right away. He put the client on hold, ran into Abramo's office and begged for help. Abramo—unperturbed by Victor's fraud—asked his business partner to "take care of it."

Abramo's partner "sold it out of that guy's account and put it into trading," Victor testified.

At Sovereign, a good crook like Victor could collect commissions as high as 35 percent. The National Association of Securities Dealers (NASD)—precursor to the Financial Industry Regulatory Authority (FINRA)—put a 5 percent cap on legal commissions.

According to Victor, Vinny Palermo told him he'd heard that Phil Abramo and one of his business partners had made $150 million on SC&T-style scams.

If things went the way I hoped, Philly wasn't going to enjoy much of it anymore.

Shortly after his apprenticeship with Phil Abramo, Victor established his own securities firm. His opening IPO would be a fraudulent company and, as Abramo advised, Victor would place the fake shares in an untraceable offshore account. Hence Victor's regular jaunts to the Bahamas.

Victor DiChiara's Wall Street banditry made a good impression on Vinny Palermo. As December 2, 1999, drew near and our impending indictment was leaked to the DeCavalcantes, the acting boss and associate were parked at Pinocchio's in Elizabeth, New Jersey, a diner just over the Goethals Bridge from Staten Island, when Vinny took Victor into his confidence.

"He said he was going to have Frank Polizzi call in Frankie Scarabino and have him killed," Victor told Mimi as she approached the end of her direct examination. "He was going to have Charles Majuri call in Frank D'Amato and have him killed. He said he was going to have Joe Sclafani call in Ralphie and have him killed."

All in a day's work.

With no hard evidence, Vinny had decided Ralph Guarino and Frank Scarabino were rats. As for Frank D'Amato, he had to die because he was hell-bent on killing Anthony Capo. Eight years had passed since Capo shot Johnny Boy, but Frank's determination to avenge his brother's death hadn't dimmed so much as a watt.

Late 1999 was probably Vinny Palermo's most active season for murder conspiracies. A few months back, in the summer, Vinny was all worked up about killing Tommy Salvata. The FBI had just raided one of Palermo's restaurants and had asked about Salvata, who according to Victor made weekly stops at the restaurant to courier loan-shark money to Palermo. Salvata "seemed nervous," Victor testified, as he had just undergone a triple bypass and didn't want to convalesce in prison. Salvata's behavior echoed Joey Garofano's nervousness in the wake of Fred Weiss's murder. It had gotten Joey a one-way ticket to lovely Marlboro, New York.

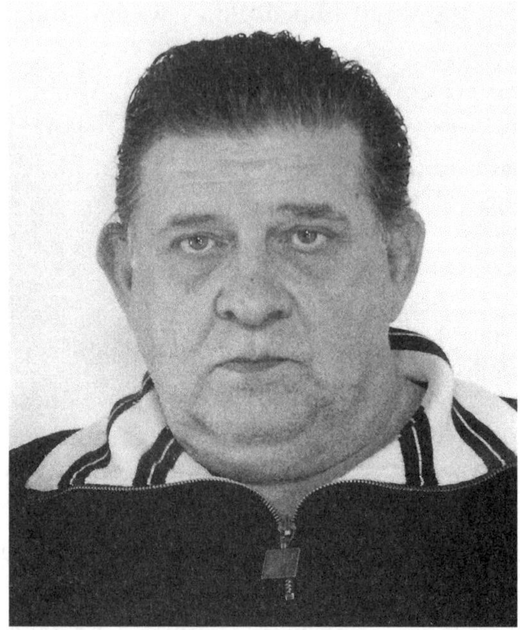

Charles "Charlie" Majuri. *Department of Justice Trial Exhibit, US Attorney's Office, Southern District of New York / FBI*

Imagine if Salvata knew that Vinny Ocean had already concocted a plan for DiChiara and Capo to kill him, either with a cheese grater or a few shots to the back of the head. Luckily for Salvata, Palermo's plan lost steam when Victor took off for the Bahamas and Anthony Capo wouldn't do the kill with anyone else.

Mimi asked Victor if Palermo had given him specific instructions about murdering Scarabino, Guarino, and D'Amato.

"He told me to go home, go get some good ratchets—which he refers to as guns—and that he would call me later on in the night and tell me what I had to get done," Victor answered. "He said that we should all go on the lam after tonight, stay away for a few days. When the arrests come down, we should surrender so that it would be easy to get bail."

Palermo was hoping Victor wouldn't get arrested. "In the case I didn't get arrested . . . he wanted me to take over his businesses," Victor testified. "And take care of his family, Capo's family, and Gallo's family."

It means something that Vinny couldn't entrust his empire to a captain or to an underboss, and by now the only guy he could rely on was an associate.

When Victor got back to his apartment, he shut off his beeper so Palermo couldn't reach him. The next day he tracked down Capo at his mother's house. Capo had just gotten out of the hospital where he'd been treated for his worsening diabetes. Victor told him about Vinny's "crazy scheme."

Anything else? Mimi asked.

"[Capo] told me that Vinny had called him in the middle of the night to come out of the hospital," Victor said. "The way he [Palermo] phrased it, Jimmy Gallo was calling him to come out of the hospital, he [Capo] thought."

Mimi asked why Victor had shut off his beeper and phone.

"At that point, I had enough," Victor said. "Vinny was looking to kill everybody."

Two days later, everybody on the leaked indictment was arrested at six in the morning.

During Victor's cross-examination on May 14, Judge Mukasey called all the attorneys into a conference before the jury entered the courtroom.

"There has been a bald-headed gentleman sitting, I believe, with Mrs. Schifilliti, who is in the courtroom," the judge told counsel.

The deputy clerk volunteered he might be Steve Vitabile's cousin.

Judge Mukasey asked Anthony Servino, "Is your client's cousin in the court?"

Servino said, "It's his son. He will be here about eleven."

Vitabile's son had no connection to La Cosa Nostra. He was in the courtroom to support his father. He was always cordial to me.

"He has apparently been perceived to be staring with a high degree of intensity at either the jury or the witness," Judge Mukasey said. "So if he could lower the intensity of his gaze."

"Will do," Servino said. "Understandably, we don't want that, Your Honor."

"I understand that," the judge said. "If we can make it a 60-watt instead of a 150-watt gaze."

"Might even put a smile on his face," Servino said.

"No, don't do that," Judge Mukasey said.

The jurors filed in, none the wiser, and the trial resumed.

The defense attorneys could have jumped on Victor as a fraud not to be trusted or believed. Instead they focused on his having smoked pot when the government had strictly forbidden him from doing any illegal drugs.

Ever the trickster, Victor justified smoking a joint while wearing a wire for the government. He had to "keep up the appearance of being an active associate," he reasoned.

It would make you look more like you were really a criminal if you lied to the government, Marty Klotz said. Maybe I'd be snide too if I were in Klotz's shoes.

Victor's response got a snort out of the jurors: "I know how to look like a criminal all on my own."

Nothing about Victor at trial was bluster. He had been an accomplished car thief. He knew makes and models like the back of his hand. I once asked him if he remembered stealing a 1989 IROC-Z on September 30, 1992. It was parked within walking distance of the East River Savings Bank near the West Side Highway. I had just taken theft insurance off the car when it got stolen. I ended up having to make the last eight payments of a four-year loan on a car I no longer owned.

Down the drain: $2,286.16 in payments. Not to mention the value of a three-year-old pristine car.

Victor said he couldn't take credit for that one.

Between April 28 and May 14, 2003, the jury in *US v. Vitabile et al.* had heard the testimony of a DeCavalcante associate, soldier, and captain. Our witnesses could have been fragile. Insecure. They were anything but. So it was ironic, to say the least, that our big-fish acting boss Vinny Ocean—the witness we relied on to bring it all home—came close to losing us the whole case.

24

THE "REAL" TONY SOPRANO TAKES CENTER STAGE

May 14, 2003

Day twenty-four of *US v. Vitabile et al.* AUSA John Hillebrecht announces, "Your Honor! The government calls Vinny Palermo!"

Wait a minute. That's not Vinny. The deputy clerk is swearing in the wrong guy.

What the hell? It *is* Vinny!

All of us who'd known Vinny Palermo in FBI custody did a double take. He'd clearly gotten plastic surgery. His lips were plumped up now. His chin looked bigger, his nose smaller. A goatee hid his jawline. Vinny had clearly upped his game to hide his mob identity. The rest of us wondered how he came up with the five or ten grand for such a makeover. Witness Security didn't include a voucher for nip and tuck.

Hillebrecht dove in. "Mr. Palermo," he began. "Can you tell the jury how old you are?"

"Fifty-seven." The voice was somber, but it was the familiar voice of the old Vinny.

"Are you married?"

"Yes."

"How long have you been married?"

"Twenty-three years second marriage. First marriage when I was nineteen."

"Do you have any children from either of your marriages?"

"Yes. Two from the first marriage. Three from the second."

Hillebrecht asked Vinny Palermo to move a little bit closer to the microphone. "And keep your voice up," he said.

The DeCavalcante acting boss—former acting boss—wasn't ready to speak above a whisper. Understandable. The trial was public and Vinny was about to break his oath of omertà, the mob code of silence he'd been sworn to for the past forty years.

It was killing Vinny to testify.

The prosecution wasted no time in getting him to name names. Identifying everyone from Frank D'Amato to Frank Polizzi couldn't have felt noble, and maybe Vinny was glad he could hide inside his own skin. Of course, Vinny—old and new—had *chosen* to turn canary. Not so long ago, he'd have expected anybody else in his predicament to shut the F up too.

When it came to ID'ing Government Exhibit 332, for example, he merely said, "Victor. He was associated with the DeCavalcante family and he was proposed to be a wiseguy."

Yeah. The guy you chose as the executor of your estate in the event you got arrested. Did you even know his last name was DiChiara?

And what about Government Exhibit 341?

"His name is Joe," Vinny testified. "He was associated with Anthony Capo and Anthony Rotondo."

Yeah. But you once knew him as that "fat kid Joey."

While Vinny could identify Government Exhibit 308 as Anthony Capo—"I was involved with him with several murders, shylock business, some sports business"—he could only call Government Exhibit 203 "Virgil"—even though "he was involved with a murder that I was involved with."

Last name Alessi. Did you remember he had a heart attack after he shot Joey Garofano? Remember he had to be hospitalized?

"Mr. Palermo, I don't want to interrupt you, but do us all a favor," Hillebrecht said. "Keep your voice up. We are having a little trouble hearing."

Government Exhibit 395 was an individual Vinny had known as Steve—"the consigliere of the family as long as I remember." Vinny had dealt with Steve over a smorgasbord of organized crime activities.

"Do you know Steve's last name?" Hillebrecht asked. He needed Vinny to confirm he was talking about defendant Steve Vitabile.

Vinny responded, "Can I come back to that?"

In all his debriefs, Hillebrecht assumed Vinny knew Vitabile's last name. Well, you know what they say about what happens when you assume.

"In going through those photographs, Mr. Palermo, you didn't tell us the last names of many individuals. Is there a reason for that?"

"Many, many years ago, I was taught not to learn last names," Vinny said.

Hillebrecht wanted to know who'd taught Vinny that.

"Sam the Plumber," Vinny said. "Sam DeCavalcante." Vinny's uncle by marriage. He was such a dominant personality that the North Jersey crime family eventually became known by his name.

Vinny wanted to expand on this answer. Hillebrecht stopped him.

"Listen to my question," he said. "Of the hundreds of meetings you had with Steve, what percentage of those meetings involved . . . in part conversations about the DeCavalcante family and Cosa Nostra business?"

Vinny said most of them.

"Do you see Steve in the courtroom today?"

"Yes."

"Would you point him out?"

"With the gray suit," Vinny said.

Vinny also had to identify Steve's two codefendants. "Can you tell us approximately how long you've known Philip Abramo?" Hillebrecht asked.

"Twenty years."

"In that twenty-year period, about how many face-to-face meetings would you say you have had with Philly Abramo?"

"A few hundred." Marty Klotz had argued that Abramo had had virtually no extended contact with the thugs who had murdered John D'Amato.

Vinny struggled to keep his agitation in check. He was about to speak when Hillebrecht advised him again to listen.

"Do you see Phil Abramo in the courtroom today?" Hillebrecht asked.

"I seen him before," Vinny said.

"Do you want to stand up and look around?"

"I can see him."

"If you see him, point him out."

"He's right behind the computer," Vinny said.

"What's he wearing?"

"He's got glasses, black suit, black jacket."

"Mr. Palermo, you also identified . . . Government's Exhibit 385 as Pino Schifilliti, a captain in the DeCavalcante family. Roughly how long have you known Pino Schifilliti?"

About thirty years.

Hillebrecht asked how many meetings had been face to face. About two hundred.

"Do you see Mr. Schifilliti in the courtroom today?"

"Yes, I do," Vinny said. "With the white hair and glasses on."

Judge Mukasey said two people at the defendants' table had white hair and glasses.

"Right there," Vinny clarified. "With the gray suit jacket and dark tie."

Vinny had identified all three defendants on trial. We were off to a good start.

We were barely an hour into Vinny's testimony when I was ready to bet Pino Schifilliti, Philip Abramo, and Steve Whatshisname were second-guessing their decision to go to trial.

As the trial progressed, Vinny did dredge up another name for Steve Vitabile. Identifying the DeCavalcante who gave the go-ahead to murder John D'Amato, Vinny said, "We got the approval from Steve Number Three, the consigliere."

"Number Three" referred to the New Jersey crime family's third in command. Not a legitimate surname, but an unmistakeable ID nonetheless.

The government attorneys put up org charts I'd created to illustrate how DeCavalcante members had moved up in the organization over time. Vinny had lived through the churn and had no trouble recalling his old *borgata* hierarchies.

Can you explain to us why the DeCavalcantes are called the New Jersey family? Hillebrecht asked.

"Well, if something needs to be done in Jersey with different companies, with unions, it would come to the Jersey family and get permission to work on a union job and not have union men working," Vinny said.

Hillebrecht knew the jury needed a simpler explanation. "As basically as you can, what is the DeCavalcante crime family?" he asked. "What's its purpose?"

Vinny was philosophical. "It's a group of people that are dedicated to each other, work with each other to make money, protect each other, and go into all different businesses, legal and not legal."

Wait a minute. Wasn't this the same guy Victor DiChiara had described as a vindictive killer? Vinny's explanation sounded like a Mafia version of *The 7 Habits of Highly Effective People.*

"The overall Cosa Nostra," Hillebrecht began. "How is that organized?"

"Five New York families and one Jersey family," Vinny said. "That's the Cosa Nostra, a group all put together."

Hillebrecht asked, "The phrase 'Cosa Nostra.' Is that Italian?"

Vinny said yes. Hillebrecht asked him to translate it into English.

"The thing of ours," Vinny said. His voice was a decibel above a whisper.

"Say it again," Hillebrecht said.

"The thing of ours."

Vinny Palermo always spoke in a low voice whenever he despaired the loss of his world.

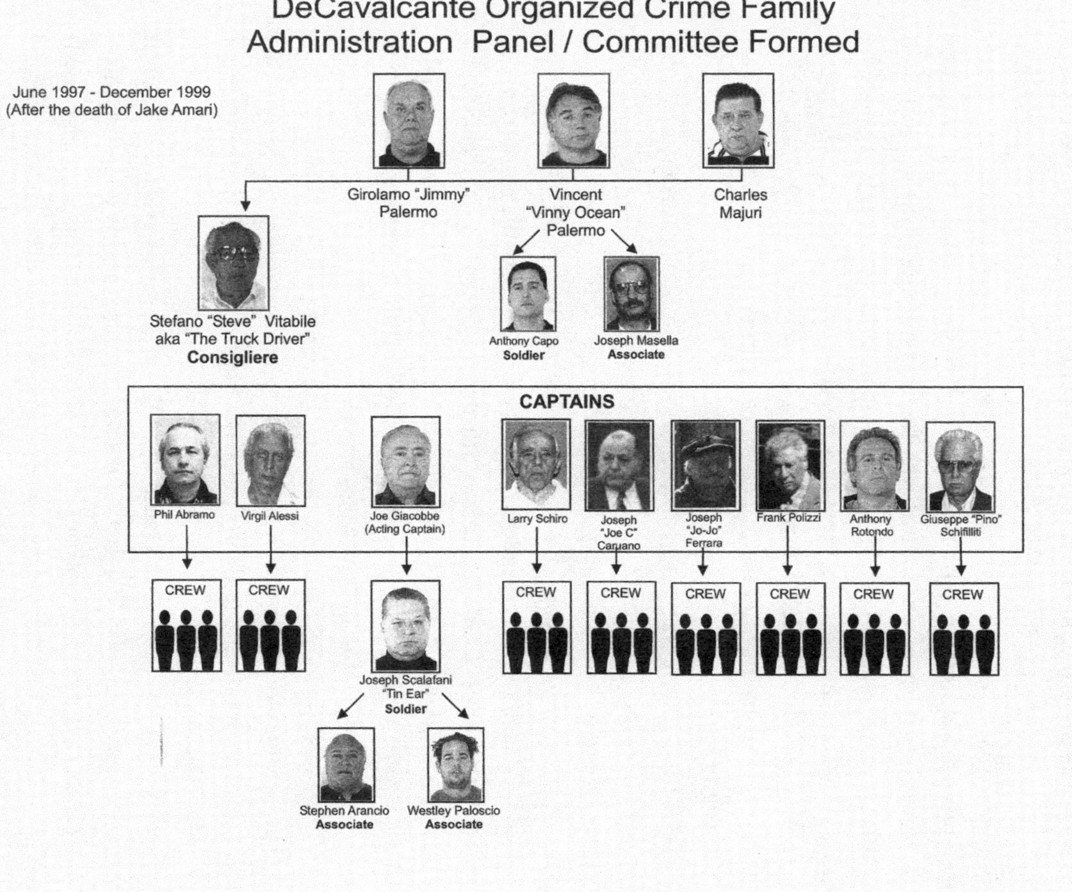

Chart of the DeCavalcante organization that I prepared for trial. *Department of Justice Trial Exhibit, US Attorney's Office, Southern District of New York / FBI*

Vinny may have done whatever he damn well pleased, but where the DeCavalcantes were concerned, he was a walking rule book. He told the court who could get made (Hillebrecht: "Can women join the Mafia?" Palermo: "No."); what businesses the Jersey family discussed at regular meet-ups in Manhattan (shylocking, bookmaking, control of unions); and what the chain of command was (soldiers at the bottom, and then captains, consigliere, underboss, and boss in ascending order). In short, he affirmed that he had been part of a racketeering operation since the 1960s.

When Hillebrecht led Vinny to the December 2, 1999, indictment and asked him to enumerate the changes against him, Vinny was suddenly vague.

"The indictment was extortion, shylocking, sports, murder, just a lot of charges," Vinny summarized. "Fourteen, eighteen charges."

"Let me cut it down for you," Hillebrecht said. "The murder you mentioned, who were you charged with having murdered?"

"Joey Masella." Vinny added that he'd also conspired to murder Charles Majuri and Frank D'Amato but hadn't executed on those plans.

"And was it explained to you by the judge the maximum penalty that you were facing if you were convicted of all the charges that you were looking at?" Hillebrecht asked.

Vinny acknowledged it was the death penalty.

The jurors, who'd already heard lots of ghastly evidence, clearly wondered what warranted the death penalty. Actually, it was the murder of Joey Masella.

Joey O was murdered in October 1998—four years after the Federal Death Penalty Act of 1994 became law. Any federally charged murders committed after 1994 exposed the alleged perpetrator to the death penalty. During his debriefings with Nora, Vinny divulged his extensive criminal history, but he vehemently denied any involvement in the murder of Joseph "Joey O" Masella.

Vinny did not plead guilty to the murder of Joey Masella. He did plead guilty to all the other charges in the December 2 indictment, though, as well as a host of other charges. To my knowledge, he spoke frankly about everything from tax evasion to the hijacking of fresh fish to loan-sharking to murder.

His tax evasion started with the sale of Ocean, the fish restaurant he opened in Queens when he was sixteen.

Hillebrecht asked, "And how did you get the money at that young age—"

"It cost me $4,000 to buy it," Vinny said. "I had most of it saved and I borrowed some money from my sisters."

"OK," Hillebrecht said. "Mr. Palermo, again, you've got to wait until I finish the question or nobody's going to understand either one of us. OK?"

"OK."

I couldn't tell if Vinny was excited about telling his story to the jury or if he was in a rush to get the hell out of Judge Mukasey's courtroom—or if he was just used to cutting people off. In any case, we learned he got at least $500,000 in cash for Ocean when he sold it two decades later. Not a penny of it went to the IRS.

The fish and seafood hijackings surely contributed to Ocean's solid bottom line over the restaurant's twenty-three-year-long existence. Back then, the FBI knew Vinny only as a corrupt restaurant owner.

"I brought a load of shrimp off some people I knew, and FBI came to me and into my store," Vinny testified. "And I wind up getting charged for that. Caught for that."

Vinny pled guilty to receiving stolen goods. He was sentenced to five years on parole and fined $5,000.

Even when Vinny himself didn't put loan-sharking money out on the street, he benefited handsomely from the financial struggles of many indebted restaurateurs. A case in point was a Frenchman named **Jacques Petit**.

Rudy Farone loaned Petit $75,000 for a seafood restaurant. Mickey Dimino, a captain in the Genovese crime family, loaned Petit $75,000 as well. Petit's extortionate interest on his mob-financed loans was north of $7,000 a week.

Hillebrecht asked Vinny to explain "points" in the context of loan-sharking. Vinny described how a $10,000 loan at two points turned into

$200 a week, $800 a month, and $10,400 a year—even while the loan recipient still had to pay back the initial $10,000.* Hillebrecht wanted to know what would happen if the loan shark customer failed to pay back the money he borrowed.

"Well, you extend it for a while," Vinny said. "And then if nothing happens, he winds up with a beating."

Jacques Petit was afraid for his life.

Vinny to the rescue. "I told him that I would sit with them"—the loan sharks in various mob families—"and work out the money for him," Vinny testified. "And in return I wanted the restaurant. But he could stay there working, with salary, and live in the building."

Petit was in deep. He didn't have a choice. He accepted Vinny's offer.

And Vinny came through. He sat down with the loan sharks and made "settlements" with them.

Hillebrecht asked Vinny to describe the settlements.

Vinny was able to "knock down" a $75,000 loan by half. His fellow mobsters also forgave all the vigorish, or interest.

"And can you explain to the jury why these wiseguys, who put Jacques in fear of his life, accommodated you?" Hillebrecht asked.

"Because I was one of them," Vinny said. "In organized crime."

At the time of his arrest, Vinny was "part owner" of various restaurants in Queens through loan-sharking rackets like the one with Jacques Petit. These "part ownerships" were handshake deals, and Vinny's name was never on paper. As part of his cooperation agreement, Vinny had had to agree to forfeit $2 million he'd obtained, directly or indirectly, from racketeering activity.

Lest you harbor hard feelings toward the government for confiscating Vinny Palermo's money—after all, Vinny had been working since he was sixteen years old—you should know about one of his topless dancers who bragged about the $25,000 she had saved up. She kept the cash in her apartment.

"And when she was dancing, I went to the apartment," Vinny testified. "I took the money."

---

* See chapter 13 for a more complete description of loan-sharking.

There's also a matter of $700,000 worth of jewelry—most of it acquired by theft—stowed inside a garbage can while Vinny and his family went on vacation.

"Well, my wife took the garbage out for the first time in twenty years," Vinny said. "And that was the end of the jewelry." Vinny related the story pretty calmly. I'd like to have been a fly on the wall for Vinny's conversation with his wife. My guess is she never took out the garbage again.

In any case, Vinny blamed the sanitation workers. He concluded they'd found the jewelry and made off with it. He enlisted Anthony Capo, Joey Masella, and another thug to beat the workers and threaten to shoot them if they didn't cough up the goods. Masella and Palermo had their fists. Capo had a weapon. The fourth man hid in one of the upstairs bedrooms.

Vinny never got the jewelry back.

The sanitation workers fared better than the mechanic at Fred Chall Marine on Long Island who was trying to fix the motor on Vinny's Wellcraft Scarab speedboat. Average price: $99,000. When he last piloted the boat, Vinny said, the motor worked fine.

"Someone must have used it," Vinny accused the mechanic.

The mechanic said he'd only put new rings on the motor. "I said, 'Someone seen you out in the ocean racing with my boat,'" Vinny told the jury. The mechanic denied it. "So I pulled out a .357 and I put it to his head. . . . And he says, 'Yes, I did. I was racing and blew the motor.' And when he said that, I was mad, and I bit his nose."

Right through the skin.

Engaging in acts of violence to achieve a desired end was a core precept of the DeCavalcante catechism. Vinny learned this in the mid-1970s when Sam DeCavalcante himself ran Vinny's induction ceremony in the basement of Pinocchio's in Elizabeth. In attendance were John Riggi, the crime family's number-two man, and Steve, the number-three man. The consigliere.

"Steve who?" Hillebrecht asked.

"Steve," Vinny answered. He mumbled something else, but it wasn't even remotely a last name. It sounded like "*Rrr-rrr.*"

The prosecution team couldn't help but look at each other. We were all thinking, *What the hell was that?*

Vinny had already testified he didn't know people's last names. Why bother saying anything? Jay Kramer and I exchanged glances. We were disgusted and amused.

Now was not the time to get into a psychopath's head. We'd have to wait until we got out of the courtroom to bust a gut.

Hillebrecht forged ahead to ask Vinny to recap the induction ceremony.

"Well, Sam spoke first," Vinny recalled. "And he said, 'Do you know all—who all these people are?' And I says yeah. He says, 'You like all these people?' I says yeah. He says, 'If they need you to take care of something or help them, would you help them?' I said yeah. 'Would you like to spend the rest of your life dealing with them and being with them?' I says yeah. And he says, 'All right, you're here. We're going to make you part of the family, and there's rules that you need to know.'"

What followed were the rules about no drugs and no sleeping with a wiseguy's wife.

"And there's no setting bombs off anywhere because you could hurt innocent people," Vinny added.

Sam DeCavalcante underscored that the gun and knife were the made man's must-haves. "He says, 'These are tools like a carpenter has a hammer and screwdriver,'" Vinny testified. "'This is our tools, gun and knife.'"

The induction was where Vinny officially learned about the Mafia Commission. "Three people from each family sit and they make up the rules," Vinny said.

The Jersey family did not have a seat at the table.

Hillebrecht asked, "So when you say three people from each family, which families are you talking about that had representatives—"

"Five New York families."

"Don't interrupt me, sir," Hillebrecht said in a curt tone of voice. "I'll try not to interrupt you. The five New York families, each of them had three representatives?"

"Yes."

Hillebrecht asked how the meeting came to a formal close.

"Just when it was all over, they just put out a lot of cold cuts and food and cookies, and everybody just eats," Vinny said.

As Anthony Rotondo had testified, the DeCavalcante induction ceremonies pre–John Gotti were declared invalid, and a decade later, Vinny had to be reinducted. The rule about no drugs was still in place. But, as Vinny testified, "it's broken all the time."

One day in the middle of Vinny Palermo's testimony, the jury arrived in the morning to find that the judge had a message for them. Phil Abramo's lawyer Marty Klotz had tried to block Mimi Rocah from telling the jury about the guilty plea of former codefendent Louis "Louie Eggs" Consalvo, on the basis that it was "unreliable," but Judge Mukasey had ruled that the plea was taken in open court and therefore could be shared with the jury. This morning, the judge told the jurors that the "securities fraud with which Mr. Abramo is charged in this case is a fraud in connection only with the operation of Sovereign Equity Management Corporation. He's not charged with fraud in connection with any of the other firms about which Mr. DiChiara testified."

Mimi expanded on Judge Mukasey's comment. She told the jury that Consalvo "pleaded guilty to violating Title 18, United States Code, Section 371, by conspiring to commit securities fraud." The rest of his plea was an admission that he had conspired to murder Louis LaRasso "in order to maintain or increase his position in the DeCavalcante organized crime family."

Judge Mukasey pointed out that the guilty plea pertained solely to Louis Consalvo, not to any of the three defendants on trial. "There's nothing in what you just heard that relates to the question of whether any defendant in this case participated in any of those activities," he said.

True. But Mimi put the idea in the jurors' minds: birds of a feather flock together.

Mimi passed the virtual baton to John Hillebrecht, and he resumed the government's direct examination of Vinny Palermo.

Hillebrecht couldn't take the chance that Anthony Servino would argue that the "Steve" Vinny Palermo knew was not his client Steve Vitabile. He began day two of direct examination by giving Vinny an opportunity to say Steve's full name.

"I want you to take us through your second induction ceremony now," Hillebrecht said. "Who was getting straightened out that night?"

This time Vinny was ready. "There was a bunch of soldiers from the DeCavalcante family," he testified. "John D'Amato, Steve Vitabile, Philly Abramo, Louis. Just a bunch of fellas."

"When you say 'Louis,' which Louis do you mean?" Hillebrecht asked.

"Louie Eggs." True to form, Vinny Palermo either didn't know or didn't remember that "Louie Eggs" was Louis Consalvo.

Hillebrecht moved on to DeCavalcante succession issues. He asked what happened to the administration panel John Riggi put together before he went off to prison. Vinny said it took six or seven months for the three-man panel to fall apart.

Anthony Rotondo had already told the jury about how Manny Riggi plotted to murder fellow panel member John D'Amato. Now Vinny told them about D'Amato's own murderous schemes. They came to a head at the administration meeting in a New Jersey catering hall, when John D'Amato accused Vinny and Anthony Rotondo of planning to kill him.

Hillebrecht asked, "How did you respond when he made that accusation to you?"

"Well, I jumped up and I got very annoyed with it," Vinny testified. "And I told him, 'If I wanted to kill you, you would be dead by now. You wouldn't be sitting here.' I said, 'That's not true.'"

D'Amato's reaction?

Vinny said, "John looked over at everybody and said, 'I told you it wasn't true.'"

And the award for Best Actor goes to John D'Amato.

Jimmy Gallo told Vinny that, in fact, D'Amato wanted to kill him, Anthony Rotondo, and Rudy Farone. Unbeknownst to Vinny, Johnny Boy D'Amato had stationed his rock-ribbed supporters outside the catering hall, and with a word from him, Vinny, Rudy, and Anthony would be full of holes.

Louie Eggs was one of the would-be assassins.

Gallo and Vinny, of course, had been shooting partners in the murder of Fred Weiss. Maybe the people who slay together stay together.

Vinny bounced the news off Steve Vitabile. The way Vinny pronounced "Vitabile," I didn't think the name was going to stick for long.

Steve tried to allay Vinny's fears. He conceded that some guys had been standing outside the catering hall to protect the administration meeting. "What they were really going to do," Vinny said, Steve just wouldn't say. In short, Steve Number Three was full of it.

Maybe Vinny wasn't so reluctant to rat out Steve the Truck Driver.

And not much point in committing Steve's last name to memory. After the trial, Vinny would never see Number Three again.

But you know how it is. One day you want to splatter somebody's brains across the backseat of a car. The next day you're ready to work with him. After the murder of John D'Amato, Steve Vitabile asked Vinny if he wanted to become the DeCavalcante consigliere.

Having just gone through the succession drama involving John D'Amato, Vitabile knew enough to head off such problems at the pass. To make sure the promotion was kosher, Steve told Vinny to talk to Joe Massino, the Bonanno crime family boss, about transitioning to the number-three spot.

Vinny couldn't reach Massino, so he checked in with Spero,* the Bonanno consigliere. "He was on his roof flying his pigeons on Bath Avenue in Brooklyn," Vinny testified.

"He was on his roof flying pigeons?" Hillebrecht asked.

"Yes, he flies pigeons."

"Did you go on the roof where he was flying pigeons to speak with him?"

"Yes."

With pigeons aflutter, Spero said it was fine with him if Vinny became the DeCavalcante consigliere. Spero wanted to check with the other organized crime families, though.

---

* Anthony Spero, Bonanno consigliere and eventual acting boss. At this point in the trial, Palermo referred to him only as "Spero."

Vinny lied when he reported back to Vitabile. "I told him that Spero said you could do it, but it's not a good idea," Vinny testified.

Vinny didn't want to be number three. He was holding out for something better.

And what was Vitabile going to do? Retire to Boca and play shuffleboard?

Nature abhors a vacuum. Something had to happen. Vinny and D'Amato-appointed captain Charles Majuri went at each other.

"Well, I got worried and phoned Jimmy Gallo, who said they were plotting to kill me," Vinny explained.

"They" meant Majuri and a couple other DeCavalcante captains. They wanted Jimmy Gallo to join the Majuri hit parade and help kill Vinny. "Gallo came and told me about it," Vinny said.

Hillebrecht asked, "When you learned about it, what did you decide to do about it?"

"Kill Charlie Majuri."

Did you make efforts to do so?

"Yes, I did." In Vinny's world, he had no other choice.

At an administration meeting in the mid-1990s at Vitabile's house, attended by Schifilliti and Abramo, Steve served as an arbitrator. Boss Jake Amari had just died, so Steve set up a ruling panel to run the DeCavalcantes.

"He picked me, Charlie Majuri, and Jimmy Palermo," Vinny said.

Before each ruling panel meeting, Vinny and Jimmy—the two unrelated Palermos—huddled together the day before. "We used to discuss what we needed to talk about, and we agreed on it together," Vinny said. Steve the Truck Driver usually joined them.

The Palermos and Vitabile could be levelheaded if they had to be. Majuri was on the ruling panel so as "not to cause any problems."

Keep your friends close. Keep your enemies closer.

Or, from Majuri's standpoint: if you can't beat 'em, join 'em.

They all deserved Brownie points for using their words instead of their guns.

On the witness stand, Vinny recounted the three murder plans he put in place in the days leading up to the December 1999 arrests.

I'm no shrink, but here's what I think. When Fritzy Giovanelli warned Vinny about the grand jury leak and Vinny's impending arrest for the murder of Fred Weiss, Vinny went round the bend. As Victor DiChiara rightly testified earlier in the trial, Vinny had been in a mad rush, first, to murder Frank Scarabino and Ralph Guarino when he decided—with no evidence—that they had cooperated with the government, and, second, to murder Frank D'Amato, who wanted to kill Anthony Capo.

Guarino was the first suspected rat on Vinny's hit list. "I told Anthony Capo I just left Anthony Rotondo and he told me that he met Fritzy, and Fritzy gave him a list of guys that are going to get arrested," Vinny half ranted. "And I mentioned that he [Capo] was on that list . . . And Anthony [Rotondo] says there's somebody around us for two years with a wire and we figure it's Ralphie. So get Victor and Jimmy Gallo. Make arrangements to meet them and try to find Ralphie and kill him."

Four years had passed and Vinny had no trouble recreating the fanatical search for his white whale(s). He recalled how he drove out to John Street in Elizabeth to get Steve the Truck Driver's permission to kill Ralph Guarino.

"What did Steve Vitabile say?" Hillebrecht asked.

"He said, 'That's fine,'" Vinny replied.

On Sunday, November 21, 1999, Vinny went to a wedding in Jersey. "I walked in and Anthony was standing up—Rotondo—talking to Steve and Jimmy Palermo and a few other soldiers," Vinny said in a rush. "And they were discussing about the list. . . . Most of the night everybody was talking about it. All soldiers in the DeCavalcante family."

Vinny couldn't just do nothing. Over the next day or so, he met Anthony Capo, Victor DiChiara, and Jimmy Gallo at a joint called the Coach Diner on Sixty-Third Drive in Queens. They talked about finding Ralph Guarino and killing him.

Hillebrecht asked, "Was there any attempt to kill Ralph, by which I mean, did anybody fire a shot at him or anything like that?"

Vinny said no.

"But just so it's clear," Hillebrecht said. "You told those guys to kill him, right?"

"Yes."

A couple days later, Anthony Rotondo told Vinny to meet him at the Tiffany Diner, once located in Brooklyn on Ninety-Ninth Street. Rotondo told Vinny that Fritzy had gotten hold of an updated list of names on computer paper. Vinny was annoyed with Rotondo for not making a copy.

Vinny heard about the list again at his daughter's wedding on November 28. He walked over to Rotondo to say hello and get an update.

Rotondo said, "'*Goombata*, got some bad news for you,'" Vinny testified. "'I don't want to ruin the wedding for you. I'll tell you later.' I said, 'You can tell me now.' He said the arrest is going to come down Wednesday or Thursday of this week."

After the wedding, Vinny moved into a friend's house in Point Lookout, a beach town along the southern coast of Long Island. He didn't want the FBI to arrest him in front of his children. The beach house was close enough to Vinny's home that he could still see his family every evening for a few hours.

Life turns on a dime when you're desperate to kill your enemies. Suddenly Anthony Capo, Vinny's reliable shooter, was out of commission. He was stuck in the hospital with complications from diabetes and too weak to kill anybody.

"I told Anthony [Rotondo] to call Fritzy and set up an appointment for me to meet him face to face to discuss what he knows about the arrest going down," Vinny told the jury.

How many times was Vinny going to worry this bone? Did he think going over the list again would change anything?

Vinny arranged to meet Fritzy and a Florida-based DeCavalcante soldier named Anthony "Marshmallow" Mannarino at a Dunkin' Donuts on Northern Boulevard and Sixty-Third Drive in Queens. When Fritzy walked in, the two DeCavalcantes got up to say hello.

"Anthony Mannarino went to give him a kiss hello, and he [Fritzy] said, "None of that! None of that! That's why everybody's in trouble."

The rotund Marshmallow tried to introduce Vinny as the acting boss. "Fritzy said, 'I don't want to hear it.' He says, 'I have my own problems. . . . I'm going to wind up back in jail where I just came from.'"

But information is power. Fritzy was willing to talk about the indictment. "He said, 'My friend, I got bad news for you. You're going to get arrested Wednesday or Thursday. . . . I just wanted you to know personally, you know, what you're facing.'"

Vinny said, "The only thing he did say about the murder—that I am going to be charged with a murder that's ten years old."

Hillebrecht asked, "As a result of the information you received from both Fritzy and from Mannarino, did you rethink any of your suspicions about Ralph?"

"I started thinking it was a fellow called Frankie the Beast, nicknamed," Vinny said. "He was on the scene of the murder of Fred Weiss, and he was gone for many years. . . . So I started thinking it was him."

Vinny clarified that Frankie the Beast—Frank Scarabino—had unaccountably shown up again in the two years before the December 2 arrest. To Vinny's suspicious mind, nothing happened by chance.

Fritzy liked being a power broker. He promised to track down Scarabino.

Vinny was restless. He drove out to Staten Island to see Anthony Rotondo. "We walked around the corner several times and I explained to him about what Fritzy said, and I explained to him about Frankie the Beast," Vinny said. "And he felt the same thing I felt: that it's Frankie, because he'd been gone for many years and then he's been around two years prior to this day."

Paranoia was all the evidence Vinny needed. "I told him that I wanted to go over to Jersey and meet Steve Truck Driver and tell him what's happening and get some help to kill Frankie," Vinny testified.

True to form, Anthony Rotondo didn't want to be an active participant, but he did rubber-stamp Vinny's murder plans, whatever they turned out to be.

Before driving out to see Steve the Truck Driver, Vinny had Victor DiChiara chauffeur him to see Capo in the hospital. Vinny told Capo about the impending arrests.

"And if you don't want to be home in front of your kids, make sure you're not at home," Vinny advised Capo.

Next stop: Elizabeth, New Jersey. Vinny asked Jimmy Gallo to meet him at Pinocchio's on Bay Street. "I explained everything to him about Fritzy, what he said about the list, about the arrest coming down Wednesday or Thursday, and about what we needed to do with Frankie the Beast," Vinny said.

Vinny and Gallo headed off to the John Street coffee shop to wait for Steve the Truck Driver. Steve showed up with a DeCavalcante soldier Vinny called Supermarket Frank, so named because he used to work at a supermarket. Gallo and Supermarket Frank stayed in the coffee shop while Vinny and Steve took a walk around the corner.

The dizzying pilgrimages from one eatery to another—to throw the FBI off his trail—ratcheted Vinny's mania up to warp speed. "I told Steve about Fritzy with the list and that we were going to get locked up Thursday or Friday," Vinny testified. "I told Steve that Fritzy said Frankie the Beast is the guy that's wired for sure and we need to find him and kill him, and I need to get hold of Frank Polizzi—Hotel Frankie."

Hillebrecht wanted to know why Vinny needed to involve Frank Polizzi.

"Because going back two years prior, Frankie showed up from nowhere after many years—Frankie the Beast—and he was with Hotel Frankie, and I was shocked to see him," Vinny said in that staccato way of his. "And when I told Hotel Frankie, 'What are you doing with him?' he said, 'He's good friends with my son and they're doing some shylock business together.' And then I told him that I have a problem because he—Frankie the Beast—was on the scene in Staten Island on a homicide and he was a witness. And Frankie [Polizzi] said to me, he says, 'Don't worry about it. If there's ever a problem, I will take care of it and I will kill him.'"

Hillebrecht paused to let the jury digest Vinny's words. Imagine if corporate America got rid of problem employees like this.

Hillebrecht asked, "After you broached the topic of involving Frank Polizzi in your efforts to kill Frank the Beast, what did Steve Vitabile say in response?"

"He says, 'Whatever you want to do, we'll do it, and we'll get a hold of Frank and, you know, when would you like to do it?' And I said, 'Right now.'"

Hillebrecht reminded Vinny that he'd assured Vitabile that Fritzy said Scarabino was "for sure" wearing a wire. "Is that what you told him?" Hillebrecht asked.

"Yes," Vinny said. "That's what I told him."

"Is that what Fritzy told you?"

"No, that's not what he said."

"Why did you lie?"

"I wanted to get it taken care of and I didn't want a doubt there."

Hillebrecht didn't ask Vinny how he'd have felt if he'd killed Frankie the Beast for no good reason. What would the jury think if Vinny shrugged off Scarabino's death as collateral damage?

At Frank Polizzi's house, Vinny, Jimmy Gallo, Steve the Truck Driver, and Supermarket Frankie had cookies and espresso.

It was too cold to go talk outside, so Vinny, Steve, and Polizzi spoke privately in the garage.

Vinny told Polizzi about Fritzy and the big arrest coming down that week. "There's somebody wearing a wire for two years," Vinny insisted for the dozenth time. "And Fritzy told me it's Frank the Beast. Frankie Polizzi got all upset. He said, 'I just gave him money to push out in the street. I just gave him the money to open a car dealership.'"

Vinny said they had to kill Scarabino "like tonight."

Polizzi suggested waiting a day so Pino Schifilliti, who was close to Scarabino, could lure him in somewhere.

I looked over at the jury. I saw they couldn't believe what they were hearing.

More driving around and then Vinny and Jimmy Gallo drove to the beach house at Point Lookout. Vinny went to visit his family. Gallo stayed at the beach house watching a TV show about John Gotti.

In the morning Vinny and Gallo showered and went to yet another diner in Jersey, where Pino and Polizzi were waiting for them. Vinny remembered how they all sat at the first table on the right side, "just talking about really nothing at the time." They had lunch.

"I ordered a bacon, lettuce, and tomato sandwich and everybody said it's a good idea. So everybody ordered the same. We ate, and when everybody was done, we said, 'Let's go out and go for a walk. We need to talk to you.'"

Polizzi griped about the cold, so the conspirators drove out in their respective cars to his hotel in Rutherford, New Jersey.

There, Vinny gave Pino Schifilliti his phony-baloney story about Frank Scarabino wearing a wire the past two years, and Pino agreed to lure him to Exit 123 on the Garden State Parkway. Meanwhile, Vinny gave Steve the Truck Driver the job of getting a hole dug for Scarabino's hefty body. In a while, Steve reported back to Vinny that the ground was too frozen to dig.

Jimmy Gallo peeled off to visit his daughter, hospitalized with a grave illness. When he returned, he had a gun.

Vinny was dogged. On Wednesday, December 1, 1999, he met again with the usual suspects to shore up his plan to kill Frank Scarabino. Various other DeCavalcantes got looped into the murder conspiracy, including Charles Majuri.

Vinny ran out of time to kill Frank D'Amato.

He did have time, however, to take care of something he'd neglected to tell SDNY prosecutor John Hillebrecht and Vinny's handler, FBI agent Nora Conley.

He transferred some $2 million in cash to a daughter and son. The money had come entirely from Wiggles, Vinny's strip club in Queens. He hadn't paid a cent of tax on any Wiggles smackeroo. Tony Soprano hadn't paid any on the Bada Bing either.

US v. Vitabile et al. could have come and gone without our knowing a thing about that money transfer if the defense attorneys hadn't tossed off a comment during a break to John about Vinny having millions of dollars socked away somewhere. They were bluffing him, but it turns out they were right.

Vinny shit the bed.

Hillebrecht confronted him. The defense says you didn't tell us about money you've got stashed away, he said.

Vinny's new face turned as white as courthouse marble. He acknowledged that while running around to coffee shops and diners to map out murder conspiracies, he'd "gifted" a couple million to his children so they could send their younger siblings to college.

"Mr. Palermo," Hillebrecht said during direct examination, with no sign of rancor. "When is the first time you told the government about that $1 million you gave to your son?"

Vinny said, "This morning."

"About how long ago?"

"Twenty minutes ago."

Vinny said he'd have told the government about the Wiggles money if the government had asked him about any monetary gifts he'd made before his arrest. "If I was asked about it, I would've said it," Vinny alibied.

What about "tell us everything" didn't he understand? We were so pissed off.

Hillebrecht was as cool as a cold beer. "And as you sit here now, do you have any understanding about what might happen with your cooperation agreement with the government as a result of your not telling them until twenty minutes ago that you gave your son a million dollars?" he asked.

"Well, I didn't know," Vinny protested. "But they said they could rip up the agreement. But I told them and I mentioned it. I didn't think—I didn't see that to be a problem."

A Hollywood casting director would never find anybody to play Vinny as well as Vinny could play himself.

I knew Vinny, though. He was sweatin' bricks.

Wiggles, Vinny Palermo's strip club in Queens. *Photo by Tess McRae, courtesy of the photographer*

Watching our four cooperating witnesses gave me food for thought. Three and a half years after their arrest, were any of them truly contrite, or did they fess up just to stay out of prison? Could these killers become genuine citizens? Were they looking back with nostalgia at their years of union tampering, bid-rigging, no-show jobs, stock scams, and loan-sharking and wish they'd never gotten caught? Did they miss the camaraderie that came with doing home invasions, even murders, together? At some point in their testimony, our witnesses spoke in present tense, as if they were still active LCN members. Could they make a clean break from the mob—and how long would that take?

How did each one feel about becoming a witness? I knew that none of them wanted to die.

Of all the DeCavalcantes, I did feel sorry for Capo's murdered friend Joey Garofano. He should have used better judgment, but as I've said, I didn't grow up in a mob-infested neighborhood the way he did. If Joey had been a little older, maybe a little better educated, he'd have taken a different path. He had a tight family, with a sister, nieces, and nephews who loved him. At least that's what Joey's sister Geralyn had conveyed when she took the stand at 2:00 PM the previous Thursday, May 8—despite a protest from Phil Abramo's lawyer Laila Abou-Rahme. She was afraid Geralyn's presence would be "inflammatory."

"No one suggests she is going to be cool as a cucumber," Hillebrecht told Judge Mukasey. But Hillebrecht had met Geralyn several times, and she'd never broken down.

"The message of this witness to the jury is this is a grieving sister whose brother has been killed," Abou-Rahme argued.

"Whose brother screwed up a murder," the judge said. "It seems to me there is a limit to the sympathy that any jury could feel in that kind of circumstance."

Before Geralyn entered the courtroom, Judge Mukasey reminded the prosecution, "We want facts, not emotions here."

Judge Mukasey wasn't kidding when he called for decorum in his courtroom. After George Hanna made a brief appearance on the stand, the judge had some stern words for Hillebrecht. "Apparently, there are members of the Garofano family seated in the spectators' section," he said. "His mother and father and there are two youngsters, I think. The mother was carrying a photograph of Mr. Garofano, about an 8" × 10" or so in a frame and holding it open. My deputy clerk confiscated it. It will be returned, obviously. But I don't know what these folks want to do or not do, or what they're here to do or not do. But I don't want any outbursts."

Marty Klotz, Abramo's other lawyer, also asked the judge to disallow Geralyn's appearance.

Judge Mukasey wasn't ruffled. "If what they are interested in is revenge of the death and they hold the people here on trial responsible, they have to know that doing something to foul up the trial isn't going to bring that about," he said.

Geralyn couldn't attest to anything about the DeCavalcante organization. And as Judge Mukasey said, she wasn't going to sway the jury into pitying a murderer. Yet fourteen years after Anthony Rotondo drove Joey to Rudy Farone's garage and stood guard while Virgil Alessi shot Joey to death, Geralyn made some kind of impression by saying she still missed her brother.

Mimi asked Geralyn to describe where she was on the last day she saw Joey. "I was in my mother's house sitting in the kitchen," Geralyn said. "And my brother came in. He went and got Burger King, and he sat down to eat the Burger King. And he got a phone call. And he got off the phone and he looked at me and he says, 'I got to go.' So I said yeah."

Mimi asked, "When he said, 'I got to go,' he whispered it like that?"

"Yeah."

"You said he got a phone call," Mimi said. "Did he say who he got the call from?"

"No."

Geralyn watched Joey get into a car with a man she knew to be close with Anthony Capo. Joey had left without a suitcase.

Mimi asked Geralyn if she'd heard from her brother again. Joey called her the day after he left. He wouldn't say where he was. They spoke several more times.

"He told me that he didn't want me to bother with Anthony or talk to Anthony," Geralyn testified.

"Who did you understand him to mean?" Mimi asked.

"Oh, Anthony Capo," Geralyn said. "And he told me if I wanted to talk to anybody, or ask any questions, to call Victor with the red hair."

What was the point of having Geralyn on the witness stand? Within fifteen minutes, Mimi established that Joey Garofano disappeared from his sister's life at about the same time he was last seen in Rudy Farone's garage.

Left hanging in the air was Joey's intuition that he could trust Victor DiChiara—Victor with the red hair. Joey seemed to be done with Anthony Capo.

Too late.

Neither Mimi nor the defense attorneys had any further questions for Geralyn. She left the witness stand rattled, but she hadn't made a scene. She was just somebody who wanted to see justice done for a misguided kid who could have gone in a different direction.

I'd driven up to Marlboro with Agent Nora Conley and AUSA Mike McGovern on the Saturday after Geralyn's testimony about Joey to speak with Phil "the Undertaker" LaMela.

No reporters and photographers from the *New York Daily News*. No *New York Post*. No *Newsday*, *Staten Island Advance*, Newark *Star-Ledger*, *New York Times*.

We had last seen Phil LaMela in December 1999, right after Anthony Capo told us that Joey and Johnny Boy were buried somewhere on LaMela's property. I had no idea if we'd find LaMela there. Nora, Mike, and I got out of my Bu-car and walked past several green dump trucks, dumpsters, and white flatbeds facing Route 9W. One of the trucks was loaded with junk.

"Creepy," Nora muttered.

The three of us headed toward the main building on the property. It was spring. Flowers were blooming. Much nicer than being out in the dead of winter in 1999.

"That's him," I said. He hadn't aged. Still a short, white-haired man.

LaMela saw us through a window and came out to meet us. He wasn't smiling.

I gave him our names. We showed our badges.

"OK," he said. "How can I help you?"

We said we were in trial against some of his friends. "We're trying to get closure for the Garofano and D'Amato families," Nora said.

"I've got nothing to say," he replied.

"Just giving you an opportunity to tell us where the bodies are buried," Mike said.

"I've got nothing to say."

LaMela walked back to the building. He leaned against the main door and stared at us.

The three of us began walking back to the Bu-car. I turned around.

"You guys stay here," I said. "I'm not finished yet."

I stood face to face with LaMela. I felt around in my pocket and pulled out an 8½" × 11" color photo of Joey Garofano. I said, "I've been looking at this picture for the past three years. It's your turn."

I crumpled up the photo and shoved it into LaMela's shirt pocket. I didn't wait for a reaction. I walked back toward the car.

"What'd you say to him?" Mike asked. "He's all shook up."

I told them. Mike and Nora said I was nuts.

"I want closure for Joey's family," I said.

I was disgusted. The bodies were buried somewhere on this huge property. We couldn't do anything about it. Meanwhile, LaMela got off scot-free.

Nora tugged at my elbow.

We got back in the Bu-car and didn't stop for lunch until we crossed over the Hudson River. Nora hit the nail on the head. "Creepy" was the right word for our foray into rural hell.

The three defendants in *US v. Vitabile et al.*—Steve Vitabile, Philip Abramo, and Pino Schifilliti—chose not to take the witness stand. It was their constitutional right not to. The burden of proof rested with the government to prove every count and predicate act charged against the defendants: nine counts in all. To arrive at a RICO conviction, the jury would have to believe that the defendants were, one, part of a criminal organization and, two, proved to be involved in at least two predicate acts in support of that larger crime.

On June 4, 2003—after forty-four days of trial—the jury reached a verdict at 3:05 PM. Because a RICO trial is so intricate, I'm laying out the counts and predicate acts against the defendants in three separate tables so you can see what each one was charged with and how the jury decided on each count.

Philip Abramo		
Count/Act	**Description**	**Verdict**
Count 1	From 1978–March 2003, conducted and participated in a racketeering enterprise through a pattern of racketeering activity (RICO)	Guilty
Racketeering Act 1	*Conspiracy to murder Fred Weiss*	*Proved*
	Murder of Fred Weiss	*Proved*
Racketeering Act 2	*Conspiracy to murder Joseph Garofano*	*Proved*
	Murder of Joseph Garofano	*Proved*
Racketeering Act 3	*Conspiracy to murder Daniel Annunziata*	*Proved*
	Conspiracy to murder Gaetano Vastola	*Proved*
Racketeering Act 4	*Conspiracy to murder Louis LaRasso*	*Proved*
	Murder of Louis LaRasso	*Proved*
Racketeering Act 11	*Financing extortionate extensions of credit before October 1995*	*Not proved*
	Financing extortionate extensions of credit in or after October 1995	*Not proved*
	Conspiracy to make extortionate extensions of credit	*Proved*
	Conspiracy to collect extortionate extensions of credit	*Proved*

Philip Abramo (cont'd)		
Count/Act	**Description**	**Verdict**
Racketeering Act 12	*Conspiracy to commit securities fraud*	*Proved*
Count 2	RICO conspiracy	Guilty
Count 6	Financing extortionate extensions of credit	Not guilty
Count 7	Conspiracy to make extortionate extensions of credit	Guilty
Count 8	Conspiracy to collect extortionate extensions of credit	Guilty

Steve Vitabile		
Count/Act	**Description**	**Verdict**
Count 1	From 1978–March 2003, conducted and participated in a racketeering enterprise through a pattern of racketeering activity	Guilty
Racketeering Act 4	*Conspiracy to murder Louis LaRasso*	*Proved*
	Murder of Louis LaRasso	*Proved*
Racketeering Act 5	*Conspiracy to murder John D'Amato*	*Proved*
	Murder of John D'Amato	*Proved*
Racketeering Act 6	*Conspiracy to murder Frank Scarabino*	*Not proved*
Racketeering Act 7	*Conspiracy to murder Thomas Salvata*	*Proved*
Racketeering Act 8	*Conspiracy to murder Frank D'Amato*	*Proved*
Racketeering Act 9	*Conspiracy to murder John Doe #1 and John Doe #2*	*Not proved*
Racketeering Act 10	*Conspiracy to commit extortion*	*Proved*
Count 2	RICO conspiracy	Guilty

Steve Vitabile (cont'd)		
Count/Act	**Description**	**Verdict**
Count 3	Conspiracy to murder Frank Scarabino in aid of racketeering	Not guilty
Count 4	Conspiracy to murder Thomas Salvata in aid of racketeering	Guilty
Count 5	Conspiracy to murder Frank D'Amato in aid of racketeering	Guilty
Count 9	Conspiracy to commit extortion	Guilty

Pino Schifilliti		
Count/Act	**Description**	**Verdict**
Count 1	From 1978–March 2003, conducted and participated in a racketeering enterprise through a pattern of racketeering activity	Guilty
Racketeering Act 4	*Conspiracy to murder Louis LaRasso*	*Proved*
	Murder of Louis LaRasso	*Proved*
Racketeering Act 6	*Conspiracy to murder Frank Scarabino*	*Not proved*
Racketeering Act 8	*Conspiracy to murder Frank D'Amato*	*Proved*
Racketeering Act 10	*Conspiracy to commit extortion*	*Proved*
Racketeering Act 11	*Financing extortionate extensions of credit before October 1995*	*Not proved*
	Financing extortionate extensions of credit in or after October 1995	*Not proved*
	Conspiracy to make extortionate extensions of credit	*Proved*
	Conspiracy to collect extortionate extensions of credit	*Proved*

Pino Schifilliti (cont'd)		
Count/Act	**Description**	**Verdict**
Count 2	RICO conspiracy	Guilty
Count 3	Conspiracy to murder Frank Scarabino in aid of racketeering	Not guilty
Count 5	Conspiracy to murder Frank D'Amato in aid of racketeering	Guilty
Count 6	Financing extortionate extensions of credit	Not guilty
Count 7	Conspiracy to make extortionate extensions of credit	Guilty
Count 8	Conspiracy to collect extortionate extensions of credit	Guilty
Count 9	Conspiracy to commit extortion	Guilty

United States of America v. Stefano Vitabile et al. was a historic trial. We rolled out cooperators at every level of a Mafia organization: associate, soldier, captain, and acting boss. As a result of their convictions, they were exposed to LIFE sentences.

The jury believed our witnesses.

25

TRIAL PREP AND RATS KILL MY SUMMER

DON'T ASK ME IF SUMMER 2003 was hot or humid or rainy. I couldn't tell you. My life from June to September was spent on the twenty-second floor of 26 Federal Plaza. Working late every night got me acquainted with the sound of rats—the four-legged, long-tailed kind—scurrying inside the walls after five o'clock when the air conditioning went off and when, it seems, the rodents gathered for their nightly administration meeting.* No vacation, no cruises for me or the DeCavalcante team; all we did was prepare for the trial of DeCavalcante ruling panel member Girolamo "Jimmy" Palermo, the retrial of Wes Paloscio for the murder of Joey O Masella,† and a raft of plea negotiations stemming from our DeCavalcante arrests on October 19, 2000, and April 19, 2001.

With all the work that lay ahead, we confined our elation over the guilty verdicts in *US v. Vitabile et al.* to a beer-and-pizza celebration in the court district. The only low note in our post mortem was the stunt Vinny Palermo pulled by shielding close to $2 million from our eyes and jeopardizing everything we'd done to put Vitabile, Abramo,

* The FBI New York headquarters has gotten better over the years, but in the early 2000s, the twenty-second floor was a shithole.

† See chapter 17.

and Schifilliti behind bars. In fact, we were so mad at Vinny for his shenanigans that on July 21 we remanded him. He'd been out in the Witness Security Program—not cloistered in prison—and we were like, you know what, Vinny? You're going back to jail. The former acting boss of the DeCavalcante crime family ended up doing a year in solitary confinement at the Metropolitan Correctional Center. Frankly, I don't know how Vinny passed the time, because I never spared ten minutes to walk from FBI headquarters to pay him a visit.

Vinny was pissed. I get that. To his mind, he had blown up his whole life by joining Team America, and while he was eating microwaved crinkle cuts or whatever crap they dish out at MCC, he was stewing in his own juices. That's where my thoughts about Vinny began and ended. Not one of our other cooperating witnesses tried to play us for fools. If you ask me, I think Vinny got off easy.

Our first order of business was the retrial of Wes Paloscio, set for August 11. What more knowledgeable, cooperative cooperating witness to call on than Anthony Capo?

In Paloscio's previous deadlocked trial, the jury couldn't decide if Paloscio had lured deadbeat bookmaker Joey Masella to the parking lot of the Marine Park Golf Course in Brooklyn and had him killed there. Defense attorney Joe Tacopina argued that the murder could have been committed by any number of mobsters, including Anthony Capo.

"I did a lot of bad shit in my life, but Joey O was my friend," Anthony told me. "I can't take credit for bad shit I didn't do."

"If the defense attorney, whoever it is, brings that up in the retrial, you'll refute it," I said.

"If I'd have killed Masella, I'd have told you, Séamus. If I knew for sure who killed him, I'd have told you."

Capo had a track record with me for admitting everything he'd done and everything he knew. He had become a good soldier for the government.

The Paloscio case diverted part of C-10's attention away from our major trial, *United States of America v. Girolamo Palermo et al.* The amount of preparation involved was almost enough to put the squad and the AUSAs on a steady diet of tranquilizers. We were lucky, though, in two regards. First, Bernardo Curra, a new agent, joined the team. Bernardo, a former assistant principal and a native Italian speaker, had testified at the Vitabile trial about the seizure of 117 bundles of Vinny's hidden cash. He was instrumental in prepping for *US v. Palermo et al.* by interacting with the witnesses and assisting the AUSAs. Second, several of Palermo's codefendants granted us a reprieve. On August 5, Frank D'Amato—the target of one of Vinny Palermo's murder conspiracies in the days leading up to his arrest—pled guilty to illegal gambling and loan-sharking. Judge Michael Mukasey rewarded D'Amato with a ten-year prison sentence. Eight days later, we had a glorious pile-on of guilty pleas from Charles Majuri, Jimmy Palermo's brother Simone, Salvatore Timpani, and Joseph Collina Sr. All told, they pled guilty to crimes ranging from gambling to construction industry extortion. We could replace the Zoloft with Tylenol.

For the Paloscio retrial, Capo showed up in Judge Lawrence McKenna's SDNY courtroom on Thursday, August 14, 2003, looking more scholar than knave. His hair was newly trimmed and slicked back. He wore dress pants, a collared shirt, and a blazer on a frame that had benefited from a prison diet devoid of rich Italian beef *tagliata*. Capo was giving an overview of his own criminal history on direct examination when the lights, air conditioning, and computers went out.

The courtroom was windowless and dark, and the federal marshals sprang into action. Two of them approached Anthony and hustled him into a rear room. I made my way back there.

"I guess somebody forgot to pay the electric bill," Capo said.

"Who knows," I said. "I don't know if it's just this building, the neighborhood, or what."

The marshals handcuffed Anthony and prepared to escort him to a WitSec facility.

"We'll talk soon," I promised. I hadn't seen Capo handcuffed in quite a while. He didn't utter a word of protest. The guy who got his best friend killed had learned to roll with the punches.

We'd had six weeks nonstop of the Vitabile trial. We now had a retrial that suddenly looked like a sideshow. And in less than a month, we were putting the DeCavalcante administration on trial, and we had to prove that the restaurants people ate in, the schools they'd studied at, the hotels they slept in, and the malls they shopped at all bore the fingerprints of Mafia kickbacks and bid-rigging.

Did I mention I was tired? I was going to use the delay in the Wes Paloscio retrial as my break. I was the happiest man in a crisis that, unbeknownst to me, had hobbled the electrical grid in eight US states and parts of Ontario. I practically galloped to the outdoor garage at Leonard and Broadway where I'd parked my car.

"How're you doing?" I called out to the parking garage attendant. I handed him my garage ticket.

He looked at it. He looked at me. He looked up at the lift.

"Your car's up there," he said.

I didn't react and he added, "The electricity's out. The lift's not working."

"Are you shitting me?" Of all days, the attendant parked my car on the lift!

The guy shrugged. What was he supposed to do?

What the hell was *I* supposed to do? Despite my relief that I was getting a night to myself, I saw that the city was in chaos. The streets were clogged with taxis and gypsy cabs prowling for desperate fares. I went from feeling happy to feeling miserable.

I called Liam. By this time, my brother had left the FBI Police and moved on to the FBI's Special Surveillance Group (SSG), the team that performs surveillance around the metro area. Unfortunately, Liam had already finished his shift for the day and had gone home. He offered to come back into the city, but I said, "It's madness. Don't bother. I'll tough it out."

What could I do but walk down Broadway and hang a left on Worth Street and retreat to 26 Federal Plaza? Where the AC and lights were off and the rats would get an early start on their travels inside—and outside—the walls.

My supervisor's office had a couch, and that's where I sat all night.

Sat. Not lay down. No way was I going to fall asleep and wake up with a rat on me! I had seen my own ungodly share of them in broad daylight. I struggled all night long to stay awake. The next day I was freakin' exhausted.

And to think we used to joke the rats would sit at our computers and run people's names through the FBI database.

Eight o'clock the next day, agents began trickling into the office. If I remember correctly, the power didn't come back on until late morning, and I didn't get my car until noon.

The Paloscio retrial resumed on August 16. Five days later, the judge declared a mistrial based on accidental juror interaction with personnel assigned to the case.

I cannot tell you how annoyed we were about having invested so much time on a mob associate in two aborted trials. A third trial would mean the use of more taxpayer money and a whole new jury. The judge asked the government, "Do you want to retry him again?"

An assistant US attorney didn't have the authority to request a third trial. We'd have to go back to the US attorney and get the OK to retry.

I put myself in Paloscio's shoes. He had to be thinking, *I got lucky twice. Am I going to get lucky a third time?* I could only hope Wes Paloscio wasn't reckless enough to press his luck.

He wasn't. Paloscio ended up pleading guilty to racketeering and gambling. He was sentenced to eight years.

We were in for another surprise, this time a good one: John Riggi, the official DeCavalcante boss, pled guilty to sanctioning Fred Weiss's murder. Riggi was in his late seventies and still in prison in Butner, North Carolina, so we hadn't insisted on bringing him up to New York. On September 4 he was allowed to plead via video conference from his cell. When he faced the government prosecutor on the screen, he wasn't quite as gracious to us.

"Oh, so you're John Hillebrecht," he said. Riggi couldn't hide his disdain.

John Riggi. *Department of Justice Trial Exhibit, US Attorney's Office, Southern District of New York / FBI*

On the screen was the very prosecutor who had decimated Riggi's crime family. And thanks in large part to Hillebrecht, Judge Mukasey was adding ten years to Riggi's time in prison. John Riggi's plea was exactly what G. Robert Blakey, the architect of RICO, had intended: the guy who pulls the trigger isn't the only guy held responsible for an act in an organized criminal operation.

It goes to show again, for the mob words speak louder than actions.

We had a couple more red-letter days just weeks before *US v. Palermo et al.* was to begin. Two more DeCavalcantes pled guilty: Bernard NiCastro back on August 8 for participating in the murder of Joey Garofano; and Anthony "Marshmallow" Mannarino on September 16 for conducting loan-sharking operations in Florida—and for leaking grand jury secrets to mobsters before their arrests in December 1999. These two pleas eliminated the "*et al.*" from our second big administration trial. Now the cheese stood alone.

Jimmy Palermo would be tried on seven counts targeting his participation in the "affairs of a racketeering enterprise." Thomas Nooter,

Palermo's attorney, would have to defend his client against a variety of charges, including involvement in a number of conspiracies: to murder Frank D'Amato; to extort money and other things of value from construction industry contractors by using threats of violence and work stoppages; and to make and collect extortionate extensions of credit. Other counts and their subsidiary acts were more direct: Palermo was also charged with financing, making, and collecting extortionate extensions of credit, especially in the construction industry.

The defense in *US v. Vitabile et al.* had been so weak we could mow all the attorneys down. We were hoping for a replay with Jimmy Palermo.

I also held out hope that Palermo would plead guilty before his trial date, September 22, 2003. But the man stood fast. He wanted his day in court. And we were going to give it to him.

Here we go again.

Jimmy Palermo. *Department of Justice Trial Exhibit, US Attorney's Office, Southern District of New York / FBI*

26

THE LAST DECAVALCANTE FACES A REFORMED MOBSTER

THE ACTORS IN *UNITED STATES OF AMERICA v. Girolamo Palermo a/k/a "Jimmy Palermo"*:

- AUSA David Burns
- AUSA Michael McGovern
- AUSA Miriam "Mimi" Rocah
- FBI SA Bernardo Curra
- FBI SA Séamus McElearney

We had to decide which cooperating witnesses we'd use to topple the third and final column of the DeCavalcante ruling panel. We nixed Vinny Palermo. We were still smarting from his efforts to hide almost $2 million from us during *US v. Vitabile et al.* We wouldn't use Victor DiChiara either. He hadn't had any significant interactions with Jimmy Palermo.

But Anthony Capo was a seasoned cooperator, at ease on the witness stand, and well acquainted with Palermo's union tampering and bid-rigging activities. We thought Anthony Rotondo would be an equally strong witness. As a DeCavalcante captain, Rotondo had a catch-up call with Palermo nearly every Friday morning, and Rotondo said he'd trusted Jimmy more than any other higher-up in the family. Finally, we wanted an additional witness who could corroborate Capo's and Rotondo's testimony. For that Frank Scarabino—the mob associate who refused to kill women and children—fit the bill.

AUSA David Burns, the new attorney on the team, would be responsible for the opening statement and direct examination of Anthony Capo. Bernardo Curra joined me at the FBI table. We'd modified our prosecution strategy because *US v. Palermo* was a different kettle of fish from *US v. Vitabile et al.*

Whereas *Vitabile* focused largely on the murders the DeCavalcantes had committed to protect their criminal enterprise from the prying eyes of law enforcement, *Palermo* exposed the violence the Jersey crime family inflicted on society, mostly via the construction industry. Palermo's "brutal, murderous organization, dedicated to making money any way that it could, including loan-sharking, gambling, infiltration of unions, and extortion of construction companies," as thirty-three-year-old prosecutor David Burns said in his opening statement, exemplified a racketeering operation that enriched the DeCavalcante upper echelon of crooks.

On September 23, 2003, just before Anthony Capo took the stand to become the trial's first cooperating witness, Burns told the jury that Palermo was charged with RICO and racketeering offenses. The charges against Palermo—conspiracy to murder Frank D'Amato and six additional racketeering acts resulting in a "decade-long stranglehold over the construction industry in New Jersey"—represented the activities that the entire DeCavalcante family carried out to profit from LIUNA Local 394 and Local 1030, the latter being the asbestos union created by DeCavalcante boss John Riggi. As the evidence would demonstrate, Burns said, Jimmy Palermo didn't hesitate to wield the "power and influence" to make construction companies bend to his will.

"You will learn that one way Palermo and his Mafia family made money was by using these unions for patronage," Burns argued. "There were rewarded members and associates of the family with lucrative union jobs, irrespective of skill, experience, prior work with the union, or intention of doing any actual work. Jobs, ladies and gentlemen, that were given at the expense of ordinary hardworking dues-paying members of the union who had to wait in line while friends of the DeCavalcantes cut in front of them and took their jobs."

What better witness to these abuses than Anthony Capo? Capo told David Burns about the referral slip he'd gotten from John Riggi and the series of no-show jobs he'd scored, up until weeks before his arrest. That little piece of paper was as good as Willie Wonka's golden ticket. It would give him entrée to a no-show job.

"What kind of work did you do from that work forward?" Burns asked.

"As little as possible," Capo answered.

"Did you get paid?"

"Yes."

"What time did you show up for work usually at the Exxon plant?" Burns asked.

"We had to be there at 7:00 or 8:00. Being that we were young men at the time, we never showed up on time."

"Did that cause you any problems?" Burns asked.

"Eventually, it did, yes." John Riggi demanded that Anthony Capo come to the union hall. Capo's captain, Anthony Rotondo, counseled him to tell Uncle John he'd meant no disrespect.

Burns asked how Riggi responded.

"He banged on the table and said, 'If it was disrespect, you would fucking know about it,'" Capo recalled. "And from that day on, we were a half hour early every day."

Getting to Exxon early didn't change a thing. Capo and everyone else with a golden ticket never had to do a lick o' work. Not that Uncle John didn't expect something in return. The Exxon job was just a gateway to a greater debt.

In the meantime, though, another benefit of Capo's no-show jobs was workers' compensation. "Did you ever get injured while you were working at the Exxon job?" Burns asked.

"Well, I didn't get injured at the Exxon job, but I did work with an injury," Capo said.

Capo explained how he and some other holders of a referral slip cut out from work one day and went horseback riding. "The horse was running," Capo said. "It was like [he had] a taxi meter in his head. He wanted to go back to the barn, or wherever he goes. As he's running, I'm punching him in the head, trying to get him to stop, and my saddle was going sideways. And he ran right into a tree, and I broke my wrist."

Capo did not seek medical help that day. "The next morning I went to work because I wanted to say I got injured on the job," he testified. He went into an Exxon tower. "There was a bunch of air hoses for the air compressors, and I told a friend of mine to punch me in the wrist," Capo continued. "When he hit it, he dislocated it more, and I just laid there like I fell."

It takes a con to know a con, but John Riggi might have fallen for Capo's ploy. After Capo sought medical attention and filed a claim, "Riggi felt so bad about the situation that I got hurt like that, he told me to stay in the tool shanty," Capo said. "I just stayed there for the next six months and didn't do anything."

While "convalescing," Capo got his regular salary plus compensation.

One day Capo told Steve Vitabile how much he appreciated the stream of no-show jobs. "He said, 'You don't have to appreciate nothing,'" Capo testified. "'It is our union. Any time you want a job or I want a job, it's ours. . . . It belongs to everybody in the family.'"

David Burns asked Capo how John Riggi could tout Local 394 as a democratic institution when it was clearly a rigged—and Riggi—operation.

"Well, there would be a vote to put the new business agent in, and we would be sure to make sure that we won the vote," Capo said. "So, by installing the new business agent, you certainly have control of the union. We were never going to lose that."

"How did the family make sure that it was going to win that vote?" Burns asked.

"By nobody running against the guy that we put up. You know, fix the vote. It was never a question who the new business agent was going to be. It just was who was going to get picked from the family. And it seems that every time you had a business agent, you had a field rep, and he in turn would get that job."

"And who determined who the field rep would be?"

"The ruling panel, or the ruling administration, of the family," Capo said.

Which, of course, included Jimmy Palermo.

Even while the DeCavalcantes had Local 394 in its pocket, they were careful about not drawing the scrutiny of the government. At one point the field rep was Larry Giacobbe, son of DeCavalcante captain Joe Giacobbe. Larry was a DeCavalcante soldier, Capo testified, but his conduct as union rep alarmed the ruling panel. Burns asked Capo what complaints he, Jimmy Palermo, and Vinny Palermo had.

"That he wasn't keeping on top of his job, going around with the car that he had," Capo said. "He had been given a car through the union that was bought through a car dealership that we controlled, and he wasn't using the car to go around [to] check jobs."

Capo delved further into the matter. "He wasn't treating the minorities in the union very fairly," he said. "He seemed to be prejudicial that way and to non-Italians. This is not something that you can have when you are supposed to be fair with everybody in that job."

"What, if anything, did Jimmy Palermo say during those meetings about Larry Giacobbe and his conduct of his position in the union?" Burns asked.

"'We can't have that,'" Capo quoted. "'We've got to get rid of him. You can't have him in that union and blow the union. The union is the lifeblood of the DeCavalcante family.'"

"Why do you say that?"

I looked at the jury. Would anyone see the DeCavalcantes as crusaders for racial justice?

"It puts everybody to work," Capo testified. "Your nephews, your son, cousins, friends. It feeds the whole town. So they certainly couldn't have this guy ruining it." To give the appearance of equal opportunity for all, Local 394 included minorities on its membership rolls.

Vinny had a candidate to replace Giacobbe. It was Anthony Capo.

"I laughed at him," Capo said. "'How are you going to put me in that job? I got the FBI on top of me all the time. I won't last a day. They would be flinging me out of there.' He [Vinny] says, 'Well, you can make a thousand, fifteen hundred a week. You can get the cars.'" Vinny told Capo that he'd gotten the go-ahead from Jimmy Palermo, Charlie Majuri, and Steve Vitabile—the rest of the ruling panel and the consigliere. As Capo testified, Vinny said, "'I'm going to put you in that job.' I said, 'All right, I'll take it.'"

Vinny and Jimmy were also worried about Charlie Majuri's misconduct. He was putting pressure on the current field representative for "special jobs" for his nephew, his sister.

Burns wanted to know what specifically Vinny and Jimmy were concerned about.

"Well, the government is always trying to take over the union as it is," Capo said. "Most of these construction unions and Teamsters, they were taken over by government officials. By Charlie going up there, with his record and his past, you blow the union."

Capo never said what distinguished his patronage jobs through Local 394 from Majuri's request for patronage jobs. Indeed, Capo admitted to having benefited from the DeCavalcantes' labor racketeering five or six times. In recent years, he hadn't even paid union dues.

The difference between Capo and Majuri: Capo had the stamp of approval from John Riggi and Jimmy Rotondo. Majuri, well, as the earlier hierarchy trial and now this one showed, Jimmy, Vinny, and Steve didn't like the guy. It was easy to pin "prejudicial" behavior on him. I mean, really, they were all "prejudicial."

As for who "deserved" the patronage more? None of them did. But, in Majuri's defense, he exhibited some old-fashioned work ethic at FedEx, where he and Capo landed union jobs in the mid-1990s, when Jake Amari was the crime family boss.

"What kind of work did Charlie Majuri do at that job site?" Burns asked Capo.

"He was supposed to have been a foreman," Capo said.

"When you first showed up at the job, what was he doing?"

"He was sweeping."

"When you saw him sweeping, what was your reaction?"

"I went over to him and I says, 'What are you doing?' He said, 'I'm sweeping.' 'Sweeping!'" Capo exclaimed. "'You're a caporegime in this family!'"

Capo said Majuri asked, "'What do you think I should do?'"

Capo had a solution: "'Let's go shopping,'" he said. "'Let's go to BJ's.'"*

Majuri liked to joke that Capo had corrupted him.

Thomas Nooter had his work cut out for him. As with the defense in *Vitabile et al.*, Nooter's cross-examination of Anthony Capo depended, first, on the wildly mistaken premise that our government witnesses colluded with each other before their arrests to come up with a single unified story. Second, it depended on ad hominem attacks.

"Isn't it true that you guys decided ahead of time that if you ever got arrested, you would cooperate?" Nooter asked.

"No, sir," Capo answered. "No way." Capo may as well have said, *Only if we'd all wanted to end up dead.*

"You never talked to Vinny Palermo about the idea?" Nooter persisted.

"No way."

If Nooter had read the Vitabile trial transcripts, he'd have gotten a picture of Vinny as a whirling dervish of paranoia. His murder conspiracies to "kill everybody," as Victor DiChiara put it, barely left time to leave the gun and take the cannoli, let alone time to collude.

"So, you now have pretty much become a professional government witness, is that right?" Nooter said.

Capo: "No, I wouldn't say that."

"Well, you are a government witness, is that right?"

"I am a government witness, but I am not a professional."

Maybe not, but Capo was getting awfully good at being a government witness.

---

* BJ's Wholesale Club Holdings Inc., or BJ's, is a membership-only warehouse club chain with outlets in the eastern United States as well as Ohio, Michigan, Indiana, and Tennessee.

Jimmy Palermo's attorney did his best to grind Capo down. And I could see how Nooter's sniping might unnerve anybody. But Capo didn't break a sweat.

Nooter was the right age to have remembered the "*Perry Mason* moment"—the turn in the 1960s TV courtroom drama when an attorney stuns the witness on the stand with a gotcha piece of evidence. "Would it surprise you to learn that you didn't even mention Jimmy Palermo until April of 2000?" he asked Capo.

Capo ran a hand through his coifed hair. "Oh, I talked about Jimmy Palermo," he said. "I would have to. He was on the ruling panel of the family."

"Would it surprise you that, at least from the notes, the first mention you made of Jimmy Palermo was on April 8, when you described him as Simone Palermo's brother?"

Burns objected, but Judge Mukasey allowed it.

"Would it surprise me?" Capo echoed. "I didn't write the notes. . . . It wasn't my notes."

"You think you might have spoken about Jimmy Palermo before April of 2000?"

All Nooter had to do was review the notes we'd sent him for discovery. They reflected information we had gotten from Anthony beginning in December 1999. And they included details about Jimmy Palermo's decision to protect Capo by murdering Frank D'Amato.

It was easy to assassinate Capo's character. Like shooting fish in a barrel. But Capo still didn't break. I'd spent I don't know how many hours prevailing upon him never to get angry in court. "The defense wants you to explode," I'd told him. "They want the jury to reject you."

So far our witness's performance was textbook perfect.

"Soldiers like yourself generally did a lot of crimes, right?" Nooter asked Capo.

"Some more or less than others, yes," Capo conceded.

"Where do you put yourself in that list?"

"I was a terrible person."

"You did a lot of crimes?"

"I was a very, very bad person. Very bad."

Nooter seized on Capo's badness. He asked Capo to talk about his murder conspiracies.

"Frank D'Amato," Capo said.

"We had heard all about that one," Nooter said.

I looked at the jurors again. A couple looked down at their hands. A guy in the back row glanced at his watch. Nooter was losing them.

In fact, Nooter was doing David Burns's work. He was only underscoring Capo's testimony: that murder and labor racketeering were part and parcel of the DeCavalcante ethic. Anthony Capo had learned how to put the defense on the defense.

Nooter: "Did you ever hear what's required if the family has decided they need to get rid of a boss?"

Capo: "Did I ever hear—you would have to get permission from the Commission to kill another—I mean, to kill another boss in another family? Mr. Nooter, I'm not following your question. Could you be a little bit more—"

Nooter: "You're following it. What's the Commission?"

As he'd done many times by now, Capo explained the power of the Commission to kill a boss. Nothing was to be gained by beating this dead horse, and Nooter cantered in another direction. "You said that when you were inducted, the ceremony started, some Italian words were said, right?"

Capo: "Yes."

Nooter: "What are they?"

Capo: "I don't know. I don't speak Italian."

Anthony was engaging in a kind of studied carelessness called *sprezzatura*. How's that for Italian?

Mr. Nooter meandered. He asked Capo what it meant when some families kissed once or twice.

Capo showed himself capable of splitting hairs like a philosopher. "I kiss my uncle," he said. "My uncle is Irish. That doesn't mean he is part of an organized crime family. That is just a sign of respect. That's the way I was brought up. So, no, it doesn't really signify anything."

Nooter looked up at the ceiling. Maybe his strategy was up there. "If you say 'This is our friend,' that means he's with you as a made man or something?" he asked.

Capo heard a dismissive tone in Nooter's "or something."

"No, we didn't say it like that, no," Capo said.

"You didn't say anything like that?"

"Not like that."

Neither Judge Mukasey nor David Burns came to Nooter's aid with an objection or a sidebar. Nooter tacked in another direction. "Was a word 'propensity for violence' something that the La Cosa Nostra used?'" he asked.

"When you say 'used,' people used that word?" When did Anthony become a linguist?

Nooter: "Correct."

"I think that was my description if someone was proposed for membership in La Cosa Nostra." Capo accentuated "La Cosa Nostra" to indicate he had omitted Nooter's redundant "the."

Nooter: "That they had to have a propensity for violence?" He went on in this vein and then disappeared down the rabbit hole of futile interrogation. "Do you remember when you learned the word *propensity*?" Nooter asked.

The old Anthony Capo would have picked up a fork and stuck it in the poor lawyer's face. The government's Anthony Capo went for a touché instead.

"I read a lot," he said. "I've got a pretty good vocabulary, so that is my word."

Jimmy Palermo's lawyer kept asking Capo for definitions as if they were defense strategy lifeboats. He asked Capo to define *conspiracy* and *associate* and asked when he'd first heard these words. He opened a new line of questioning and asked Capo if Anthony Rotondo had ever talked about who killed his father. When Capo said Rotondo thought it might have been John Riggi, Nooter asked Capo to speculate why Riggi would have killed the father and promoted the son.

I waited for Burns to object. Silence. Finally, Nooter asked Capo to interpret what Frank D'Amato meant when he once asserted, "If somebody killed my brother—the way somebody killed Anthony Rotondo's father—they would have to kill me too."

Capo's answer would have made my twelfth-grade English teacher proud. "He was making a comparison," he said.

Nooter argued that Frank D'Amato didn't literally say, "I would take revenge."

Capo said, "Oh, that's what he meant."

Nooter: "How do you know what he meant if that's not what he said?" It was a question only a lawyer could ask. Everyone else on the planet knew meaning comes from both the literal and the nonliteral.

"That's the way I took it," Capo said.

"So you can tell what people mean even when they say something different?"

Finally, Judge Mukasey said, "May I see counsel at the side?"

"Do you want to break for the day?" he asked Nooter.

Nooter said he got a little flustered and didn't know why. "Could we maybe just take an afternoon break?" he suggested.

"It is a stressful situation," the judge said. "I did this once. I can remember."

Judge Mukasey dismissed the jury. I'd never seen him be this merciful. "They are surly, but not yet rebellious," he said of the jurors and their wish for a speedy trial. "See you tomorrow. Feel better, Mr. Nooter. Get a good night's sleep."

If Capo had known he could bring a grown man practically to tears without resorting to violence, who might he have been if he hadn't taken up with the Jersey boys?

I wasn't about to pity Jimmy Palermo for hiring a lawyer ill prepared to run circles around Anthony Capo.

27

"THE BEAST" GIVES A LESSON IN LABOR RACKETEERING

As if one humiliation for the defense weren't enough.

Five days before Frank Scarabino took the stand, AUSA Mike McGovern asked permission of the court to read a stipulation into the record, entered as Government Exhibit 500. This stipulation—a written agreement about a settlement in a different court case germane to the current trial—concerned a guilty plea by Joseph Collina Sr., the DeCavalcante soldier who pled guilty six weeks earlier in the SDNY to "conspiring to participate in the affairs of a racketeering enterprise through a pattern of racketeering activity."

In other words, Joseph Collina conspired "with others" to extort individuals and companies doing business in the construction industry and to threaten them with labor unrest if they didn't ante up.

The stipulation included various scenarios already familiar to the jury in *US v. Palermo*:

> Judge Mukasey: Mr. Collina, could you please tell me in your own words what it is that you did that makes you believe you are guilty of the crime of extortion.

COLLINA: The contractors that I got jobs for paid commission and/or a fee for the job that they received.
JUDGE: What would have happened if they hadn't paid the fee or commission?
COLLINA: Probably would stop the job on them.
JUDGE: Did you participate with others in getting them to agree today to those commissions?
COLLINA: Yes, Your Honor.
JUDGE: And were the others associated with the DeCavalcante crime family?
COLLINA: Yes, Your Honor.

When McGovern finished speaking, Judge Mukasey had to tell the jurors, in essence, *Pay no attention to the man behind the curtain*: "There is nothing in what you heard that answers the question whether this defendant was a participant or not one way or the other," he cautioned the jury. "As to that question, whether the defendant on trial here—Mr. Palermo—was a participant is something as to which you will have to look at other evidence in the case. There is nothing in this stipulation that relates to that."

Not technically. It's just that Jimmy Palermo and Joseph Collina had been business partners. The day before, Anthony Capo had testified that he met Joseph Collina's son at the Cheesequake rest stop on the Garden State Parkway, and that Joseph Jr. bragged about the union official who gave his father and "Uncle Jimmy" a lot of work with townhouses and condominiums down the Jersey Shore. And just that afternoon, a New Jersey–based FBI agent testified that the voices on an FBI consensual recording* belonged to Jimmy and Collina.

Here's the thing: when a defendant, be it Joe Collina or Jimmy Palermo, pleads guilty, he doesn't name the people he committed crimes with, he accepts guilt only for his own crimes. In the Collina plea agreement, though, "and others" unmistakably implicated Jimmy Palermo.

On with the show!

---

* The cooperating witness on the consensual recording was a DeCavalcante named Joseph Cofone, who began working with the FBI in Newark in January 1998. The FBI agent who testified was Wes Rigler.

Now for the debut of Frank Scarabino.

Despite being deaf in one ear, and decked out in suit and tie, Frank "the Beast" Scarabino looked every bit the muscleman he'd been when he reached out to the FBI from prison to say he'd been ordered to kill Anthony Capo's wife and kids. Within minutes of beginning her direct examination, Mimi Rocah got Scarabino to talk about growing up in a Brooklyn neighborhood crawling with La Cosa Nostra. When he joined the Brooklyn faction of the Jersey crime family through his childhood friend and DeCavalcante soldier Michael DiPietro, Scarabino was already an old hand at shylocking. By the time he appeared in Judge Mukasey's courtroom on the last Monday of September 2003, he had added extortion, illegal gambling, assault, and murder to his bio. Scarabino made no secret of the person he'd been most of his adult life: "If they sent me after you, I came relentlessly and ferociously until I got you," he testified.

"If you could first turn to Government Exhibit 384," Mimi said. "Mr. Scarabino, do you recognize who is pictured in those two photographs?"

"It looks like my mug shot," he said. "I remember taking those pictures.

"I am going to ask you to keep your voice up," Mimi told him. "Lean into the microphone a little bit."

John Hillebrecht had needed to tell Vinny Palermo to speak up too. Vinny spoke quietly from the shame of ditching omertà. Scarabino spoke quietly as if he swam in a sea of shame and hadn't yet reached the shoreline. Anyone who'd been at both trials could hear the difference. Fascinating what three years of sitting in prison can do to a man.

As with all our cooperators, the government asked Scarabino to talk about his history in organized crime.

Not long after his role in the murder of Fred Weiss, and his role in the conspiracy to murder Danny Annunziata and Corky Vastola, Scarabino participated in the murder of a guy named Michael Shapiro as a favor to a Colombo family captain. "I drove the two shooters to his house," Scarabino offered up. "We waited for him to come home. As he entered his driveway and got out of his car, **Twiggy**, the guy with the Colombos, chased him in the backyard and shot him in the head. Killed him." Shapiro had an attack dog with him. He had ordered it to attack **Vincenzo**, the other Colombo shooter. Vincenzo shot the dog dead.

Moving on to the late 1990s: Frank Polizzi—the DeCavalcante who'd ordered Scarabino to kill Capo's family—ordered the Beast to kill a bookmaker and loan shark named **Vito Cello**. Mimi asked why Polizzi wanted Cello dead.

"Because somebody brought him [Polizzi] information saying that Vito Cello was an informant," Scarabino said.

Scarabino did his "homework" on Cello, and in his "judgment," Cello wasn't an informant. "The people that were accusing him of being an informant, I found [they were] the people who owed him money and in my judgment, they just didn't want to pay him back. It was easier to kill him." Polizzi called the murder off.

Scarabino wasn't always this level-headed. In the early 1980s, he got involved in the attempted murder of **Little Freddy**, a neighborhood guy who shot Scarabino's friend **Armand Calabro**.

"In retaliation, Armand Calabro asked me to help him kill Little Freddy," Scarabino testified. "We found out that Little Freddy frequented a club, the 22 Club in Brooklyn. I drove Armand to the club and we waited about a quarter of a block up on the street. Armand was in the backseat. He had a rifle. And we waited for Little Freddy to come out."

Little Freddy never showed up. And that was the end of that.

In the mid-1980s, Scarabino helped a guy named **Joe Baldi** do a favor for a Genovese crime family member named Sally Fish. Joe Baldi said some guy was walking around the neighborhood trying to take Sally Fish's shylocking and bookmaking businesses away from him. Sally asked Joe to help him get rid of this guy. Teach this guy a lesson.

"I agreed to help Joe," Scarabino said. "I drove him to where the guy lived. We waited for the guy to get out of his car. As he walked up to his house, Joe got out of his car and shot him five times."

Joe got back in Scarabino's car. "He handed me the pistol he shot the guy with," Scarabino testified. "I drove Joe home and I kept the gun with me. And I went to work in the fish market."

These unprosecuted crimes—and a slew of pipe beatings and brass knuckle attacks—served as vocational training for Scarabino's career in extortion.

"Explain what you mean by 'extortion,'" Mimi said.

"Well," Scarabino began. "If a soldier or a captain in the family decides that an individual or a company is making a lot of money, and they want to get a piece of that company, they'll send someone like me in there to intimidate that person, either with words of violence or actual violence."

The construction business was a profitable target. Scarabino's first extortions came about when Anthony Rotondo asked John Riggi to let Scarabino into Local 394. "My cover position was that I was a laborer," Scarabino said.

Mimi wanted to know what Scarabino meant by "cover position."

"I was really there to be at the beck and call of John Riggi or Jimmy Palermo or any of the captains or soldiers that were there in the union, like an enforcer," Scarabino explained. "If they need me, I would take care of things for them. If not, I would show up on the job site."

Mimi asked for an example.

"Well, for instance, there came a time when I went to the union hall, like I usually do," Scarabino said. "I went into John Riggi's office, and Jimmy Palermo was there with Simone Palermo, Joe Colletti, and Johnny Riggi, and they were discussing a concrete contractor that was balking at coming up with his end of a contract. They had given him or awarded him a contract and he had agreed to pay John Riggi and the family a cash kickback, and now he was coming up saying that he couldn't do it."

Scarabino's job during this meeting was to watch the door to make sure nobody else came in. The Beast eavesdropped on the conversation. "The contractor was really giving them a hard time, saying that he couldn't do it, that it would be hard for him, that the law would be all over him," Scarabino testified. "Maybe there was a better way to do it. But Johnny Riggi wouldn't have anything—he wouldn't hear about [it]. Johnny Riggi said, 'The guy knows without us he wouldn't have that contract. He agreed, he got the contract. He made the money. He has to pay the money. He knows he's got to pay it. Just tell him to pay it!'"

Jimmy Palermo had a solution for John Riggi. "'We might have to use Frankie,'" Scarabino quoted.

"What did you understand that to mean?" Mimi asked.

"That, if necessary, I would beat the guy up. Do whatever I had to do to make sure the guy understood that he was not going to renege on his deal."

Less than two weeks after the meeting in the union hall, the same team showed up again, only this time the concrete contractor was in the room. Joe Colletti and Simone Palermo were asked to leave.

"Jimmy Palermo told me outside the office to be prepared," Scarabino testified, "that if this guy didn't do what he was supposed to do, that this guy could get hurt today. And it was my job to do this. He said, 'Did you realize that's what you're here for?'"

Scarabino assured Palermo he had no problem with smacking this guy around. He knew he was an enforcer for the family. "My job was to make the guy very uncomfortable," Scarabino explained. "To let this guy know, without putting my hands on him, that he could get hurt."

Scarabino said he stood directly behind the contractor and let out a heavy sigh every time the guy complained he couldn't come up with the kickback.

"I was there, like, looking over the guy," Scarabino said. He then reenacted the scene by looking over his own shoulder. "And the guy was, you know, going on and on how he was afraid of the law, and that the government would be on top of him because he had to take all this cash," Scarabino continued. "And Jimmy said to him, 'Since when in New Jersey do we have to worry about the law?' And John Riggi confirmed that. He said, 'We're the law in New Jersey. You never had to worry about this before. You're only saying this now because you don't want to come up with the money.'"

The contractor caved. Scarabino said the guy ponied up whatever he'd agreed to pay Jimmy. Frank Scarabino's role in the affair was over.

Scarabino told Mimi that he repeated this sort of extortion nearly every day from the late 1980s to 1992. Quite often the extortions involved contractors working at big housing projects. Anything concerning construction at Starrett City in Brooklyn, for example—painting, changing lightbulbs, etc.—was under soldier Mickey DiPietro's control.

"So I would go to the job site on any given day," Scarabino said. "Go to an electrical contractor or a carpenter contractor or somebody that was working on the complex and make them pay Mickey a percentage, a kickback, whatever he wanted. If he wanted $100 a week, if he wanted $500 a week, if he wanted $200 a month, if he wanted a piece of any materials that came in, whatever, it was my job to go there and make these people pay."

The DeCavalcante top brass rewarded Scarabino with a no-show job at Exxon in Jersey. "Most of the time I was there, we did nothing," he said. "I did nothing. There was a few soldiers there and associates there that we would get together and play cards, drive around in the truck all day. But every once in a while, it would be necessary for me to pick up a shovel, jump in a ditch, put a little dirt on myself and a little dirt on the shovel and make it look like I was working, and make the local inspectors happy."

Scarabino got paid for full-time work. To his superiors, he was worth every penny. DeCavalcante soldiers and associates often asked the Beast to keep an eye out for a "good score" that would help them in their work. "Maybe copper comes in or something valuable may come in," Scarabino said. "Something right away that can be taken and sold and we can make a few dollars, because most of the time, key associates or soldiers would be placed in key positions at Exxon. Guys who could be trusted to be bagmen. Guys, you know, when there were kickbacks being given, they would get the money. They would be the guys holding the money to bring it back to the union or to either give it to Jimmy, give it John, or whoever they were told to give it to."

The lower-downs in the Jersey crime family didn't actually make much money. A "good score" was their due.

Through the DeCavalcantes, Scarabino himself had control over six other buildings known as the Roberto Clemente Houses. This affordable rental housing in the Williamsburg section of Brooklyn had largely been funded by the US Department of Housing and Urban Development (HUD), and as Scarabino described it, the fox had been sent in to guard the chickens.

"I was in charge of buying all the material for the complex," he testified. The tenants, he said, "were entitled to refrigerators and washing machines and stoves, and they also were entitled to get their apartment painted, and any upkeep of the complex was totally under my control under Mickey DiPietro." If Scarabino had to order, say, two refrigerators or stoves or washing machines for the complex, he would order two more for himself and DiPietro.

Scarabino would also sell union memberships. "There was a very big Polish immigrant population in that area," he said, "and I had a few Polish guys that worked for me, and I gave them key positions. I made them foremans on the crew. They would bring me Polish guys to come to work. I charged them $1,500 apiece. They paid to get into the union. I guaranteed them thirty days on the job. And then I would call my office and say, 'We don't need this guy here anymore, but he is in the union.' And they would place him on another job site."

But how did these Polish workers enrich the DeCavalcantes?

Scarabino testified that he would have one of these foremen give him names and Social Security numbers of people who wouldn't have to show up at a job site. "So what I would do is I would keep twenty guys physically on the job site and five guys would be just ghosts, names on the payroll that we would take their checks," Scarabino said. "I would kick a portion back up to Mickey DiPietro, including all the money I was charging to get into the union."

Shylocking brought in another couple thousand dollars a week. Scarabino testified he kicked it all up to DiPietro. A lot of associates and soldiers didn't kick up the way they were supposed to, but the Beast was a DeCavalcante Boy Scout.

Frank Scarabino discovered how pervasive the DeCavalcantes were in the field of Jersey labor when he met with John Riggi at Newark Airport. According to the Beast, he was on his way to California to strong-arm some entertainment executives into giving Tony Bongiovi—Jon Bon Jovi's cousin—a record deal, and he stopped off at Riggi's office.

"I says to him, 'I can't believe you have an office here,'" Scarabino testified.

Scarabino recalled that Riggi's office was in the United Airlines terminal. Riggi had come out of a back room there carrying food. He offered some to Scarabino, but Scarabino didn't like to fly on a full stomach.

Mimi asked what the office looked like.

"Like an executive office," Scarabino said. "It was nice. It had a desk. It had a rug, tables, chairs. I mean, it looked like he belonged there."

Scarabino already knew that everything to do with baggage handling—"all the freight that went in and out," and "all internal operations belonged to the DeCavalcante family. It belonged to us."

"I said, 'I can't believe it,'" he told Mimi and the jury. "'Between construction—and now we own the airports too?'" Riggi responded by reaching into his pocket and withdrawing $3,000. He offered Scarabino the whole fat wad. "'Here, take this with you,'" he said.

Scarabino refused Riggi's generosity, just as he refused Riggi's offer to send some muscle along with him. "He put the money away," Scarabino said. "I kissed him and I left."

And yet it came to pass that Frank Scarabino let the DeCavalcante good times roll without him. Mimi asked him to explain why.

He said that by 1992, Mickey DiPietro had a habit of abusing cocaine and alcohol. One day Scarabino dropped by DiPietro's apartment with a Columbia University–educated friend, **Marco Polo**.

"He was already whacked out," Scarabino said of DiPietro. "There was cocaine on the table. There was one bottle of vodka already finished, another bottle opened. We sat down and we started a conversation with him."

DiPietro took an instant dislike to Polo. He couldn't understand why a guy with a Columbia master's degree wanted to hang out with him and Scarabino. "He said to him, 'I think you're a rat,'" Scarabino testified.

DiPietro told Polo he'd kill him if he ever tattled to the government. "As he [DiPietro] said that," Scarabino went on, "he swiveled around in his chair, and behind him was cabinets and drawers. . . . He reached in, spun around with a .25 caliber pistol, and shot my friend in the head. Then he turned to me and pulled the trigger, but the gun jammed. It stopped. And then he [DiPietro] passed out."

Marco Polo prayed to Jesus, Mary, and Joseph. "When I realized he wasn't dead," Scarabino testified, "I took him to the hospital."

A couple days later, Scarabino went back to DiPietro's place. "I said, 'I have to die, I gotta die, but I gotta fuckin' die like a man. You're not going to abuse me no more. . . . I'm not answering to you anymore and I'm not answering to anybody anymore. I'm walking away. If I got to, I'll go get a regular fuckin' job.'"

DiPietro promised to "fuckin' destroy" his old childhood friend. "'Listen,'" Scarabino said, as he reenacted the conversation. "'I ain't going to hunt nobody because I got to respect the thing—the Mafia, La Cosa Nostra—I got to respect that. I'm not going to fight everybody . . . But I'll tell you this right now: if I see somebody two times where they don't belong, you remember that my guns don't shoot rubber bullets either. But I won't hunt nobody.'"

The Beast walked out of the life.

But he availed himself of his old contacts. He created new ID documents for himself and asked "someone in California" to make up a birth certificate and driver's license for him under a new name. Frank Scarabino became James Christian. He got himself set up in California and went back to Staten Island to collect his wife and kids.

"If the DeCavalcantes were looking for me, they were looking for Frank Scarabino and they wouldn't be able to find me because I was living as James Christian," Scarabino testified.

Mimi asked why he chose to live under an assumed identity. "Because you can't just walk away from the Mafia," Scarabino said. "And you can't just tell a made soldier that if it need to be, you would kill him or anybody else associated with the Mafia. . . . If they were looking for me, they would have to really look."

Mimi asked, "Why didn't you tell your wife the truth about why you were moving to California and the assumed identity?"

"Because my wife didn't really know that I was part of organized crime," Scarabino said. "She had no idea."

If Scarabino's wife had understood why her husband transferred the family clear across the country, she probably wouldn't have insisted on going back to Staten Island. But she hated California. "She cried every day," Scarabino told the jury. "The phone bill was, like, $1,000 a month because she kept calling her mother."

In the late 1990s, Scarabino moved himself and the family back to Staten Island.

Every once in a while, DiPietro would make his presence known. "He would have a few guys around him and they would try to intimidate me," Scarabino said. "They would go to places where I was working, show up there, let me know that they knew where I was. But I had no association with them whatsoever."

Scarabino went totally legit. He drove a truck for a moving company. He drove a truck for an oil company. He worked construction.

If you're already guessing that the Beast's attempts to go straight led him right back to the DeCavalcantes, go get yourself a cappuccino and biscotti. You deserve it.

While Scarabino was working construction, he met **Ian O'Donnell**, a guy with a construction company that did small jobs in Manhattan. Some guys from the Laborers' Union came by and insisted he become a union shop. Ian told Scarabino he couldn't afford to do that.

The Beast's first thought: *This might be a way for me to make a few extra dollars.*

Scarabino told Ian he'd go to the work site, talk to these union guys, and make a deal with them. His only proviso: "You've got to let them understand that I'm your partner and I control the company," Scarabino said. That was fine with Ian.

Scarabino put on a suit and went to Ian's Manhattan work site. He waited for the union reps to come and shake Ian down. When they arrived, Scarabino spoke to them as if he were the company owner and he had organized crime behind him.

Scarabino suggested working out a deal for Ian.

"And it turned out they said yes," Scarabino testified. "All they wanted to do was put one laborer on the job and make it look good."

Ian was so grateful to Scarabino he paid him $15,000 in cash. "And he said to me at one point, 'Instead of me paying you all the time to do this for me, why don't you just really become my partner in the company?' And I did."

Ian announced he was going to do a big deal with **Sebbie Delvecchio**, the owner of **Level Development** in Linden, New Jersey. But Ian was afraid of him. "I said, 'Why?'" Scarabino told the jury. "He said, 'Because the guy wants to do this big deal but he don't want to sign no paperwork. He wants me to sign all the paperwork, and he keeps making me believe that he's a gangster.'"

Ian asked Scarabino to come with him and talk to Delvecchio, just as he had talked to the union people. "I went to Level Development," Scarabino said. "And we went upstairs and I had a meeting with Sebbie Delvecchio."

Scarabino was freaked out at the sight of Delvecchio: He had an "uncanny resemblance to John Riggi," he said. But that's where the resemblance ended. Scarabino thought Delvecchio was full of hot air. He talked the gangster talk, but somehow he didn't walk the gangster walk.

"It sounded to me like he just wanted to take this kid Ian, who was very naive, and abuse him," Scarabino said. "Get some contracts, make some moves, take the cash, and leave the kid holding the bag."

Scarabino asked Ian to leave the room. The Beast confronted Delvecchio with his suspicions. Delvecchio admitted he wanted to take advantage of the "kid."

"So I said, 'Well, you can't do that. I'm the kid's partner. You really won't be hurting him. You will be hurting me, and we can't have that happen.'"

Scarabino felt Delvecchio out to see if maybe he really did have some La Cosa Nostra contacts. He called his bluff.

"So I said to him, 'Listen, are we going to have to go further with this? Are we going to have to make another introduction? Or is this conversation going to be enough?'"

Mimi asked, "What did you mean by that?"

"I was letting him believe that I was a made guy," Scarabino explained. "That I was associated with a crime family, and that if he had somebody he was associated with, was it going to be necessary to go through them to have this conversation. Or could we straighten it out, just me and him. And he said, 'No, no, no, it's not necessary. We can do this just between us.' And that's what I did."

Scarabino still had time to do the right thing by Ian—his trusting and "naive" business partner. But old habits die hard.

Scarabino looked through the dollar signs in his eyes and addressed Delvecchio. "I said, 'Why don't we do this. Instead of all of this nonsense, you become my partner with all these contracts. And instead of Ian being my partner, you be my partner.'"

Scarabino said he didn't want to hurt Ian. "'I'm here because the kid brought me here,'" he told Delvecchio. "'So let's give him some work and eventually we will phase the guy out rather than telling him to hit the road.'"

And so it came to be. Scarabino and Delvecchio gave Ian some work and phased him out. Basically, Scarabino horned in on the construction partnership with Delvecchio the way Vinny had horned in on Jacques Petit's restaurant. "It was just me and Sebbie," Scarabino concluded.

In due time, Delvecchio introduced the Beast to Frank Polizzi. Delvecchio was the guy who wanted to burn Vito Cello and asked Polizzi for help killing him. Maybe if Scarabino hadn't come along, Vito Cello would have ended up hog-tied in the trunk of car.

Every cloud has a silver lining.

It was too late for Frank Scarabino to turn back. That's why when Vic Moretti showed up at Level and told Scarabino that Frank Polizzi sent him, Scarabino had no choice but to get in the car with him.

"'You're a great man,'" Scarabino quoted Moretti, as the two of them headed to the Meadowlands Hotel, one of Polizzi's properties. Moretti said Polizzi was "really very happy." He wanted to talk to Scarabino.

Scarabino was glad to get Frank Polizzi's stamp of approval. "But some part of me inside thought, you know, I was being driven to be killed. But I went."

At the hotel, Polizzi walked up to Scarabino and hugged and kissed him. "'From today on, all your problems with the DeCavalcante family, with Anthony Rotondo, or anybody else, is done,'" Scarabino quoted Polizzi. "'From today on, you answer to me.'"

That's how it went for about the next three years. Scarabino helped fuel Polizzi's bookmaking and loan-sharking businesses. Polizzi loaned Scarabino money to open up a car dealership on Staten Island as a money-laundering outfit for Scarabino's illegal earnings. In fact, Polizzi was so satisfied with his mob intern he submitted Scarabino's name to Jimmy Palermo and Steve Vitabile "and told them that he was formally proposing me to be a member of the family," as Scarabino testified.

"Vinny Palermo hugged me and kissed me and said, 'You really deserve this,'" Scarabino continued. "'I'm in total agreement with it. Just be patient.'"

One person could have stood as a reminder that when you lie down with the DeCavalcantes, you wake up with fleas. That one person was Marco Polo. But he was tucked away from view in California with a bullet permanently in his head.

At least Polo had survived. With the DeCavalcantes, Scarabino would never know if he'd be able to say the same about himself.

Much of Scarabino's testimony revealed his financial interactions with Jimmy Palermo. For example, a 1-800 sports-betting number in Costa Rica that Scarabino operated with Mimmo Marzullo and another DeCavalcante on behalf of Jimmy Palermo, Frank Polizzi, Pino Schifilliti, Charles Majuri, and others. Bettors could place illegal bets on "any kind of sports action." Why Costa Rica? "No office, less scrutiny from the government," Scarabino said.

In fact, when US-based bookmakers got busted, Scarabino would alert Jimmy Palermo, and they scooped up new customers. "You can get rid of an 800 number quick and get another 800 number right away," Scarabino said. "By the time the government finds out where the number is located . . . you're moved already. Also, you never open up the 800 number in your name. It is, of course, under a whole assumed person who doesn't exist."

Scarabino's loan-sharking operation used Frank Polizzi as a point of contact, but quite often, some big money came from Jimmy Palermo. Shortly before Scarabino's arrest, Polizzi handed Scarabino $90,000 in cash from Palermo to "put out on the street."

"There were times when I had upwards of $350,000 to $500,000 at any given time on the street," Scarabino told Mimi.

Mimi wanted to know if Scarabino ever had to threaten violence when he went around to collect interest on the loans from his debtors.

"Yeah, on occasion," he said.

Mimmo Marzullo was also a partner in Scarabino's loan-sharking operation, but Mimmo caused problems by lending money out quickly, not keeping track of his customers, and then having a hard time collecting the interest.

One time in particular, Mimmo talked to Scarabino about a guy who owned a pizzeria and another guy who owned a printing company.

"I went with him to the two establishments," Scarabino said. "I went with him to the pizzeria . . . and I put the owner's head in the oven." Scarabino promised the owner that he would cook him if he didn't pay up. The owner opened the cash register and paid Scarabino.

"Then we went to the printing guy's place," Scarabino said. "I grabbed him and I told him, 'I know you're under the impression that you owe this money to Mimmo, but you're under the wrong impression. Mimmo gave you my money and I guarantee you will either pay me my money or I don't want my money back.' And he paid me."

What Scarabino meant was that he'd chalk the printer's debt up as a loss, but he'd put him in the hospital.

Scarabino testified that he resorted to violence rarely. "My reputation proceeded [*sic*] me," he said. "Whoever took my money knew that they had to pay."

Frank made around $100,000 a month from gambling and loan-sharking. Even after the December 2, 1999, arrests, which could have served as a warning to lay low, Scarabino continued to put money out on the street.

In fact, the Beast really came into his own once Vinny Palermo and Anthony Rotondo were in prison. "I had proven myself to be someone who was a good earner, someone who was counted on, to be capable of handling any situation that came up, whether violence or money or whatever it might be," Scarabino said. "I also proved myself to be a capable leader."

Scarabino said he, Polizzi, and the other DeCavalcantes read in the newspapers that Vinny Palermo and Anthony Capo had agreed to cooperate with the government. They were all in a panic.

"Frank Polizzi said to me that Vinny Ocean knew almost everything, that Jimmy Palermo, Charlie Majuri, Frank himself, and other members of the family were involved with," Scarabino testified. "That he has been around for a very long time. He was very powerful and he could do a lot of damage to those individuals and other individuals in the DeCavalcante family if he wanted to."

With the Jersey family headless, Frank Polizzi declared himself to be boss. Jimmy Palermo would be underboss. Scarabino had definitely earned his DeCavalcante wings by now, but, as he told Mimi, "it was too risky to have a ceremony to formally induct me into the family."

Polizzi, however, gave Scarabino de facto authority to act as a captain, "to sit down with other families, to press the rights, if it was necessary, in the street and to meet with other families outside the DeCavalcante association," he testified.

Indeed, in the months after Vinny Palermo's arrest and cooperation, Scarabino became something like a minister without portfolio. Jimmy Palermo and Charles Majuri thought it prudent to pare down operations and funnel them through Scarabino.

"So Charlie said that they would give me this money in $250,000 increments," Scarabino testified. "We would put it out for 8 percent, and he would get 2 percent, Frank Polizzi would get 2 percent, Jimmy would get 2 percent, and Pino Schifilliti would get a point, and I would get the balance to split with my partners."

Frank Scarabino was eager to put the DeCavalcante investment out on the street. But Frank Polizzi's health was deteriorating. He was suffering from cancer and had become paralyzed from the waist down. In September 2000, after a brief hospitalization, he was sent to Kessler, a New Jersey–based rehabilitation institute, for a couple of weeks. Either Polizzi would learn to walk again or he'd learn to get around in a wheelchair.

As a patient at Kessler, Polizzi told Scarabino about his plan to import "ghost soldiers" from Sicily—"nameless, faceless people who could come in, do a piece of work, and get out of the country with no problem," Scarabino told Mimi.

The "piece of work" meant killing a cooperator's family. From his rehab bed, Polizzi had convened a meeting of Jimmy Palermo, Steve Vitabile, and Charles Majuri to agree to using these ghost soldiers to punish the informant.

While the "rat" was "living in the lap of luxury somewhere," Scarabino testified, "he would be tortured every day knowing that because he cooperated with the government, somebody in his family was hurt. . . . That may be a brother, may be a sister, may be a cousin, a father, a mother, whatever, whoever the family decided was easiest to get. Then you would have to sit with that every day, knowing that it's your fault that your family member got hurt. So at least if they couldn't get you, they would torture you in your heart every day."

Polizzi didn't hold back. "He used this Judge Falcone as an example," Scarabino said, "that we were going to target anyone who was a threat to the family, whether it be a judge, whether it be an FBI agent, whether it be a prosecutor, whether it be a local cop, anybody that posed a threat to the welfare and the well-being of the DeCavalcante family in general. . . . The shield would be taken off them."

Polizzi said the real power of the DeCavalcante family came from Jimmy Palermo, Steve Vitabile, and Charles Majuri having relatives back in Messina, Ribera, and Palermo.

On Sunday, October 15, 2000, Polizzi ordered Scarabino to kill Anthony Capo's wife and children. Scarabino was arrested on Thursday, October 19. So were Jimmy Palermo, Charles Majuri, Louis Consalvo, Gregory Rago, and Frank Polizzi, among others.

Until he was locked up in the Metropolitan Correctional Center, Scarabino didn't know he and his family had landed on Polizzi's hit list too. I don't want to think what could have happened if we hadn't arrested Scarabino and the others when we did.

Hard work brings good luck.

Thomas Nooter was skeptical. "You want us to believe that basically you had a change of heart about the life you had been living your whole life, correct?" he asked Scarabino during cross-examination.

Scarabino said yes.

Nooter pointed out that once Polizzi gave Scarabino the ticket to kill Anthony Capo's family, Scarabino did nothing more to save them than stall.

"You jeopardized their lives by guessing how long you might be able to get away with putting off doing this job while you did nothing, right?" Nooter charged.

"Well, that's not exactly right, counsel," Scarabino said. "The forte of my life in the Mafia was that I know how to do homework on people. And my reputation for getting the job done, I believed, afforded me at least two or three weeks before somebody would realize that I wasn't doing the job."

"So you're saying that you felt that your reliability was so well known as a killer that you could get away for several weeks without jeopardizing Anthony Capo's family, correct?"

"Right. Because my reputation wasn't only as a killer, but as someone who when I was told to do something got the job done and got it done right."

Scarabino testified that an FBI agent had approached a DeCavalcante acquaintance named Mark with a question: Did he know Frank Scarabino? The agent left Mark his business card. Mark gave it to Scarabino.

"I took that card and I placed it in my office," Scarabino testified. "I hid it underneath some—"

"Let me understand," Nooter interrupted. "When did you get this card?"

"In those four days." Scarabino was talking about the time from October 15, when he was ordered to kill the Capos, and October 19, when he was arrested.

"During the four days, someone came and actually gave you the name of an FBI agent?"

"Yeah."

Nooter was incredulous. "You didn't call them, but you put the card away someplace?" he asked. Nooter had backed the Beast into a corner—and inadvertently got him to make one of the most honest admissions in the trial.

"I am sorry," Scarabino said. "It all sounds very black and white, that you call the FBI and say, 'Hi, I'm Frank Scarabino and I was supposed to kill somebody's wife and kids. Let me talk to you.' It's not that black and white. At least in my mind it wasn't. I was conflicted in my mind about how to go about doing—what jeopardy I was putting my own family in and everything around me. It was overwhelming for me as a person and I did not—it was just very overwhelming for me. That's all I could say."

I looked over at the jurors. No tears of sympathy—but they were rapt. They couldn't sympathize with the trickery Scarabino had used on business partners or with his "propensity for violence." But they could connect with the feeling of being trapped in a bad situation and not knowing what to do. They could connect with feeling overwhelmed by fate. By people more powerful than they were. By marriage. By life.

Scarabino was believable.

Even when Mr. Nooter had a legitimate point, he ended up painting himself into a corner.

You couldn't fault Nooter for reminding the jury that the government witness on the stand—this contrite father of five—had been up until recently no better than a thug. A business partner of Scarabino's, for example, was skilled at submitting fraudulent paperwork to get loans from the community-based Jefferson Bank. Scarabino had even suggested to Jimmy Palermo that he rely on this guy to put in a loan application for Rockafella's, Palermo's seaside restaurant. Palermo was to think of the Jefferson loan as "free money," because—*wink wink, nod nod*—he wouldn't have to pay it back.

"Let me understand," Nooter said. "If you could get these loans, what did you need the restaurant for?"

Scarabino explained. "You need an entity to get—to attach the loan to. So we were going to use the restaurant as that entity."

Even if the restaurant already had a loan against it?

Scarabino said third-party moneylenders, such as his own mortgage company, "don't really care about all that stuff. . . . If you miss a payment with them, they can foreclose on you. There is ways for them to get their money."

"Well, they can't foreclose if there is already a mortgage ahead of them, is there? Is there a way?"

Scarabino said, "You are asking me technicalities about the mortgage business that I can't answer you intelligently. So I would rather not."

"So you didn't get involved in those details?" Nooter asked.

"No."

I worried that Mr. Nooter had won the jury back. As easily as they had sympathized with Scarabino when he was "conflicted" in his mind, they just as easily reviled him now for helping financially unqualified people get loans and mortgages. Jurors could have lived in a New York City co-op or rental apartment, and surely some of them had filed for loans and been rejected.

Fortunately for Scarabino—and for the government in its case against Jimmy Palermo—his fraudulent loan business was only just getting on its feet when he was arrested.

We had to hope the jury took Scarabino's remorse seriously.

"To be honest with you," the Beast said. "In over these last three years, seeing how everything is, and the conditions that you live in, the crimes that I committed, I wished that I was just the guy who took out the laundry. Then I wouldn't have to worry about life in prison."

In her direct examination, Mimi had highlighted the close relationship between Jimmy Palermo and Frank Scarabino. One evening at Rockafella's, Scarabino offered, Palermo introduced him to his wife: "And Jimmy put his arm around me and he said to his wife, 'This is a real friend. Frankie's my friend.' And he had mentioned to his wife, 'You have all his numbers. If anything happens, if you need anything, if I'm not around, you can always call Frankie.'"

Suddenly, Judge Mukasey asked to see counsel briefly at the side. The judge looked out over his eyeglasses at Mr. Nooter and said, "It has actually happened on more than one occasion, but just now your client turned around to his wife and they engaged in a whole series of face expressions meant to suggest that what the witness testified to hadn't happened. I don't want to have to give an instruction. I don't want to have to throw her out of the courtroom. So if you could see to it that that doesn't recur, I would appreciate it."

Nooter had no choice but to be deferential.

"OK, I will," he said.

"Thank you," the judge said.

"Thank you," Nooter repeated.

Maybe we didn't have to worry so much about the effect of Frank Scarabino's testimony on the jury. Jimmy Palermo was doing a bang-up job being his own worst enemy.

28

THE DECAVALCANTE "SCHOLAR" HITS A HOME RUN

We made Anthony Rotondo our clean-up hitter in the trial. As the highest-ranking DeCavalcante to testify in *US v. Palermo*, he corroborated what Anthony Capo and Frank Scarabino had testified to regarding the Fred Weiss murder; the Frank D'Amato murder conspiracy; the corruption in union locals 394 and 1030; the shakedown of construction industry contractors; the extent of loan-sharking operations; and, indeed, the reality of the DeCavalcantes as a racketeering enterprise. Rotondo specifically called out Jimmy Palermo—one of the few top-brass DeCavalcantes he trusted—as his conduit to nonunion contractors he could shake down for kickbacks.

Mike McGovern began the direct examination of the highest-ranking member of the Jersey crime family to testify at this trial. "To your knowledge, where did all that money go?" he asked.

"To the committee, consigliere, to a kitty that was supposedly going to receive it," Rotondo answered. "But to my understanding, it never really made it to the kitty for the family."

McGovern asked where the money actually went.

"It never got into the kitty, and it was shared amongst the three members of the committee and the consigliere," Rotondo said. "Four people."

The four people who profited from a fund designed to pay for a member's legal fees, or support his family if he got incarcerated, or serve as seed money for a loan-sharking business—these four people were Charles Majuri, Vinny Palermo, Steve Vitabile, and Jimmy Palermo.

But Rotondo explained that the self-dealing went back further than this ruling panel. In 1996, when Jake Amari was still underboss, he used the lion's share of the pot for himself. "Jake was building a large house out in Millstone, New Jersey, on Steve's property, and I visited there," Rotondo testified.

McGovern asked for a description.

"It was tremendous," Rotondo said. "Maybe five thousand square feet."

"Where were you and he having this discussion?" McGovern asked.

"The job was about three-quarters done and we were on the job site."

"What did you say to Jake Amari?"

"I told him how beautiful I thought the house was, that he had done a great job. And he told me, 'Do you think I got this money by working for 394? I got it from that thing.'"

McGovern asked Rotondo what he understood Amari to mean.

"That it was extortion payments he received between 1030 and 394," Rotondo said.

McGovern asked Rotondo if Amari's high life was the norm for an upper-level member of La Cosa Nostra.

"There is a general understanding among DeCavalcante family members that we are to fly below law enforcement radar," Rotondo said. "To act legitimate. Be as legitimate as we could."

"What does that mean in terms of how conspicuous you are with your money?" McGovern asked.

"Try to live modestly, decent size house, don't flaunt the cars, don't go out spending large amounts of money."

Who lived that way, McGovern wanted to know.

"John Riggi, while he was the boss, he wore his First Communion clothes," Rotondo said, tongue in cheek. "Everybody—Paul Farina, Jimmy Palermo, most of the membership—conducted themselves that way."

McGovern asked if this was also true for Nick Delmore. He'd already asked Rotondo several questions about Delmore, Sam DeCavalcante's uncle and predecessor. He'd been the Jersey crime family's boss from the late 1950s to the early 1960s.

"Nick Delmore, he used to take the train into Manhattan and my father would pick him up at Penn Station while he was the boss of the family," Rotondo said.

Delmore and the Jersey mobsters of his generation were a low-profile crowd. Sounds like Jake Amari didn't get the memo.

Jimmy Palermo (left) and John Riggi.
Department of Justice Trial Exhibit, US Attorney's Office, Southern District of New York / FBI

Anthony Capo, Victor DiChiara, Vinny Palermo, and Frank Scarabino had each presented a picture of the DeCavalcantes as a nest of vipers. A conversation with Jimmy Palermo convinced Rotondo that the biggest viper of all was . . . John Riggi.

"And what did Jimmy Palermo say he believed the problems of the family to be at that point in '97?" McGovern asked.

"He said there was a lot of problems going on among the individual members and crews," Rotondo testified. "That Johnny Riggi had screwed up the family. He looted the kitty. That he was a backstabber and a snake."

In addition to robbing the union, Rotondo said, Riggi had tried years back to have Jimmy Palermo killed by the Lucchese family. The two lifelong DeCavalcantes had actively despised each other since the 1960s. No honor among these thieves.

The accusations among the DeCavalcantes ricocheted around Judge Mukasey's courtroom like bullets.

I was confident Anthony Rotondo had begun to envision a life different from his mob life. Still, it wasn't easy for him to sit across from Jimmy Palermo, recount their weekly Friday 11:00 AM meetings at the Monmouth rest area* on the Garden State, and air Uncle Jimmy's dirty linen.

Indeed, more than the two earlier witnesses, Rotondo put the nail in Palermo's coffin when he testified that Joseph Collina was a topic of conversation nearly every Friday. Yes, the same Joseph Collina who had pled guilty to extorting kickbacks from contractors—and whose plea Mike McGovern had read into the court record. We were connecting the dots for the jury to convict Palermo.

"What did Collina have to do with your business affairs with Jimmy Palermo?" McGovern asked.

"We were both interested in bringing Joey back into the family as a soldier," Rotondo resumed. "Joey years ago had been in the crew with my father, and then he had been switched over to Elizabeth in the early '80s, I think. And just that Joey was out there grabbing contractors, shaking guys down."

McGovern wanted to know why Palermo wanted to take Collina "off the shelf" and bring him back into the family.

* The Monmouth rest area is now called the Judy Blume Service Area.

"Well, he was another gun," Rotondo said. "He was a tough guy. He could do a piece of work, if needed."

Palermo knew Collina was extorting a landowner down the Jersey Shore. "He had a large tract," Rotondo said of the landowner. "And he was considering developing a large roller-skating rink, a strip mall, possibly some housing."

Palermo told Rotondo that Collina had "grabbed this guy" and was shaking him down. Collina told the landowner, "'You're not doing anything without me,'" Rotondo quoted.

McGovern asked Rotondo to explain what he meant by "grabbed."

"Not necessarily physically, but implied threats, yes," Rotondo said. If the contractor didn't play ball, he could go pound sand.

Because he and Palermo were on good terms, Rotondo got all the glass work for the development. Palermo said any of Rotondo's "people"—his soldiers and associates—could bid on the plumbing and electrical work.

"Someone could possibly grab a pizzeria or something there," Rotondo testified. Meaning, someone in Rotondo's crew could extort "protection money" from a business.

Palermo wasn't just being a pal. He needed a favor from Rotondo. Would Rotondo be willing to put soldiers Joe Collina and Joseph "Tin Ear" Sclafani together so they could patch up their differences with each other? They'd had a falling out over money from a construction job years ago, and they hadn't spoken since.

Rotondo testified that Palermo was trying to rebuild the family that Riggi had left in tatters—and Uncle Jimmy had ambitions for the top job. His campaign slogan could have been "Make the DeCavalcantes Great Again."

The reconciliation between the two sparring DeCavalcantes took place in summer '99 at the Monmouth rest area. "Jimmy and I went inside into the food court, and he instructed the two Joeys—Joey Sclafani and Joey Collina—to go outside and iron out their differences," Rotondo said.

Just like that, the "two men were friends again," Rotondo said. "The past was the past, and they were interested in building the family back up to what it was."

Pretty sweet of the FBI's SO-2 squad to capture the two Joeys on camera. Rotondo—usually so attuned to being tailed by an FBI agent—was unaware that members of Joe Sconzo's surveillance team had been watching and photographing the DeCavalcantes for more than two years straight. Stacy and I had catalogued hundreds of these photos, and this particular one was entered into the trial as Government Exhibit 486.

"Please tell us what you recognize the scene to be," McGovern said.

"Well, from left to right, it's Joseph Collina Sr., Joseph Sclafani, myself, and Jimmy Palermo on the right," Rotondo said.

"Do you recognize the location that this picture was taken?"

"I believe it was the parking lot of the rest area."

"Is that the Monmouth rest area?"

"Yes."

SO-2 had snapped twelve photos. They captured the half hour or so Sclafani and Collina spent together burying the hatchet.

They say the road to hell is paved with good intentions, and the day came when Jimmy Palermo regretted getting back in touch with Joseph Collina. He expressed his second thoughts to Rotondo at the Monmouth rest area.

"Jimmy said that Joey was just out there going crazy, shaking down contractors," Rotondo testified. "And that he had grabbed this kid that, I believe, was a plumber, and that Joey had been collecting cash off this guy . . . extortion money."

Palermo had to question Collina's common sense when he sent "this kid"—the plumber—to his restaurant, Rockafella's, with an envelope of kickback money.

Palermo was not happy. Collina was supposed to be the "buffer" between extorter and extorted. Payoffs were not supposed to arrive at Palermo's legitimate place of business in the hands of an extorted contractor. Palermo was worried that Collina was shooting off his mouth to "this kid," telling him that Jimmy Palermo was boss of the New Jersey crime family.

Collina swore up and down he never whispered a word about kickbacks. "And he winked and he said, 'It's legal money anyway,'" Rotondo dramatized with a wink. "'It's finder's fees.'"

Nah. It was shakedown money.

McGovern wanted to know if Rotondo had information that, in fact, Collina was running off at the mouth.

Rotondo heard from Charlie "the Hat" Stango, the DeCavalcante associate based in Elizabeth, that "Joey was baloneying Jimmy, giving him a line," as Rotondo testified. "That, in fact, Joey Collina told this fellow, that Jimmy was the boss, that Joey was a soldier, that wherever this guy went in the state, he would have the power of the DeCavalcante family, Jimmy's connections [behind him]."

McGovern moved Rotondo on to various other subjects dealing with the role Jimmy Palermo played in inter-family sit-downs and union-related business.

"Did you also discuss murder?" McGovern then asked.

Rotondo said, "At times, yes."

"Your Honor," McGovern addressed Judge Mukasey. "This may be a convenient break point."

The judge told the jurors to take a short break and told Rotondo to step down.

With the jury and witness out of the room, Judge Mukasey addressed "Mr. McGovern": "Since I get to do so little around here, let me call the recesses," the judge said.

McGovern looked as if he'd stepped out of the choir to do a solo without his priest's blessing. But I could see how the brilliant line of questioning Mike had crafted, as well as the stipulation he'd read into the court record, made him feel on top of the world and—momentarily, if mistakenly—in charge of the courtroom.

No other DeCavalcante was better placed than Anthony Rotondo to implicate Jimmy Palermo in the conspiracy to murder Frank D'Amato. And as a stickler for procedure, Rotondo could even point to La Cosa Nostra rules permitting Palermo to authorize the murder of a DeCavalcante associate or member. Like Rotondo, Jimmy Palermo knew that a made man—Anthony Capo—was within his rights to take revenge against an associate—Frank D'Amato—who wanted to kill him. All Capo needed to do was put his request to kill D'Amato before Capo's captain, that is, Rotondo, and the ruling panel.

"What was your vote?" McGovern asked.

"To kill Frankie D'Amato," Rotondo said.

"What was Vinny Palermo's vote?"

"Same. To kill Frankie D'Amato."

"What was Jimmy Palermo's vote?"

"Also, yes, to kill Frankie D'Amato."

At Rotondo's weekly meeting with Jimmy Palermo at the Monmouth rest area, Palermo asked Rotondo to weigh in on Anthony Capo's request.

"I told him there was merit to it," Rotondo testified. "That I heard from other people that Frankie was getting revenge for his brother's killing, and I felt Anthony was telling the truth, and he [D'Amato] had this coming to him."

"What was Jimmy Palermo's response?" McGovern asked.

"He said, 'Fine, let's do it.'"

The plan to whack Frank D'Amato got under way. The DeCavalcante administration invited Jimmy Gallo to the meeting at Steve Vitabile's house in Millstone, New Jersey. As the prospective shooter, Gallo had gone into Manhattan on Vinny Palermo's orders to meet with D'Amato, to get a fix on where he hung out, to see how he was earning money. Gallo reported that D'Amato was acting "kind of nervous."

"But he [D'Amato] was trying to appear friendly with Jimmy," Rotondo testified. "And he [D'Amato] told him the only way he was surviving now was picking up Philly [Abramo's] money and selling packages. Which is heroin. Junk."

Gallo reported that he hadn't felt comfortable killing Frank D'Amato out in the middle of the street. Gallo was a no-go.

Vinny Palermo was getting impatient with all the time, energy, and resources put into the conspiracy to murder John D'Amato's brother. "I told him that I had heard Joe Sclafani was now recruited, and Joey was looking to get on a motorcycle, driven by Ralph Guarino, and shoot Frank D'Amato, or inject him with a needle, or something like that," Rotondo said.

I couldn't blame any of the jurors for laughing outright.

"What was Jimmy Palermo's response when [you] told him about this plan?" McGovern asked.

"He didn't say anything," Rotondo responded. "He just nodded."

Rotondo wanted Jimmy Palermo to take Vinny Palermo's impatience seriously. "I told him Vinny was getting disgusted with the amount of time it was taking, and he [Vinny] told me he would have Frank D'Amato lured to Elizabeth where he would strangle him [D'Amato] himself," Rotondo said.

The motorcycle plan to murder Frank D'Amato came to a screeching halt on December 2, 1999.

A task common to all of our government cooperators was identifying La Cosa Nostra members in the hundreds of photographs I'd collated for the trial. Anthony Rotondo had been acquainted with the DeCavalcantes since he was a kid, and he was a de facto historian of the crime family. He could come up with the names of some four dozen DeCavalcantes who had gathered in the late 1970s or early '80s—brashly—for a group photo inside the Ribera Club, a meeting place in Elizabeth, as Rotondo put it, for the DeCavalcante family. McGovern asked Rotondo to go through the photo, starting with the individuals in the top row, and tell the jury who they were.

"These six or seven individuals here I recognize them as associates, friends of the family," Rotondo muttered. "I don't recall any of their names."

"Please keep your voice up," McGovern said.

It was not easy for Anthony Rotondo to dishonor his father by working with us, the enemy.

Jimmy Palermo was in the second row from the back. Several Local 394 bigwigs stood nearby. Joseph Colletti was in there, as were Charlie Majuri, Lou LaRasso, Jake Amari, Steve Vitabile, and an elderly soldier Rotondo called Mr. Corsentino. "He was an undertaker by trade," Rotondo said. He thought Mr. Corsentino, who owned a funeral parlor in Elizabeth, had lived to be a hundred.

"It was kind of ironic that the two oldest members of the American Mafia had about fifty bodies between them," Rotondo said, and noted that they "lived to receive congratulatory letters from President Clinton."

The two oldsters had lived through Prohibition "and they saw a lot," Rotondo testified. "In fact, I heard rumors that Mr. Corsentino was one of the originators of the double-decker coffin."

"What's a double-decker coffin?" McGovern asked.

"During the '20s and '30s, when there were a lot of Mafia murders committed, the family would put the body of the murdered victim below the regular customer, thus disappearing forever," Rotondo explained.

"What happened when they went to carry out that coffin?" McGovern asked.

"Everybody would kind of look at one another," Rotondo said. "There were six grown men carrying somebody's eighty-pound grandmother and they looked like they were having a problem."

Rotondo's testimony was the shot heard round the world.

The *New York Post* announced on October 7, 2003:

BURY CLEVER MOBSTERS
TWO-DECK COFFINS HIDE DEAD

On October 8, the Newark *Star-Ledger* went with:

MAFIA TURNCOAT TELLS OF 'OVER/UNDER' COFFINS

The same day, across the pond, London's *Daily Telegraph* used a tamer headline:

MOBSTERS 'USED TWO-TIER COFFINS'

The double-decker coffins were the sensation of the day, but one of Rotondo's last Ribera Club identifications was more important to the trial. "This fella is Gaetano Alessi, also known as Guy, a soldier in the family," Rotondo said. "And he has a company called Durable that builds JCPenneys and malls."

Don't forget, jurors: labor racketeering was the mainstay of DeCavalcante wealth.

Anthony Rotondo's most quoted testimony had nothing to do with the Frank D'Amato murder conspiracy or charges of labor racketeering lodged against Jimmy Palermo. It had to do with *The Sopranos*. Writer-producer David Chase, who created Tony Soprano and his fictional New Jersey crime family, maintains to this day that he took his inspiration from Richie Boiardo, a Genovese captain who lived in his mother's Newark neighborhood.* I take the man at his word. But like everyone else on C-10, I marveled at how perfectly the show's characters aligned with the real-world DeCavalcantes. Not only did Jake Amari die of stomach cancer as the fictional Jackie Aprile did, but Corky Vastola was allegedly a concert promoter for Ray Charles and Aretha Franklin, like *The Sopranos*' Hesh Rabkin, a mob associate who founded a record company promoting black musicians.† Coincidence?

What matters is that on March 3, 1999, the DeCavalcantes believed they were the basis for *The Sopranos*, which aired its first episode on January 10, 1999. Ralph Guarino, wired up earlier that late winter day by George Hanna, got three other DeCavalcantes on tape expressing their glee and amazement that a screenwriter must surely be getting intel from somebody inside the DeCavalcante family.

Ralph's recording entered the trial record as Government Exhibit T-7. Mike McGovern played it for the court to hear. He let the jury know Rotondo had already listened to the recording and identified the four speakers as Joseph Sclafani, an associate named Billy Perrotta, and Ralph Guarino. The fourth voice belonged to Rotondo.

---

* When DeCavalcante boss John Riggi died, the *New York Times* spoke with David Chase. Chase said he'd never heard of Riggi until he began filming *The Sopranos*. See "John Riggi, Who Led New Jersey Crime Family, Dies at 90" by Sam Roberts, *New York Times*, August 11, 2015, https://www.nytimes.com/2015/08/12/nyregion/john-riggi-former-head-of-decavalcante-crime-family-dies-at-90.html.

† Anthony Rotondo testified in *US v. Palermo* that cooperating witness Frank Scarabino had also gotten into the entertainment business. He reportedly got magicians and musicians gigs at resorts in the Pocono Mountains.

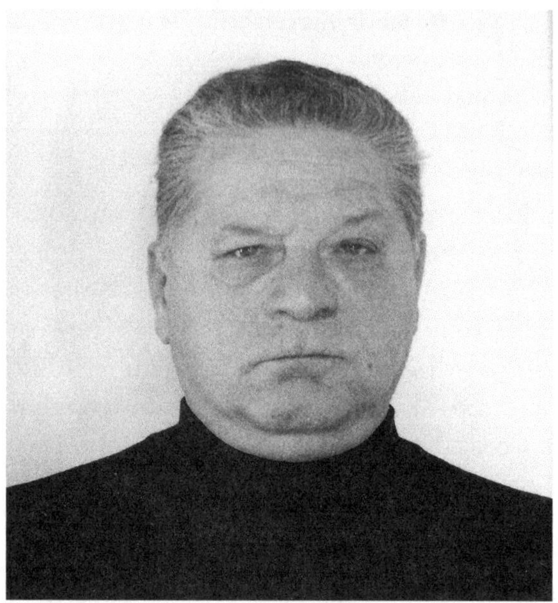

Joseph "Joe" Sclafani. *Department of Justice Trial Exhibit, US Attorney's Office, Southern District of New York / FBI*

SCLAFANI: Hey, what's this fucking thing, What the fuck are they . . .

GUARINO: You ever watch it?

SCLAFANI: Is that supposed to be us?

ROTONDO: You're in there.

GUARINO: (*Laughs*).

ROTONDO: They mentioned your name in there.

SCLAFANI: Yeah, what did they say?

PERROTTA: "Watch out for that guy," they said. "Watch that guy."

ROTONDO: Every show you watch, every show you watch, more and more you pick up somebody. Every show.

SCLAFANI: Yeah (*unintelligible*). I'm not even existing over there.

ROTONDO: Corky.

SCLAFANI: Yeah.

ROTONDO: One week it was Corky. One week it was, from the beginning it was a, was a, was Don Giacomino.

SCLAFANI: Yeah.

ROTONDO: The guy that died and had stomach cancer.
PERROTTA: They had the guy die with stomach cancer?
SCLAFANI: Yeah, but where do they get this information from?
ROTONDO: Ah, where?
PERROTTA: Joey, there's somebody close to you there, Joe.

Anthony identified "Corky" as Corky Vastola and "Giacomino" as Jake Amari, the DeCavalcante underboss who died of cancer two years before *The Sopranos* went on the air. A priceless consensual recording for the jury to hear: the "real-life Sopranos" comparing themselves to the fictional Sopranos.

McGovern asked, "At the time that you had this conversation, did you think it was funny that your life in the Mafia was being fictionalized on TV?"

"At that time, yes," Rotondo said.

"At the time you had that conversation, did you know that Ralph Guarino was wearing a wire and recording your conversations with him?"

"No."

Me with actor Vincent Pastore, who played Salvatore "Big Pussy" Bonpensiero on *The Sopranos*. *Séamus McElearney*

The rest of the trial was no laughing matter. Rotondo spoke about his father as a killer. He didn't seem angry at him. He didn't seem perplexed. When you're in the life, you might have to kill. That's just the way it goes.

"And he [Jimmy Rotondo] sat down and told you this story about how he had done a murder, correct?" Mr. Nooter asked.

"He was part of a murder, yes," Rotondo said.

"And is that the first time you ever heard that your father had been involved in a murder?"

"From him, yes."

"Is it that you heard it from other people?" Nooter asked.

"I had heard that my father was a very capable guy during the Gallo war. . . ."

Nooter asked Rotondo to explain.

"There was a war between the Gallos and Colombos and the Persicos,"* Rotondo said.

"And you heard stories about your father being involved in those battles?"

"Yes, that he was very capable."

"Did you admire him for that?" Nooter asked.

"Yes, I did."

"And when he told you he was involved in this killing back in 1958, did you admire him for that?"

"I don't know if I admired him that night," Rotondo answered. "I was more upset that he wasn't promoted to underboss."

"You weren't upset that he was involved in killing someone?" Nooter asked.

"I was a member of Cosa Nostra at that time," he said. "I wasn't upset."

I knew Anthony Rotondo was not going back to a life of organized crime, but even three years in prison wouldn't turn him against his father.

In fact, he paid Jimmy Palermo the ultimate compliment. "I trusted Jimmy like a father, yes," he told Nooter.

These were just about the last words he was ever going to say to his old mob boss.

---

* The Gallos and the Persicos of the Colombo crime family violently jockeyed for power in the 1960s and early 1970s.

I leaned back to steal a glance at Jimmy Palermo. His face showed no emotion. Our DeCavalcante scholar had just put the nail in Palermo's coffin.

At 10:13 AM on October 9, 2003—after eighteen days of trial—the jury filed back into Judge Mukasey's courtroom. They had reached a verdict. I'm laying out the counts and predicate acts against Jimmy Palermo in a table so you can see what he was charged with and how the jury decided on each count.

Girolamo Palermo		
Count/Act	**Description**	**Verdict**
Count 1	Conducted and participated in a racketeering enterprise through a pattern of racketeering activity (RICO)	Guilty
Racketeering Act 1	*Conspiracy to murder Frank D'Amato*	*Proved*
Racketeering Act 2	*Conspiracy to commit extortion*	*Proved*
Racketeering Act 3	*Financing extortionate extensions of credit, conspiracy to make extortionate extensions of credit, and conspiracy to collect extortionate extensions of credit*	*Not proved*
Count 2	RICO conspiracy	Guilty
Count 3	Conspiracy or agreement to murder Frank D'Amato	Guilty
Count 4	Financing extortionate extensions of credit	Not Guilty
Count 5	Conspiracy to make extortionate extensions of credit	Not Guilty
Count 6	Conspiracy to collect extortionate extensions on credit	Not Guilty
Count 7	Conspiracy or agreement to commit extortion related to the construction industry	Guilty

Each juror answered "yes" when asked if they had voted in favor of the verdict.

Mike McGovern asked that Palermo's bail be revoked.

"Bail is revoked and Mr. Palermo is remanded pending sentence," Judge Mukasey announced.

Defense attorney Nooter had done the best he could.

What a punch in the gut that must have been for Jimmy Palermo. You get convicted. The government remands you. Reality sets in. You're not going home.

I don't remember where on the Lower East Side the AUSAs, Bernardo, and I went out for more than a few beers to celebrate. I do remember a couple of other things, though. I remember Agent George Wright congratulating me for doing a whole year of trials without a break.

I also remember working with the federal marshals to get Anthony Capo out on bail before Christmas. After everything he had done to help us put the DeCavalcantes behind bars, he deserved to spend the holiday as a free man.

If you think it was simple for me to say that, it wasn't.

Do you know the optical illusion that looks equally like a curvy vase and two faces in profile turned toward each other? The images kind of flicker, and in one second you see the vase, and in the next you see the profiles. That's what my mind was like. The two sides of Anthony Capo's personality went in and out of focus, and when I thought of all the testimony he'd given to help the government dismantle the DeCavalcantes, I also thought of the Anthony Capo who could kill upon the orders of his "superiors." Seeing him in this dual way was at the root of my being an FBI agent.

Capo's current life was an optical illusion too. Becoming a law-abiding citizen didn't mean the DeCavalcante in him withered away. To quote Capo himself, he was "a work in progress."

Sometime after the Jimmy Palermo verdict, AUSA John Hillebrecht said of Capo, "Séamus, you transformed that guy."

I asked John if he'd worried that Capo was going to snap.

"It crossed my mind," Hillebrecht said. "I was surprised to see him debate the defense."

"Think about it," I said. "Words speak louder than actions in the mob. Capo had to listen closely to whatever the boss said."

"That belongs in a book!"

I happened to agree.

29

I MEET THE FAMILY ON THEIR TURF

MY YEAR OF LIVING LEGALISTICALLY was almost over. I still had one more loose end to tie up, though, before going back to my everyday life. My dad had asked me to resolve the problem with the family farm in Ireland. But first I had to help Anthony Capo get bail.

Bail wasn't only a matter of rewarding Capo for a job well done. After four years in prison, most of them in a Witness Security facility, I believed Capo was ready to start his life over.

"I want you to get up at seven o'clock," I used to counsel him. "Make like you have a job and you can't stay in bed until ten."

"I want to be a success story," Capo would tell me. "For you."

He needed a decent role model. Better me than Vinny Palermo.

"Anthony, you could sell steamed shit to a blind man," I told him. He cracked a smile.

Some time after the Jimmy Palermo trial, I drove to Capo's WitSec facility. He greeted me with a present. "From your favorite snitch," he said.

I unwrapped the box and found a handmade Pittsburgh Steelers figurine inside. Varnished yellow pants, black shirt, black helmet. I loved it.

"I gotta bust your chops," I said. I pointed out the Steelers decal, incorrectly placed on both sides of the helmet. "Right side only," I said. "Proof you didn't make this!"

Capo took the figurine and angled it to catch the light. "Hard to get good help around here," he said.

He'd asked some guy in the prison workshop to make this thing for me. I don't know what it cost him. A week's worth of candy bars? I didn't ask. I just kept busting his chops.

"Anthony, what's the team's name?"

He was baffled. "What do you mean?"

"Look at this," I said. "Steelers" was missing the letter *R* on one side of the helmet.

"You can always root for the Cowboys," Capo said.

"Not a chance in hell."

"Next time I'll get you Yankee tickets."

"You know I can't accept gifts that have monetary value," I said.

I took back my figurine. I said, "This is awesome."

The figurines Anthony Capo had made for me in his WitSec prison workshop.
Photo by Séamus McElearney

The misspelling made it all the more precious to me. Eventually, he made up for the error by giving me a Yankee figurine with no misspellings.

Capo asked me for the umpteenth time when he could get bail. Whatever you tell a witness, they'll always fixate on what you said. Don't make promises you can't keep. You risk losing your witness's trust.

Two months went by and he got bail. The marshals moved him somewhere in the country—I didn't know the location—on December 23, 2003. He got to spend Christmas Eve with his own TV and an Italian hero. Definitely an improvement over lights out at ten and prison cafeteria fare. Anthony was alone, but free.

The family finally pushed me over the edge.

Not the DeCavalcantes. The McElearneys. The latest chapter in our family saga had started about a year after my dad's death, when I had to fly with my mom to Ireland. Earlier that year, I had tried to sell my grandparents' farm privately, but, well, I'm not a true-born Irishman and I didn't know how to do that. Now we agreed to hold a public auction—another formality I knew as much about as taking out my own gall bladder. I'd hired an auctioneer to run this show, and I prayed that by day's end, I'd have fulfilled my father's dying wish.

My mom and I stayed with her sister in Abbeylara, a village in County Longford once known for its old monastery. A picturesque place where a Bronx boy would lose his mind if he had to live there. I drove us in a rental north to Ballybay in County Monaghan, where, I hoped, we'd sell the McElearney property to a person who'd care for the estate. We wouldn't have had to do that if my Aunt Kathleen had offered us a fair price, but Aunt Kathleen insisted she should get the place for nothing. She even filed a civil suit against us.

The auctioneer, an old Irish gentleman, was about to initiate the proceedings when one of my cousins stood up. He was a chap about my age, one of Aunt Kathleen's sons, who began talking about the property as if he'd grown up on it. He hadn't.

"This land has been in the McElearney name for a hundred years," he said. I swear he thought he was Richard Harris in *The Field* fighting the "outsiders" who "took the meat from the tables while we [Irish] lay in the ditches with the grass juice running green from our mouths." My cousin wasn't even a McElearney by name. So what was he talking about?

The people in Ballybay didn't share my cynicism. They got my cousin's message loud and clear: don't bid on the McElearney farm.

No one in Ballybay would buy the property.

Four years later, my mom and I ended up in an Irish court with my father's sisters. What a waste of my time. I was disgusted.

I was at home in a Southern District of New York courtroom, but what did I know about Ireland's judicial system? My father's will didn't seem to have any standing in it. I defy anybody to go to their ancestral home and talk about their legal claim to so much as a pebble. My mom and I were simply two Americans come to rob the faithful Irish of their soil.

We were outside the courtroom waiting to go in for the hearing. On one side of the vestibule were my aunts. On the other, my mom and I. The two sides communicated only through our solicitors. After hours of haggling, I agreed to give my Aunt Kathleen additional funds to settle the lawsuit. You heard right. I would do just about anything to end this ordeal.

The whole affair left me bitter. I'd come to Ireland to honor my dad's wishes and ensure my mom's financial stability. I hadn't come to make a land grab. I had a life in America I loved. My every waking minute was consumed with the work C-10 had done to rid one state in *my country* of an organized criminal enterprise that enriched a few at great cost to the rest of us. I resented coming to Ireland on behalf of my father and being seen as a traitor to the family. The irony was, the longer I was mixed up in this Jarndyce vs. Jarndyce fiasco, the more money I lost. I threw up my hands. I sold them the land.

We've yet to see a single euro. The estate solicitors said all the profits were depleted. How'd that make me feel? Like I was being extorted by a foreign government.

If you ever pass through Ballybay, look for the McElearney farmhouse that's gone to wrack and ruin. My father's sisters didn't love the place. They just didn't want my dad's family to have it.

Dad, I did my best.

As for Ireland, I gave it an Irish exit and never said goodbye. I vowed one day to come back and be on better terms with ye olde McElearney homeland.

On January 5, 2004, sixty-nine-year-old Bernard NiCastro, a participant in the murder of Joey Garofano, surrendered and started his ten-year prison sentence. NiCastro's the guy who fled Rudy Farone's garage during Joey's murder because he did not have the stomach for killing.* In the early 1990s, NiCastro moved to Miami to oversee the crime family's loan-sharking, illegal gambling, and extortion operations there—and to put thirteen hundred miles between himself and the scene of the crime. Having demonstrated his "cowardice," NiCastro never got made. You have to wonder what he got out of the DeCavalcantes other than their scorn. And money.

The cascade of sentences continued apace:

- January 30: Joe Collina, forty-one months
- February 6: Simone Palermo, twenty-one months
- February 27: Sal Timpani, eighteen months, followed by deportation to Italy
- March 19: Charles Majuri, seventy-seven months

The sentencing flurry† neared an end with the trial of Federico "Fritzy" Giovanelli, the Genovese captain who leaked our December 1999 arrests. Prepping Capo for this trial was going to be more complicated

---

* See chapter 19.

† Mimmo Marzullo was arrested by FBI Newark in July 2003. He and others were named in a fifteen-count indictment charging them with conspiracy, extortion, illegal gambling, and transporting stolen checks. Marzullo pled guilty in February 2004 on illegal gambling and loan-sharking charges.

than any other pretrial meeting. Now that he had gotten bail and was living "somewhere in America," he basically belonged to the federal marshals. The marshals would let me know a week in advance where to show up to meet with him.

Capo couldn't say where he was living, but he was sly enough to drop hints. "I'm a Lions fan now," he'd say when we spoke by phone. I assumed he was living in Detroit or nearby. I couldn't ask.

"I'm rooting for the Browns," he'd say another time. That meant Cleveland, but I wasn't privy to the details.

I told Capo, and all our WitSec cooperators, that their marshal was their new best friend. Even if the marshal hated them. Their strange new life in someplace like Akron or Tacoma or Bismarck, hundreds or thousands of miles from everything familiar, wasn't going to be easy, and they needed to build a relationship with their government handler.

I was relieved to see how well Anthony Capo 2.0 was doing. He'd put on some weight and looked good. He had a job selling cars. That was a coup. At age forty-three, with a work history of murder on demand, he had turned himself upside down, shaken out the habit of beating, maiming, and extorting people, and become a regular working stiff.

We sat at a conference-room table at a local hotel. "You raised the bar for me, Séamus," Capo said after we ran through the probable questions Fritzy's defense attorney would ask about his life in La Cosa Nostra.

"You raised the bar, Anthony," I said. "You're the one living your life."

He mimed a whisper. "I got a split personality. I'm a before-and-after."

I nodded. I never discounted the DeCavalcante he once was. But I decided a long time ago to treat Anthony as newly minted, newly made.

"It's one thing to go after me," Capo said. "But to go after my kids?"

It didn't matter that his old beef came out of nowhere. Knowing the DeCavalcantes would have used his children to punish him was never far from Capo's mind.

"I know better than to ask who else is testifying," Capo said. That was his coy side.

"Let me hear your sales pitch," I said.

"How're you doin' today?" he asked in an exaggerated salesman's voice.

I had to laugh. "None of that 'How can I help you today?' bullshit from you," I said.

"I know what I can do for you today," he said. "Why waste time with bullshit? Life is short."

I had a plane to catch. Nowadays, Anthony and I had to leave more unsaid than said.

"See you in two weeks," Capo said.

"I'll meet up with you with the marshals."

"Séamus, you have a safe flight. I'll be jumping on my *Con Air* flight with these guys." He nodded at the marshals who would transport him.

I was home in several hours. Capo? He was somewhere over America.

A month before the Fritzy trial, the New Jersey State Law Enforcement Officers Association gave five C-10 members its Meritorious Service Award. Stacy Bowery, Nora Conley, Jay Kramer, Eileen O'Rourke, and I—all of us under forty—were cited for enacting or facilitating the arrests of some seventy mobsters in the course of our DeCavalcante investigation.

We were dumbfounded. New Jersey doesn't ordinarily recognize the civic contributions of "outsiders." We were especially grateful to FBI Newark, represented at the event by several agents, for not pelting us with tomatoes when we got up to get our plaques. The evening would have been perfect but for George Hanna giving me about five seconds' notice to give a speech. All I could think to say was trite—but heartfelt: "I'm proud of our team, and speaking for the whole squad, we're extremely grateful for the recognition." Just wished my dad had lived to see me deliver my first award acceptance speech.

Fritzy Giovanelli had stood trial four separate times for the 1986 murder of NYPD undercover detective Anthony Venditti, but he was never found guilty. The witness who saw Fritzy running away from the murder scene pointed him out at the first trial, recanted after having his leg broken at the end of the second trial, testified *for the defense* at the third trial, and was dead by the fourth.* All of that is just to paint a clearer picture of a mobster who might otherwise have come off as just passing along some confidential information. In fact, Fritzy was a captain in the Genovese crime family as well as a financier of a multimillion-dollar gambling empire that included sports betting and horse racing from New York to Florida. He also ran a bodega-based numbers game in Black and Hispanic neighborhoods. He was a serious player who'd already done prison time in the 1990s for violating parole.

At his new trial in April 2004, Fritzy was seventy-two years old. He was charged with extortion, trafficking in stolen auto parts, and three counts of obstruction of justice. A jury trial had worked for him in the past. Why couldn't it work for him again? All he needed was one sympathetic juror to get a hung jury. At his age, what could he possibly gain from pleading guilty? He might as well roll the dice and go to trial.

We'd go straight for the jugular and put Vinny Palermo first in our witness lineup.

None of us were happy about that. Vinny had blown smoke in our faces during *Vitabile et al.*, and we weren't eager to see what new fire we'd have to put out. But Fritzy's defense had boxed us into a corner. We knew from Palermo and Rotondo, and tangentially Capo, that Fritzy had given Rotondo and Palermo a list of arrestees. If we only put up Capo and Rotondo, the defense would have us for breakfast. Why won't the government put up the former DeCavalcante acting boss, who supposedly had direct conversations with Fritzy? What is the prosecution afraid of?

We were afraid Vinny Palermo would come across as deceitful. Not credible. But we had no choice. In a jury trial, all it takes is that one juror to say, "The defense makes a plausible argument. What's the government hiding?"

We had to rely on our most tainted cooperating witness to put Fritzy behind bars.

* The investigation into Fritzy Giovanelli's trials comes from "The Cop-Out" by Russ Baker with Malene Jensen, *New York Magazine*, December 12, 1994, https://www.russbaker.com/archives/New%20York%20Magazine%20-%20The%20Cop%20Out,%20December.htm.

To our surprise, Vinny delivered powerful testimony.

Capo and Rotondo were admirable, as usual. They were working hard to dissociate their new selves from their criminal selves. It's not nothing what they did to change themselves over.

I told myself to remember all three of the trial's cooperating witnesses just as they were in Judge Jed Rakoff's courtroom. They looked healthier than they had in 1999, but anxiety and the passage of time had left them with dark circles under their eyes. Amazing, though, that even with years of erratic sleep and decades of greasy-spoon meals, the three of them had retained some aura of youth. Even Vinny, who was about to turn sixty.

I planned on seeing Anthony at his sentencing hearing one day, but that probably wouldn't be soon. I had encouraged him, and all of our witnesses, to defer sentencing as long as possible. Living out in the world for years without committing any crimes would show the judge Anthony had been rehabilitated. I wanted him to get time served. Anthony's sentencing would probably be the last day I'd ever see him.

I knew I'd never see Vinny Palermo on the witness stand again. He was trial kryptonite. But I would attend his sentencing, whenever that was going to be.

I'd see Anthony Rotondo again only if we needed him as a trial witness. Now that Lou Vallario had entered a plea on April 23, 2004, Rotondo might never have to testify again. Vallario, an aide to Gambino boss John Gotti and underboss Sammy Gravano, got sentenced to ten years for conspiring to murder Fred Weiss and for concealing the murder from federal law enforcement authorities. As it turns out, quite a few other La Cosa Nostra members were in on the Fred Weiss murder. The complete tally of conspirators and killers makes the Weiss murder one of the most indicted organized crime murders in FBI history.

After three weeks of trial, a jury found Fritzy not guilty of extortion.* Fritzy nodded at the verdict. The jurors were on his side.

Until they weren't.

Judge Rakoff asked the jury foreperson for the verdict on the obstruction of justice charges. It was a no-brainer: Federico Giovanelli had alerted Vinny Palermo and Anthony Rotondo, and indirectly dozens

* The extortion charge was brought by the FBI's Genovese squad, not by C-10.

of other DeCavalcantes, that the government was coming to get them. The foreperson said *guilty*.

Fritzy's lawyer shrugged off the verdict by saying his client could get up to eighteen months. "But prosecutors are expected to ask for as much as 20 years," a *Daily News* reporter wrote.

"I'm going back to play handball," Fritzy himself said, about spending time in prison again.*

In September 2004, Judge Rakoff handed down a ten-year prison sentence.

Ten years in a federal penitentiary for a seventy-two-year-old man? I'll take it.

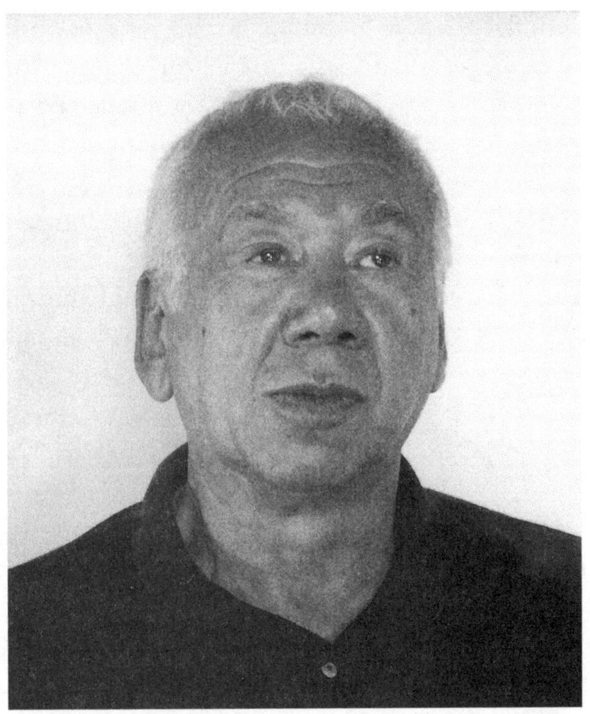

Federico "Fritzy" Giovanelli. *Department of Justice Trial Exhibit, US Attorney's Office, Southern District of New York / FBI*

* "Mob Guy Beats Extort Rap" by Robert Gearty, *Daily News*, May 14, 2004, https://www.nydailynews.com/2004/05/14/mob-guy-beats-extort-rap/.

Meanwhile, the other half of C-10 had done a stellar job of dismantling the Bonanno family. In January 2003, Jeff Sallet, Jim McGoey, and Kim McCaffrey's years-long investigation had culminated in the arrest of official boss Joseph Massino. I assisted on that arrest.* The next time I saw Massino was at his trial in May 2004 in the Eastern District of New York. The trial lasted ten weeks. No sooner did he get convicted on July 30 than he came crawling to the government to cooperate.

Jeff, Kim, and lead prosecutor Greg Andres were ticked off. All the time and money that had gone into mounting a RICO case against him that included charges of murder, extortion, illegal gambling, and money-laundering, and now he thinks he can wriggle out of a life sentence? Moreover, he still had to stand trial for ordering the murder of rival Gerlando Sciascia, the Bonanno captain connected with a heroin distribution gang in Montreal, whose wake I'd surveilled. If convicted on that charge, Massino faced the death penalty. Kim and Jeff didn't want to see the "last don" set a precedent for other convicted mobsters.

Nora Conley—now C-10's supervisor—was ecstatic. So was I. Massino had to have some gold nuggets he could trade for leniency. Nora hoped he had something on Vinny "Gorgeous" Basciano, his replacement at the top of the Bonanno heap.

What Massino had on Vinny Gorgeous—and on the fallout of the FBI's "Donnie Brasco" undercover investigation that infiltrated the family in the 1970s—blew the roof off the Bonannos. Massino and Basciano were in the same Brooklyn jail. We got Massino wired up. On tape, Basciano admitted to ordering the murder of a Bonanno associate and Bronx construction contractor named Randolph Pizzolo.

Massino had more to spill. The FBI knew about the disappearance of three Bonanno captains in 1981. In fact, the Bureau had caught a break on Thursday, May 28, 1981, when a boy playing in an empty lot in the Ozone Park section of Queens spied a human hand sticking up out of

---

* As part of that arrest team, I made an appearance in Selwyn Raab's book *Five Families: The Rise, Decline, and Resurgence of America's Most Powerful Mafia Empires*. My colleagues razzed me pretty good when Raab described me as a "strapping six-foot-tall FBI agent."

the weeds. The police arrived at the grisly scene and found the rest of the semi-decomposed corpse wrapped up in a mover's blanket. Fingerprints confirmed the corpse had once been Alphonse "Sonny Red" Indelicato, one of the three disappeared captains. But we never knew what happened to the two others—Dominick Trinchera and Philip Giaccone—until Massino told us they were rotting in the same empty lot.

Armed with Massino's intel, the FBI raced over to Blake Avenue and Ruby Street in Queens to secure the lot lest the bad guys get there first and start turning over the dirt. I volunteered to do a guard shift with fellow C-10 agent Lauren Regucci, who was doing collateral duty with the FBI's Evidence Response Team. We passed the overnight shift talking about our cases, but we did our rounds often to make sure no intruders infiltrated the grounds.

That was one of my twenty-four-hour Bonanno days.

The official dig for bodies began on October 4, 2004, when Harvey Pincus, the FBI's jack-of-all-trades contractor, showed up in Queens with his men, a steam shovel, and backhoes. We were hopeful that Harvey would unearth something, but not overly optimistic. We knew from our dig in Marlboro, New York, that we'd be lucky to uncover so much as a human bone, let alone three recognizable bodies in such a massive area.

Harvey hit pay dirt. Lodged inside a slurry of mud and concrete were human bones. Over the course of our three-week excavation, water from the water table and days of hard-driving rain had seeped into a pit the size of an Olympic swimming pool. Harvey persevered. He uncovered more remains, a wristwatch, and a pair of eyeglasses. DNA testing showed the bones to be Dominick Trinchera's and Philip Giaccone's.*

Not bad for a twenty-three-year-old cold case and a heap of lousy odds.

The discovery of the second and third murdered captains probably helped save Massino's neck. Instead of signing on for a lethal injection, he was headed to life in prison.

---

* We also received intel that the body of John Favara had been dumped in the lot. Favara was John Gotti's neighbor. He accidentally ran over and killed Gotti's twelve-year-old son. Gotti reportedly had him murdered. Favara's body, however, was never found.

To say I was disappointed when Massino's life sentence got knocked down to time served after ten and a half years is an understatement. Maybe the show of leniency in 2013 stemmed from his help in getting a murder conviction against acting boss Basciano. Now I felt the same as Kim and Jeff. Massino was not going away for life, even though his execution list included the hit on Dominick "Sonny Black" Napolitano, the Bonanno captain who brought "Donnie Brasco"—a.k.a. FBI agent Joe Pistone—into the Bonanno circle, and went all the way back to the 1960s with the murder of a Bonanno associate named Tommy Zummo.*

Ed McDonald, one of Massino's lawyers, once said, "If [Massino] had to make the decision again, if he was 18 or 19, years old, he wouldn't go into the Mafia." The New York newspapers went with a different narrative. They recalled Massino saying, "We was okay until I got pinched. . . . We was on top of the world."†

We had a sweet moment in November 2004 when C-10's DeCavalcante team received the Executive Office for United States Attorneys' Director's Award. We're talking national recognition for what FBI New York and the Southern District of New York did to bust up the New Jersey DeCavalcantes—thereby "protecting the American people and upholding the Constitution," as our citation read.‡ The awards ceremony in DC was memorable because it was our first federal award, but also because I stood next to James Comey, the deputy attorney general of the United States. At a hair over six feet, I'm not a shrimp, but alongside Comey's six-foot-eight-inch trunk, I was a sapling.

* Joe Massino reportedly died at a rehab facility in the New York City area on September 14, 2023.

† For McDonald's quote, see "Former Mob Boss Massino Set to Go Free" by Selim Algar, *New York Post*, July 10, 2013, https://nypost.com/2013/07/10/former-mob-boss-massino-set-to-go-free/. For Massino's, see "Mafia Legends 'Turning in Graves' as Ex-Bonanno Boss to Rat Out Vinny Gorgeous at Trial," *Daily News*, April 9, 2011, https://www.nydailynews.com/2011/04/09/mafia-legends-turning-in-graves-as-ex-bonanno-boss-to-rat-out-vinny-gorgeous-at-trial/.

‡ See the appendix for a list of award recipients from FBI New York and the Southern District of New York.

While I stood in the shade of the Comey oak, a stray thought crept into my brain: *What goes up must come down.* I didn't flatter myself that C-10 had eradicated organized crime from New Jersey and New York. I knew that if law enforcement failed to build on what we'd accomplished, the DeCavalcantes, or some other predator, would extort, set up illegal gambling dens, or demand no-show jobs. *Crime ye shall always have with you*, you could say, unless you keep a watchful eye on it.

Two weeks after the award ceremony, my bosses decided they wanted me to keep a watchful eye on the Colombo organized crime family and named me acting supervisor of C-38. I declined the honor. I'd been at the Bureau a relatively short time, and I didn't feel qualified.

"Think about it over the weekend," my bosses said.

When I got to 26 Federal Plaza on Monday, I realized they hadn't given me a choice. I'd been "voluntold."

Got it. I was going to head an OC squad branded as the FBI's red-headed stepchild. In eight years, C-38 had had eight supervisors. They'd all bailed after a year. I was unnerved when I heard that Mike Gaeta, an agent on the Genovese squad, had been asked to run C-38 and flat out said no.

C-10 was a dream job. How different could C-38 be?

30

WE HAVE ANOTHER VICTORY AND AN UNEXPECTED SETBACK

FIVE YEARS BEFORE I GOT TO C-10, at least twenty-six locals in the Laborers' International Union of North America had connections with organized crime. Back in the Reagan administration, the President's Commission on Organized Crime revealed how La Cosa Nostra had been defrauding LIUNA's benefit funds, insisting on no-show jobs, extorting the construction industry, and gaining access to government officials since the 1940s. With pressure from President Reagan's Department of Justice, LIUNA established an internal reform program designed to root out Mafia racketeering practices throughout its constituent locals.

As the de facto liaison between C-10 and LIUNA, I began sharing our cooperating witnesses' intel with Doug Gow, a retired FBI deputy director in charge of investigating ethical violations in union locals—an extremely respected government servant. Doug's probe into LIUNA's election procedures had already resulted in the direct rank-and-file secret-ballot election of the union president and secretary-treasurer, a transparent set of job referral rules to prevent discriminatory hiring practices (i.e., no no-show jobs), and the use of an independent accounting firm to audit LIUNA's finances.

Doug knew the laws and violations of LIUNA like nobody's business. The first thing Doug and his team did was suspend, remove, and ban any union members associated with organized crime. Next, if necessary, they would place the corrupted union into trusteeship, an eighteen-month government supervision followed by free union elections. Thanks to info we'd gleaned from Anthony Capo and our other cooperating witnesses, I could give Doug, and attorney Pat Slevin, many examples of patronage jobs and kickbacks at Local 394 that had benefited DeCavalcante top brass, members, and associates. I also had two trials' worth of testimony pointing to endemic corruption in New Jersey's construction industry. And John Riggi had made it easy for us to cite Local 394 as part of a racketeering enterprise: the same individual who was boss of the DeCavalcante organized crime family was also Local 394's business agent. Riggi helped our reform efforts further by admitting to authorizing the murder of Fred Weiss.

By June 14, 2006, when I testified at the LIUNA hearing into corruption inside Local 394, I'd been knee-deep in C-38's Colombo squad for more than a year and a half. As I was seen as the DeCavalcante expert, I'd been called back to put together a Complaint for Trusteeship, a document describing how La Cosa Nostra controlled Local 394 through no-show jobs, no-work jobs, threats of labor strikes, theft of union funds, and pension benefits as well as extortion of legitimate construction contractors. The paper itself could've been the basis for an episode of *The Sopranos*.

The LIUNA hearing at a New Jersey hotel was open to the public. Pat warned me that the large hall would be filled with Local 394 members. "Don't be surprised if they try to intimidate you," he said.

I didn't realize until I got to the hotel that intimidation can be a two-way street. When Pat asked me to talk about, say, Pino Schifilliti, Pino's Local 394 supporters were taken aback by how much we knew about him. They were stunned to hear me, an Irishman, spell Pino's complicated last name as if I was competing in the Scripps National Spelling Bee. I could speak just as knowledgeably about Jimmy Palermo, Charlie Majuri, Sal Timpani, Joe Giacobbe, Joe Collina, and other

DeCavalcantes—with each letter falling trippingly off my tongue. If we knew so much about these guys, what did we know about the men in the audience?

We knew enough to help LIUNA put Local 394 into trusteeship for eighteen months. At the end of that term, the local would have free and open elections.

I testified at the LIUNA hearing as if I were reading from my own personal DeCavalcante encyclopedia. Steve Vitabile, Pino Schifilliti, and Phil Abramo—in separate prisons since their arrests—had gotten sentenced to LIFE right before the hearing.* Jimmy Palermo got sentenced to eleven years a scant month later, on July 13, 2006. Finally, I could put the DeCavalcantes behind me and turn my attention back to rebuilding the Colombo squad.†

I spoke too soon. In September 2008, the Second Circuit Court of Appeals overturned the convictions of Vitabile, Schifilliti, and Abramo.

Shocked to the core.

I'm not a lawyer, but the way the AUSAs explained it to me, an excessive number of guilty pleas from noncooperating gangsters—eight altogether—were read into the court record as evidence during the *US v. Vitabile et al.* trial. These stipulations were deemed prejudicial to the defendants, because the evidence could not be cross-examined by the defense. Hence, it was ruled that the defense attorneys couldn't adequately represent their clients.‡

Convictions aren't finalized until all appeals have been exhausted. That can take years.

---

* Schifilliti was sentenced in April 2006. Vitabile and Abramo were sentenced in June right before I testified.

† And rebuild we did. On June 4, 2008, in partnership with the Eastern District of New York, C-38 executed its first big arrest. That day, we arrested the Colombo acting boss, underboss, two captains, two soldiers, and six associates. Our arrests were the beginning of the end for the Colombo family.

‡ See the Second Circuit's decision at https://cases.justia.com/federal/appellate-courts/ca2/06-1280/920080904/0.pdf.

Everyone involved in the *US v. Vitabile et al.* trial—prosecutors and FBI agents—had been reassigned to other geographical locations or were no longer government employees, except for Mimi Rocah and me. We had two choices: we could either redo the trial or enter into plea negotiations with the defense attorneys.

All parties were able to come to a plea agreement. This time around, Vitabile, Schifilliti, and Abramo realized numbers were better than letters: Their LIFE sentences were significantly knocked down. Now they had a chance of walking out of prison.

Neither Mimi nor I felt too bad. The reduced sentences of the three DeCavalcantes were more or less equal to prison terms they would have gotten if they'd accepted plea agreements from the get-go. Given their age and health conditions, we didn't worry that these gentlemen would jump back into the game any time soon. Vitabile got resentenced to fifteen years, Schifilliti to sixteen, and Abramo to eighteen.

Once Anthony Capo began cooperating with us—and once he set off what I call a *spiral effect of cooperation*—these three high-level DeCavalcantes weren't ever going to slip the net completely. It was up to them how they would live out their remaining years. The way I see it, if you're destined to go down in flames, go down with a highball and a silver cigarette holder, not with a match and a canister of fuel.

The one DeCavalcante with grace was Steve Vitabile. Expensive suit. Flashy necktie. Boutonniere. I couldn't like a man who ordered murder on demand, and I couldn't respect the business model he lived by. But when Steve knew he'd come to the end of the road, he didn't holler. I can still see him in an SDNY courtroom, his hands outstretched toward the sergeant at arms as he prepared to head back to his prison cell in handcuffs. I admired him. He took it like a man.

31

ANTHONY CAPO STANDS ON THE DOORSTEP OF FREEDOM

C-10 WAS A SQUAD OF ALL-STARS. We were the '98 Yankees. The '69 Mets. And, it pains me to say, Jeff, the 2004 Red Sox.* Our bosses must have been psychic, because they drafted one outstanding player after another. Our team of mostly thirtysomethings pulled together to pull down one organized crime family invisible to government for a hundred years and another dominated by "the last don." No other law enforcement body had ever come close to doing what our band of brothers and sisters did in under five years.

How many times in life do you get to do something historic?

My education, street life, and auditing jobs, and my dad's work ethic—all of which I had the dumb luck to have—prepared me to show up at a mobster's house, arrest him, and have him flip within a week. My year of transcribing Ralph Guarino's tapes and studying the DeCavalcante ecosystem of associates, soldiers, captains, underbosses, and bosses

* Boston native Jeff Sallet and I attended game 7 of the American League Championship Series at Yankee Stadium, Yankees vs Red Sox. The Yankees went into game 4 leading 3–0, but—the horror—the Red Sox came back and won four games straight.

accounted for my readiness. Scut work isn't heroic. It's not a fascinating way to spend a day. But, as I've tried to show, it honed me—an Irish American boy from Bainbridge Avenue in the Bronx—into an FBI agent who could map out a Mafia empire that began in Elizabeth, New Jersey, and fanned out to Montreal and Miami. In the process, I learned how perps think, and I learned to treat them like human beings no matter what. I never forgot my mission: do everything possible to be a thorn in the side of organized crime.

There's no silver bullet for flipping criminals. It's more art than science. How else to explain that my pleading with Mike Massa to flip ended up nowhere but in disaster for him, while my bantering about sports ultimately gave Anthony Capo a get-out-of-jail-free card. For me, Massa was a mini course in flipping Capo.

Lesson learned #1: Drop a fact here and there that lets the perp know we have the goods on him. No point in lying to us. We already know quite a bit. And that's a fact.

Lesson learned #2: Position yourself as an ally. Capo could see how he could have been me and I could have been him.

Lesson learned #3: However you got made, you can remake yourself. You've just got to get on the train before it leaves the station.

My C-10 story is sort of over. "Sort of" because trials end only after all our made men have gone on to meet their maker. Look at what happened with *US v. Vitabile et al.* They were convicted in June 2003. Their sentences were overturned in 2008. They pled guilty and were resentenced in 2009. After serving their reduced prison time,* they had the rest of their lives—admittedly not very long or healthy—to live in freedom. As I've written, several of my colleagues were PO'd that these men didn't spend the rest of their lives behind bars. I learned not to take offense when the outcome isn't a hundred percent to my liking. The FBI gives you a job to do. You do it, and you don't make it personal.

---

* According to the Bureau of Prisons, Steve Vitabile was released in November 2013, Pino Schifilliti in July 2015, and Phil Abramo in January 2018.

I've talked a lot here about rehabilitation. Lots of people don't believe in it. Lots of people don't believe in using bad guys to knock down other bad guys. During our big trials, for example, a newspaper columnist here and there railed against the FBI and the Southern District for using perceived lowlifes to prosecute La Cosa Nostra. I always wanted to throw the question back: How can an Irish American infiltrate La Cosa Nostra? That "thing of ours" is theirs. It's a secret society. It's easy to lecture us. It's hard to investigate, build relationships, and connect the dots—something that good law enforcement and good journalism do. Some people get it.

I never forgot just how much havoc Anthony Capo and his ilk wreaked in the world. I don't give anybody a pass for committing atrocities. I saw up close and personal how victims and their families suffered. But I wouldn't let myself think of Capo and our cooperating witnesses as lowlifes. Once they came over to our side, it was our job to set them on the right path. Not one of them committed another crime. Two or three might not be living the most upright lives, but even they never got arrested again. You'd be within your rights to say that our cooperators had committed unforgivably heinous acts and didn't deserve the second chance we gave them. One day they will answer to a higher power. But I can tell you more than one witness has thanked me for liberating them from the mob. Nothing but the FBI, the SDNY, and the US Federal Marshals could have gotten them out of the Mafia Roach Motel, where they could check in but not check out. With leniency from the sentencing judge, they could start a business, raise a family, repent in religious or civic ways, and stop victimizing America's people, industries, and consumer habits.

We did indeed reward them for being witnesses.

Victor DiChiara was sentenced in 2004 to fifty-four months. He was released two months after sentencing.

Vinny Palermo was sentenced in 2009. He'd already done about two years in prison, but now he got slapped with another eighteen months. The judge didn't forget how Vinny hid money from us.

Anthony Rotondo and Frank Scarabino got sentenced to time served in 2015 and 2013, respectively.

Life isn't uncomplicated. C-10 didn't eliminate organized crime. No one could. It'll always be with us. We did set the DeCavalcantes and Bonannos back years, though. To this day, they're still trying to recover.

I won't deny I had the time of my life. As a bank auditor, I was on a middle-class path to making money and being bored batshit. As an FBI agent, my finances were always constrained, but every minute of every day had meaning—and I include the days I was on Frank Polizzi's Sicilian-style hit list. When law enforcement attracts the right people, it attracts idealists. All of us, in the FBI and the federal court system, got out of bed each morning to make our society a safer place to work, make money, grab a burger, watch a ball game, shop, and live a beautiful life. On C-10, I belonged to a corps of people who felt the way I did. I knew back then they were the best of the best. They still are.

Late in the afternoon of January 21, 2012, I was at my desk when that special number popped up on my phone. I had a feeling Anthony had some last-minute questions for me. His sentencing was coming up in a week.

"Séamus, I'm sorry to deliver the news," the marshal said. "Anthony Capo suffered a heart attack. We believe he died a day or two ago."

Dead? Anthony?

He and I had just spoken two weeks earlier. We discussed the 5K letter the prosecutors would submit to the sentencing judge. I'd also offered to give a statement in court about everything Anthony had done to help the government bust up the "real Sopranos." I was going to talk about the courage it took for Anthony to shed his life of crime in favor of living an ordinary life. Now the guy who spurred the downfall of the DeCavalcantes was never going to have his day in court. And I wouldn't see Anthony Capo one last time after all.

By 2012, I'd been supervising the Colombo squad for nearly seven years, and I confess weeks would pass without my thinking overly much about Anthony. Spearheading the dismantlement of the Colombo family didn't leave time for anything else. C-38 was on the verge of solving another cold case.

I put the phone back in its cradle and picked it up again to call Liam. My brother had been an agent for almost three years by now, and he had planned on attending Capo's sentencing. He'd gotten intensely curious about the guy I'd been talking about since my early days at the Bureau. I had to give him the news that Capo had just passed.

I couldn't talk long with Liam. We were both busy. On my end, the Colombo squad needed constant attention, to put it mildly, but just then I didn't have a head for work. I threw on my down jacket and took the Duane Street exit out of 26 Federal Plaza. I walked east to Foley Square and sat down on a bench facing the Southern District of New York. So much of my drama with Capo had taken place there, beginning with his arraignment and ending with his testimony in the Fritzy trial. Anthony and I had met in a kind of DMZ between crime and punishment, and I believe our encounter there changed our country for the better. C-10 would never have tunneled its way into the Jersey crime family without Anthony's cooperation. Undoubtedly, Anthony would have gone on to kill and extort people if he hadn't met me.

Damn New York winters! It wasn't even three thirty in the afternoon, but it was cold and getting dark. I had my cellphone with me and called my wife to give her the news. As I'd told Anthony, I'd met a great girl and married her. Despite the load of trouble I dealt with every day on C-38, my own life kept getting better and better. I hoped Capo had also found some serenity in his world of Witness Security.

I called Capo's mom to offer my condolences. I had a brief conversation with Capo's sister too. They both invited me to attend Anthony's wake. I used my phone app to find the funeral home. I'd filed my Hagstrom maps away in a file cabinet a couple years back.

At the funeral home, I made my way to the casket. I kneeled down and said a prayer. I kissed my fingers and touched Anthony's hand. I could only thank him, silently, for the monumental role he'd played in our investigation of the DeCavalcantes.

Anthony's parents saw me. His mom kissed me. His stepdad, a retired court officer from the Kings County Criminal Court, shook hands with me. I said I was sorry for their loss. His mom, neat and petite as always, teared up when she saw me. Anthony's sister came over to say hello. She pointed out Capo's ex-wife. I walked to the back of the funeral home and hugged her. She introduced me to her three children. The last time I saw them, they were little. I remember how Capo's youngest daughter told me, just after her father decided to cooperate, "You know what FBI stands for? Forever Bothering Italians." She was a young lady now. All three kids were poised. Respectful.

I looked around the room. Attendance was scarce. I saw Capo's brother, a city employee. And then I saw the other brother, who lived out of state. He was standing beside a print of the Savior. I'd had exactly one interaction with him, and it wasn't good. Back in 2003, I was in Florida with John Hillebrecht doing trial prep for the Vitabile case. Hillebrecht and I were working round the clock. We took a break to watch the Super Bowl at a bar, where, incidentally, we saw the comedian Jackie Mason.

That's where the jokes stopped. I no longer remember who called to tell me that the out-of-town brother said he'd been assaulted. I had to leave trial prep to Hillebrecht so I could look into this claim. It turned out to be a total fabrication. Capo's brother wasted my time. I wanted to assault him myself! The next time I saw Capo, I told him, "Never mention this brother to me again."

At the wake, I couldn't hide the disgust on my face. I'm sure my expression warned this guy to keep his distance from me.

I said goodbye to the family. They told me how glad they were that I'd come. Everything that had happened, from Anthony's arrest to his living in Witness Security, had forged a bond between us. We'd grown together.

I got behind the wheel of my Bu-car. I sat for a minute and did something I hadn't done in a while. I reflected on our investigation of the DeCavalcantes. I had a plaque from John Hillebrecht—and from "your friends at the United States Attorney's Office, Southern District of New York"—that succinctly summarized the case:

> Seven trials.
> Seventy-one defendants convicted.

Eleven murders solved.
And untold mayhem.
DECEMBER 1999–JULY 2004

Anthony, before you, no made member of the DeCavalcantes had ever cooperated with law enforcement. Almost one hundred years of omertà.

Because of you, C-10 had an unprecedented five-year run. We flipped every level of the DeCavalcante family: four associates, one soldier, one captain, and an acting panel boss. We thwarted New Jersey's organized crime family. No other DeCavalcante made member to date has agreed to become a cooperating witness for the government.

I don't think there's ever been another squad like C-10. Our special group of agents and support personnel brought down two organized crime families at the same time.

Anthony Capo had traveled a distance further than anyone else in his family, and not only because he'd lived God knows where or because he'd transformed himself from a ruthless killer to a killer salesman.

I put my Bu-car in gear. Before I could back out of the parking lot, I had to respond to a text on my cell. A C-38 rookie was telling me about the latest fire we had to put out.

"I'm on the bridge," I said, the way George Hanna used to. "I'll be right there."

ACKNOWLEDGMENTS

Séamus

My deepest gratitude to Jack Garcia, one of the FBI's best undercover agents, for guiding me through this crazy book process, and for connecting me with Michael Levin, who introduced me to my coauthor Barbara "Brook" Finkelstein. Brook, it has been quite a ride. We spent endless Sunday mornings at the Riverdale Diner in the Bronx discussing my thoughts and getting them down on paper. I just want to say a sincere thank-you. *By now, you are well versed in organized crime!*

Thank you to our literary agent Jill Marsal of Marsal Lyon Literary Agency, who believed in this story before it found its voice; and to Jerry Pohlen and Devon Freeny of Chicago Review Press for your passion, trust, and countless ways you made this book better.

Thank you to my friends for always keeping me grounded. A special shout out to Billy Treanor for his kindness when my dad passed away.

To my C-10 squad mates: You were nothing less than a cast of all-stars. I tried to include everyone who worked on the squad during the time period in the appendix that follows. My sincere apologies if I missed anyone; it was purely accidental. To the ladies of C-10: You are the hardest-working women I ever teamed up with, especially my partner Stacy Bowery. I am deeply grateful to ASAC Kevin Donovan for drafting me, SSA Jack Stubing for believing in me, and George Hanna for taking me under his wing.

My deepest respect to our talented DeCavalcante investigative team: FBI Agents Nora Conley, Eileen O'Rourke, Stacy Bowery, George Hanna, Jay Kramer, Bernardo Curra, Anthony Zampogna, Doug Leff, Andre Cicero, Intelligence Analyst Josephine Mauro, and the NYPD's Detective John DiCaprio.

The Southern District of New York prosecutors assigned to this case were simply amazing: AUSA Maria Barton, who passed the torch to John Hillebrecht, Mimi Rocah, Mike McGovern, Dani James, Lisa Korologos, and David Burns. Watching the brightest minds in action and learning from them was priceless. Quite frankly, they spoiled me for the rest of my career. They set the bar so high that I've always expected the same excellence from everyone else.

Thank you to the US Marshals Service for the constant shuffling of cooperating witnesses for trials and the countless neutral site debriefings across the United States.

Most important of all, a big thank-you to my family, because you are what truly matters. I will start with my mom for always guiding us in the right direction, and then my sisters for putting family first.

Thank you to my brother, Liam, who exemplifies the spirit of perseverance. Liam began his career as an FBI mechanic, advanced to FBI police officer, and then Special Surveillance Group (SSG), all while earning his bachelor's degree at Manhattan College. In March 2009, Liam graduated from Quantico, where I had the distinct honor of presenting his credentials. We later worked together on a white-collar squad, which he now supervises. I am so proud of him and his relentless determination to become an agent.

Lastly, I never thought about marriage, but that changed the day I met my wife. I cannot thank her enough for the unwavering support and encouragement, and her never-ending sarcasm, which made sure I never took myself too seriously.

I am truly blessed to have been part of the historic dismantlement of three organized crime families: the DeCavalcantes, Bonannos, and Colombos.

Barbara

Grateful acknowledgment to Michael Levin for connecting me with Séamus and for providing invaluable editorial guidance; to our agent Jill Marsal of Marsal Lyon Literary Agency for representing *Flipping Capo*; to Jim Gardner and the late Victor Navasky for their generous help with publicity and promotion; and to Chicago Review Press for letting us work with the talented editorial team of Devon Freeny and Jerry Pohlen. Above all, my heartfelt gratitude to Séamus for inviting me along on a journey that was often exhilarating and only occasionally maddening. I couldn't have gotten an honorary degree in organized crime from a better teacher.

Appendix

THE PLAYERS

Law Enforcement

FBI C-10 Squad

December 1998–December 2004
(any omission of a C-10 squad member is entirely accidental)

Special Agents (SAs)

Elizabeth Baren–RIP
Joseph Bonavolonta
Stacy Bowery
Michael Breslin
Andre Cicero
Nora Conley (SA / SSA)
Bernardo Curra
Courtenae Druker
Frank Gasper
Christine Grubert
George Hanna (SA / SSA)
Pat Kern
Jay Kramer
Douglas Leff

Gregory Massa
Kimberly McCaffrey
Séamus McElearney
James Meskill–RIP
Scott McGaunn
James McGoey
Wayne McGrew
Eileen O'Rourke
Joseph Phelan–RIP
William Powell–RIP
Lauren Regucci
Jeffrey Sallet
Michael Trombetta
George Wright
Anthony Zampogna

Supervisory Special Agent (SSAs)

John Louis "Jack" Stubing
John DiStasio–RIP

Assistant Special Agent in Charge (ASAC)

Kevin Donovan
Keith Trace–RIP
Matthew Heron

Analysts

Josephine Mauro
Deborah Morales
Dan Melore (forfeiture contractor)
Ken Zoeller

Support Employees

Hector Deliz
Bernadette MacMillan–RIP
Barbara Montana

NYPD

Detective John DiCaprio

Southern District of New York (SDNY)

Assistant United States Attorneys (AUSAs)

Maria Barton
David Burns
John Hillebrecht
Dani James
Lisa Korologos
Michael McGovern
Miriam "Mimi" Rocah

Other SDNY Employees

Legendary investigator Kenny McCabe–RIP
Paralegal Richard Stephan

Indicted Individuals

Initial Indictment of Alleged Members and Associates of the DeCavalcantes and Other Organized Crime Families

December 2, 1999

(in the order in which they appear in the indictment; for *italicized* individuals the charges were dismissed, with the court docket reflecting "filed *nolle prosequi*")

Vincent "Vinny Ocean" Palermo (a.k.a. "the Uncle," "Oscar")
Joseph Giacobbe
Joseph "Tin Ear" Sclafani (a.k.a. "Little Joey")
Anthony Capo
Stephen Arancio
James Gallo
Westley "the Kid" Paloscio
Joseph "Joey Cars" Migliorato
Thomas DiTorra
Thomas Salvata
Joseph Abruzzo
Stephen Keenan
Anthony Greco
Anthony Rotondo
Frank "Chickie" Leto
Frank Melia
Joseph "Jo Jo" Muraca
Stefan Redulovich
John Campanella Jr.
John Campanella Sr.
Philip Caracappa
Vincent Cerchio
John Maggio
Robert Pinsky
Robert Volpe

Richard Boothe
Stanley Gash
Christopher Cheddie
Harold Ponton
Mark Capichana
Anthony "Coco" Antoniello
Joseph "Sonny" Juliano
Vincent Romano
Louis Tufano
Ralph Castore
Anthony Stropoli
Salvatore Borgognone
Felix Rivera
Peter Kaminski

DeCavalcante Hierarchy Indictment

October 19, 2000

Giovanni "Uncle John" Riggi
Girolamo "Jimmy" Palermo
Charles Majuri
Stefano "Steve" Vitabile
Philip Abramo
Francesco "Frank" Polizzi
Anthony "Marshmallow" Mannarino
Louis "Louie Eggs" Consalvo
Gregory Rago
Frank D'Amato
Bernard NiCastro
Frank "Frankie the Beast" Scarabino
Giuseppe "Pino" Schifilliti*

* Schifilliti was indicted on October 19, 2000. He fled to Italy and was arrested there on January 8, 2001. He was extradited back to the US on March 9, 2001.

Additional Indictments, Including for the Murder of Joseph "Joe Pitts" Conigliaro

April 19, 2001

Giovanni "Uncle John" Riggi (a.k.a. "the Eagle")
Girolamo "Jimmy" Palermo
Charles Majuri
Stefano "Steve the Truck Driver" Vitabile
Philip Abramo
Giuseppe "Pino" Schifilliti
Francesco "Frank" Polizzi
Anthony "Marshmallow" Mannarino
Louis "Louie Eggs" Consalvo
Gregory Rago
Frank D'Amato
Bernard NiCastro
Simone "Daddy" Palermo
Joseph Collina Sr.
Salvatore "Little Sal" Timpani (a.k.a. "Sal the Barber")
Charles "Charlie the Hat" Stango (a.k.a. "the Mad Hatter")
Joseph "Big Joey" Brideson
Americo "Mike" Massa
Martin "Marty" Lewis
Reuben Malave

May 10, 2001

Detective Michael Silvestri

August 1, 2001

Federico "Fritzy" Giovanelli

Recipients of 2004 United States Attorney Director's Awards

(for the DeCavalcante investigation)

New York FBI (Special Agents)

Stacy G. Bowery
Nora Conley
George Hanna
Jay Kramer
Séamus McElearney
Eileen O'Rourke

Southern District of New York (AUSAs)

Maria Barton
David Burns
John Hillebrecht
Lisa Korologos
Michael McGovern
Miriam "Mimi" Rocah